The House of Blackwood

The House of Blackwood

Author-Publisher Relations in the Victorian Era

DAVID FINKELSTEIN

The Pennsylvania State University Press
University Park, Pennsylvania

Library of Congress Cataloging-in-Publication Data

Finkelstein, David, 1964–
The house of Blackwood : author-publisher relations in the Victorian era /
David Finkelstein.
p.   cm. — (Penn State series in the history of the book)
Includes bibliographical references and index.
ISBN 978-0-271-05836-8 (pbk: alk. paper)
1. William Blackwood and Sons—History
2. Publishers and publishing—Great Britain—History—19th century.
3. Authors and publishers—Great Britain—History 19th century.
4. Great Britain—Intellectual life—19th century.
I. Title.   II. Series.
Z325.W58 F36 2002
070.5'0941—dc21   2002000501

It is the policy of The Pennsylvania State University Press to use acid-free
paper for the first printing of all clothbound books.
Publications on uncoated stock satisfy the minimum requirements of Ameri-
can National Standard for Information Sciences—
Permanence of Paper for Printed Library Materials,
ANSI Z39.48—1992.

Contents

List of Illustrations

Acknowledgments

This book presents the results of more than ten years of work in the Blackwood archives at the National Library of Scotland. It started in 1990 with an idle question posed to the then head of the Department of Manuscripts, Patrick Cadell. I asked, Why had the vast collection of papers donated or purchased since 1942 from the Edinburgh publishers William Blackwood & Sons never been studied in depth by anyone in recent years, aside from those interested in individual authors? Because, he replied, much of it remains uncataloged and scattered in a variety of temporary holdings and accessions, out of range and unknown to most researchers. He then went on to ask whether I would like to take on the job of cataloging this material. He couldn't offer me much in the way of a salary, but he thought the experience could prove of use to me in any future career. Young and foolish, I thus began a journey into the unknown, spending a year creating a temporary catalog and finding list that members of the Department of Manuscripts are now starting to turn into a more permanent and more accurate catalog record. More than ten years and several jobs later, my knowledge of the Blackwood material barely scratches the surface: the collection, one of the most inclusive of any publishing archive to be found in Britain, is so vast it would take a lifetime to excavate fully. I doubt I will accomplish this task on my own, but I wish anyone caring to follow in my wake the best of luck in their travels!

It is appropriate that in my acknowledgments the first group of people I must thank are the staff of the National Library of Scotland's Department of Manuscripts, who have put up with me in various forms: first as a member of staff, then as a British Academy Research Fellow attached informally to the department for three years, and subsequently as an ordinary reader ceaselessly demanding bulky ledgers and large quantities of bound and unbound letters and odd material. Many thanks to them for their patience and support of my quest. I would like to thank the late Wing Commander Douglas Blackwood and his son Michael Blackwood for permission to use Blackwood material. Thanks also to the National

Library of Scotland for permission to quote from the Blackwood archives, and to the King's College Library for permission to quote from the E. M. Forster papers. I am also grateful to the following people for their comments, advice, and help: William Baker, Tom Barron, Laurel Brake, Iain G. Brown, Robert and Vineta Colby, Sondra Miley Cooney, Linda Dryden, Simon Eliot, Mary Ann Gillies, Robert Hampson, Steven Jobe, Aileen Kristianson, Patrick Leary, Carol A. Martin, Alistair McCleery, Colm McLaughlin, Liz Morrison, Pete Murray, Robert L. Patten, Douglas Mark Peers, John Sutherland, Dale Trela, and James L. W. West III.

References from the unpublished letters of E. M. Forster have been included with the kind permission of the Society of Authors as agent for the Provost and Scholars of King's College Cambridge. Material from the Blackwood Papers has been reproduced with the kind permission of the National Library of Scotland, Michael Blackwood, and the late Wing Commander Douglas S. Blackwood.

Over the past ten years, time for my research has been made possible by the following awards: a Bibliographical Society of America Research Grant, a British Academy Postdoctoral Research Fellowship, a Carnegie Trust for the Universities of Scotland Research Grant, the National Library of Scotland Ratcliff Award, a Newby Trust Grant, and a Scottish Arts Council Writer's Grant. I am grateful to these sponsors for their faith in my work.

Finally, while this book is the product of original research, some material has appeared previously: a variation of Chapter 3 was published as "Breaking the Thread: The Authorial Reinvention of John Hanning Speke in His *Journal of the Discovery of the Source of the Nile*," in *Text: An Interdisciplinary Annual of Textual Studies*, 9 (1997): 280–96; Chapter 4 appeared in slightly different form as "*A Woman Hater* and Women Healers: John Blackwood, Charles Reade, and the Victorian Women's Medical Movement," in *Victorian Periodicals Review*, Winter 1995, 330–52; and a portion of Chapter 6 formed the article "Scottish Cultural Identity in Nineteenth-Century Publishing Memoirs," in *Interfaces: Image Texte Langage* 15 (1999): 221–29. My thanks to the editors for permission to reproduce these sections here.

Setting the Scene

On a warm, sunny day on 8 November 1879, the body of publisher and editor John Blackwood was interred in Old Calton Hill Cemetery in Edinburgh, overlooking the city in which he had spent much of his working life. Passing by the tomb of David Hume on one side, the pallbearers brought the casket to the family vault, where it was placed next to that of his father, William Blackwood, founder of the Blackwood publishing firm and the famous monthly *Blackwood's Magazine*. Among those who helped carry the remains to its final resting place were some of John's most trusted friends and literary contributors: General Edward Bruce Hamley; historian John Hill Burton; John Skelton, author and critic; and Colonel James Grant, African explorer and J. H. Speke's overshadowed companion in his famous search for the source of the Nile River.

Weeks later, men with lists swarmed through the firm's premises on 45 George Street and 32 Thistle Street in Edinburgh. They measured rooms; they counted shelves; they counted chairs, desks, tables, light fixtures. They counted stock on the 275 shelves in the front shop, investigated the firm's ledgers, noted copyright values. Equipment in the printing office was fingered, valued, and listed in a twenty-eight-page report; among the notable items in its eighteen rooms were boxes filled with varying types and fonts, including:[1]

Wood Type	Metal Type	Book Type
76 pieces 20-line pica	94 12-line pica Roman	10,395 English
68 pieces 17-line pica	100 8-line pica Clarendon	6,490 pica no. 28
94 pieces 16-line pica	43 7-line pica Grotesque	1,669 pica no. 4
76 pieces 18-line pica	77 4-line pica Roman	5,740 small pica no. 28

Also listed were thirty-eight double crown letter boards, sixty-seven brass galleys, thirty-six composing sticks for use on *Blackwood's Magazine*, and one Double Deny Albion proof press with inking table and three rollers, along with other printing presses and heavy machinery. The final estimated value of all this printing office stock and equipment was £5,870.

The numbers men counted, they added, and then they summarized, in the end producing a financial report that detailed to the last brass molding and brass farthing the total worth of the Blackwood publishing firm. The resulting remarkable document is one of the most complete commercial and financial statements one is likely to encounter of any British publishing firm operating in the nineteenth century. It was used to settle family interests and establish John's nephew, William Blackwood III, as the new head of the firm. Its value, however, extends beyond that of the personal, allowing us a snapshot view of the Blackwood firm at the peak of its success.

When Alexander Blackwood (head of the firm following his father William Blackwood's death in 1834) died in March 1845, a similar accounting exercise placed the firm's value at £41,633. Of this sum Alexander's share as a company director came to £12,004, which, combined with income withdrawn by both his brothers, Robert and John Blackwood (both also partners in the firm), accounted for almost half the total value of the family business. The final sum also included £14,814 in copyright values (that is, the value of the firm's intellectual property rights in its publications) and £7,361 in capital free for further investment.[2] The spread of income looked like this:

	£	s	d
Mr. A. Blackwood's share	12,004	3	7
Cash withdrawn by J. & R. Blackwood	7,453	17	6

	£	s	d
Estimated value of copyright	14,814	0	0
Capital at 21 March 1845	7,361	13	9
Total balance at 21st March 1845	£41,633.14.10		

Thirty four years later the value of the firm had almost doubled to £80,509, and the balance sheet now read more complicatedly like this:

Assets	£	s	d	Liabilities	£	s	d
Cash Edinburgh & London	502	8	0				
Bills receivable	2197	10	1	Bills payable	1,768	2	6
Amounts due to W. B. & Sons	16,760	11	3	Amounts due by W. B. & Sons	12,225	0	2
Amounts due to W. B. & Sons per cash	3,160	9	5	Amounts due by W. B. & Sons per cash	23,334	11	3
Ledger				Ledger			
Stock	15,938	8	6	Maga contributors	431	18	0
Furniture	357	8	8				
Printing office	8,495	14	1	Printing office	2,578	0	10
Property	18,900			Salaries, misc. accrued	691	18	1
Copyright	14,197			Capital	39,479	19	2
Total	£80,509.10.0				£80,509.10.0		

What is significant about this welter of statistics is that while copyright valuation had not increased greatly since Alexander Blackwood's death, stock, printing office assets, and general property since accumulated now accounted for more than half the firm's value. More important, the capital available to the firm—the clear profit—had increased more than fivefold in thirty-four years, from £7,361 to £39,479. Even allowing for inflationary factors, the result is a clear statement of the role John Blackwood played in energizing and expanding the firm's lists and profitability during his tenure as director, validated in the manner in which this capital sum was subsequently divided between the two main partners of the firm: John Blackwood's estate received four-fifths (£34,043), while William Blackwood III held on to the remaining 20 percent stake (£5,436).

William Blackwood III had much to live up to when he dutifully took over management of the firm in 1879, and his path was not made smoother over the next three years by the retirement of key personnel and the death of various family members who might have contributed to its development. His solution to this loss of support, a solution that has remained hidden until now, is revealed in documents from 1913, when, following his demise, the counting men were once more dispatched to assess the value of the firm. This time, however, there was a hidden agenda to satisfy. In this case, sums were calculated and worth assigned in order to establish how much to pay off the silent member of a secret partnership that had run the firm between 1903 and 1910. Cataloged in the legal document subsequently produced is a detailed breakdown of the firm's assets and liabilities, with columns of profit and loss neatly recorded and balanced in order to arrive at the amount necessary to remove David Storrar Meldrum from the firm's directorship (Meldrum was the first non–Blackwood family member ever to be allowed such a role) and to return full control of the firm to family hands, in this case William's nephews George William and James Hugh Blackwood.[3] How Meldrum became such a privileged insider is a story that will be detailed later in this book. Why he was accorded privileges denied to earlier and equally valuable Blackwood employees, such as Joseph M. Langford (London office manager from 1845 to 1882) and George Simpson (Edinburgh office manager from 1842 to 1878), will also be discussed more fully in later chapters.

The 1913 legal document charting the end of this relationship reveals a story about the firm that is different from the story in the 1879 documents. Reading through the balance sheets, one sees distinct signs of financial slowdown and decline, evinced by the final evaluation of the firm's worth, which now stood at £67,783. As the balance sheet below shows, the firm's fortunes had peaked and, while not down to the provincial levels of publishing solvency seen in its accounts in 1845, the firm was decidedly in a spiral of decline that would be temporarily halted only through the intervention of the First World War.

Assets	£	s	d	Liabilities	£	s	d
Cash	132	0	11.25				
Bills receivable				Bills payable			
Amounts due	10,235	19	6	Amounts due	9,081	4	6.5
Amounts due per				Amounts due per			
cash ledger	617	0	8	cash ledger	41,664	13	3
Stocks	13,206	8	0	Accrued interest	316	7	11
Interest on				Printing office	471	11	0
partners a/c	376	6	2				
Property	24,285			Reserve a/c 1909	3,000		

				Undivided profit			
				1909	160	6	2
Copyright	11,374	9	7	Capital	10,000		
				Profit 1909–10	4,088	19	1/4
Total	£67,783.1.10 3/4			£67,783.1.10 3/4			

Copyright values had remained static over the period of William Blackwood III's direction, and a substantial proportion of the excess capital/profit recorded in 1913 came from reserves built up from past years. The capital and profits sum divided among the firm's beneficiaries (who now totaled four) was £17,249, half the equivalent sum dispensed in 1879. Once again, the division of the spoils reflected the shifting balance of power within the firm: William Blackwood's estate was accorded 40 percent of the capital (£6,899), while David Storrar Meldrum, George William, and James Hugh Blackwood each received 20 percent of the total (£3,449). Once the debt to Meldrum had been discharged, partnership in the firm was devolved equally upon James Hugh and George William, an arrangement that continued until the 1940s.

The information to be gleaned from such legal documents forms a small part of the new material uncovered for this work. This book is concerned with the firm's history before, during, and after the snapshot moments represented by the 1879 and 1913 inventories. More specifically, it focuses on the activities of the firm and its directors between 1860 and 1910, using unpublished archival material as well as information gained from a variety of published sources. It charts the firm's history from a point of preeminence in mid-nineteenth-century British publishing and cultural history through to a marginalized position as publisher of popular works for colonial and special service interests audiences at the start of the twentieth century.

Reasons for focusing on this period have as much to do with what past studies have included as with what they have left out. Work on Blackwood's has invariably focused either on its early history or on specific authors whose lives intersected with the Edinburgh firm. The literary history of the firm, and more particularly the careers of William Blackwood I, John Blackwood, and William Blackwood III, have provided background information for exploring the lives of such illustrious literary figures as John Wilson, Thomas DeQuincey, John Galt, George Eliot, Margaret Oliphant, and Joseph Conrad. Of less interest has been an analysis of the firm, its staff, and their publishing careers in unliterary contexts: of viewing them less as "handmaidens to literature" (a position adopted even in the firm's "house" histories) and more as individuals working within volatile and competitive business arenas, whose energies were directed as much at publishing financially remunerative prose and nonfiction texts—biographies, memoirs, catechisms, atlases, school primers, dictionaries, and so on—as it was in fostering the careers of literary geniuses. Similarly, scholarly interest in the firm's operations dissipates once it moves into the twilight years of the nineteenth century and away from the dominant literary culture of the period. Its retreat into niche marketing of popular novelists and a diet of colonialist-centered publications, and its complacency and seeming failure to adjust to changing tastes and markets, leaves little for those accustomed to the excitement of its earlier days. I hope to suggest otherwise in the chapters that follow.

The foundations of the firm were laid down by William Blackwood I at the turn of the nineteenth century, during a period of great change and development in the Scottish publishing and book trade. Blackwood and his contemporaries benefited from Edinburgh's long-standing reputation and tradition as a center for publishing and printing. Such eighteenth-century pioneeers as Allan Ramsay (initiator of the circulating library concept), Gavin Hamilton, William Creech (publisher of Robert Burns, Henry Mackenzie, Adam Ferguson, and the philosopher Dugald Stewart), and William Smellie (creator and publisher of the *Encyclopedia Britannica*), had in their time established Edinburgh as a potential rival to London as a source of important, well-printed books. The general diffusion of ideas in the late eighteenth century during what has been characterized as the Scottish Enlightenment, was in great part due to the access Scottish authors had to this efficient and localized print network that could generate and disseminate their texts on a wide scale.

The landmark decision in the English courts in 1774 of the trial of *Donaldson v. Becket*, which "established the statutory basis of copyright," as one study notes, and broke the stranglehold of London publishers on copyright and reprint privileges in Britain, led to a surge in Scottish publishing activity that built upon the successes of such Scots pioneers.[4] During the first quarter of the nineteenth century, new figures emerged whose publishing innovations transformed Edinburgh into the second literary city in Britain, a role diminished only by the fallout and subsequent reorganization and consolidation that followed the English stock market crash of 1826. Firms were founded in Edinburgh, Glasgow, London, and Cambridge by Scots whose lists were to dominate the nineteenth-century literary marketplace. Such figures as Archibald Constable (publisher of Walter Scott), Daniel Macmillan, Robert and William Chambers, and Thomas Nelson followed similar career paths and were motivated by similar desires (if one is to believe later house histories) rising from modest circumstances to become major players in British publishing.

William Blackwood I was no exception. The founder of the firm and its monthly *Blackwood's Magazine* was born in Edinburgh in 1776, the son of a silk merchant. At the age of fourteen he took his first steps into the book trade, beginning a six-year apprenticeship with the Edinburgh booksellers Bell & Bradfute, located on Parliament Square in the heart of the city. Such a start was standard practice for those with an interest in selling and publishing books for a living. Blackwood's near contemporary Archibald Constable, for example, began his career in 1788 apprenticed for six years to Edinburgh bookseller Peter Hill, former associate of William Creech and "highly respected," as Constable recalled, "as possessing gentlemanly manners beyond most others of the trade."[5] Likewise, those who followed afterward did not neglect such early training: William Chambers endured five years as an Edinburgh bookseller's apprentice before opening his own office near his brother Robert on Leith Walk in 1819, while the Arran-born Daniel Macmillan spent seven years apprenticed to an Irvine bookseller and bookbinder before moving on in 1831 to establish himself across the border in London and finally in Cambridge.

After completing his apprenticeship in 1796, William subsequently worked his way through other areas of the book trade, superintending the Glasgow branch of the Edinburgh publishers Mundell & Company for a year, serving as a partner with the antiquarian bookseller and auctioneer Robert Ross for another year, and completing his years of training in London in the antiquarian department of the booksellers Cuthill. In 1804 William returned to Edinburgh, opening a shop at 64 South Bridge, in front of the Old College quarters of the University of Edinburgh, where he specialized in selling and trading rare and antiquarian books. Its success allowed him the financial security to marry Janet Steuart in 1805, and they were to have nine children, including seven boys, of whom four were to play important roles in the future of the Blackwood firm.

By 1810 William had begun branching out into publishing, producing historical and religious works for Scottish markets. Movement beyond the regional became possible in 1811, when he was appointed the Edinburgh agent for the publisher John Murray, becoming an important link in the distribution of the latest works from London. The connection also allowed Blackwood a foothold in the London market, and he was to build on this in subsequent years. A further link was made in 1813, when William became the agent for James and John Ballantyne, printers of Walter Scott's novels. This arrangement paved the way in 1816 for Blackwood and John Murray to co-publish Walter Scott's *Tales of My Landlord*, comprising the novels *Old Mortality* and *Black Dwarf*. Blackwood's attempts to suggest improvements to Scott were not met with approval: "Tell him and his coadjutor," Scott is reported to have written to the printer James Ballantyne, "that I belong to the Black Hussars of Literature, who neither give nor receive criticism."[6] Scott's connection with the House of Blackwood was terminated soon afterward.

William decided to shift his business locations in 1816, taking the plunge into the New Town, a recent expansion by the city planners based on an architectural model and style designed by Robert Adams. Such a move, while it drew Blackwood away from the historical center of Edinburgh publishing around the High Street, allowed him more space for development. He established himself at 17 Princes Street and began concentrating his business on publishing. In April 1817 Blackwood started what was to become the flagship publication of his firm, having been approached earlier by James Cleghorn and Thomas Pringle to edit and produce a monthly journal under the title the *Edinburgh Monthly Magazine*. While general consensus has it that Blackwood envisaged creating a Tory alternative to his rival Archibald Constable's Whig orientated quarterly, the *Edinburgh Review*, recent scholarship suggests that in fact the magazine was originally directed to challenge the monthly *Scots Magazine*, also published by Constable. As Maurice Milne notes, the rival to the *Edinburgh Review* at the time was more clearly John Murray's Tory *Quarterly Review*, published in London. Murray's Scottish counterpart Blackwood saw his opportunity to attack Constable's dominant position in the periodical market from another angle, in this case moving in on the tottering *Scots Magazine*, whose sales and literary reputation were weak.[7] He contracted Pringle and Cleghorn to become editors of the new journal, paying them £50 a month and agreeing to divide with them any profits accruing from sales.

The first few issues, however, were anything but exciting. Terminating Pringle and Cleghorn's contracts after six months, Blackwood relaunched the journal in October 1817 as *Blackwood's Edinburgh Magazine*, with editorial input and contributions from members of his literary coterie, including John Gibson Lockhart, John Wilson ("Christopher North"), and James Hogg. The first few issues, with their attacks on local and national literary figures, their brand of personalized satire, and their blend of anonymously authored literature, politics, fiction, and poetry, established the reputation of the Blackwood firm. Lawsuits brought against the firm by those attacked added welcome publicity, but it also frightened off some of Blackwood's trade connections: both Baldwin, Cradock & Company (Blackwood's London agents) and Oliver & Boyd (Blackwood's printers) severed their connections with the firm based upon the furor caused by the new journal.

Bringing home the first number of his relaunched journal, William is said to have presented it to his wife with the words "There's ma Maga-zine." In affectionate parody, the journal became known to future generations of contributors and readers as "Maga." Maga's rising reputation and sales swiftly eclipsed the *Scots Magazine* while at the same time attracting competition from London. *The London Magazine*, for example, was begun in 1820 specifically in response to the journal. Blackwood, however, consolidated his initial success by using the journal to attract a core of well-placed writers to the firm. These included the Irishmen William Maginn and Samuel Ferguson, and the Scots John Galt, Douglas M. Moir ("Delta"), and Thomas DeQuincey. The magazine also featured occasional reviews by Walter Scott, fiction by Samuel Warren and Susan Ferrier, and work by Samuel Taylor Coleridge. Blackwood also began attracting commissions to publish other journals, such as the *Edinburgh Christian Monitor*, begun in 1818, and various legal, medical, and theological texts.

Maga was used both as a showcase for new talent and as a method of attracting potential contributors to the firm's book lists. A technique pioneered by Blackwood was the publication in book form of works first serialized in the magazine, predating Henry Colburn and Richard Bentley's use of such marketing strategies by several years. Works featured in this way included Susan Ferrier's *Marriage* (1818) and *Inheritance* (1824), John Galt's *Ayrshire Legatees* (1820–21), and Douglas M. Moir's *Autobiography of Mansie Wauch* (1824–28). At other times Maga was used to drum up interest in texts not yet realized, as in the sly case of John Gibson Lockhart's *Peter's Letters to His Kinfolk* (1819). In February 1819 there appeared in Maga a positive notice of this book, a collection of letters supposedly written by a Welsh doctor and published in Aberystwyth. The following month a Maga review heaped further praise upon it, going on to attack booksellers who had not yet stocked up on this virtuoso text. Needless to say, the work did not exist—not, that is, until it was brought out shortly afterward by Blackwood as a "second" (that is, first) edition due to "popular demand." Such a *jeu d'esprit*, while coming close to barefaced self-promotion, was an aspect of early experimentation in marketing by the firm that was refined in future years by other Blackwood directors.

Throughout the 1820s and early 1830s, Blackwood turned his small firm into a thriving concern, becoming one of the leading Scottish publishers of the period. His success allowed him to expand and move premises to 45 George Street in 1830. But his was still a firm yet to make the transition from regional dominance to national preeminence. On his death in 1834, his sons Alexander and Robert Blackwood took control of the business, with the aim of developing the national reach and reputation of their book lists and publications. Alexander concerned himself with the magazine and publishing and editorial matters. Throughout his short tenure, however, he was dogged with ill health, suffering from bouts of asthma and tuberculosis, complications from the latter of which were to kill him in March 1845. Robert concentrated on the firm's financial arrangements. One of Robert's legacies was the establishment of a London office in 17 Pall Mall in 1840, which he coordinated and then set the young John Blackwood to managing.

John Blackwood's entrance into the family business heralded a major shift in the fortunes of the firm. John Blackwood, the sixth son of William, was born on 7 December 1818 in Edinburgh. Educated in Edinburgh, on graduation from the University of Edinburgh in 1835, he undertook a three-year tour of continental Europe, spending much time in France and Germany. On his return in 1838, he followed family tradition by beginning an apprenticeship in the trade, in this case spending two years with the London publishers George Whitaker & Company. On the opening of the Blackwood office in London in December 1840, John was made a partner of the firm and London office manager. Over the next five years he established the firm's presence in the capital, making close personal connections with prominent authors (William Thackeray, Laurence Lockhart, Edward Bulwer-Lytton), politicians (Lord John Manners, Lord John Russell), and editors (John Delane, editor of the *Times*). Delane, with whom John shared lodgings for several years, was to prove an important contact. Through him Blackwood recruited a core group of contributors to Maga and the firm's lists, including Generals Edward Bruce and William Hamley, Frederick Hardman (French correspondent for *The Times*), George Finlay (Greek correspondent for *The Times*), and Laurence Oliphant, explorer and writer. These contacts in turn led to other sources, forming a vital cultural and information network for the firm.

In October 1845, seven months after Alexander Blackwood's death, when it was clear that Robert could no longer both edit the magazine and run the Edinburgh office all at once, John Blackwood returned to Edinburgh to take over as editor of *Blackwood's Magazine*, leaving Joseph Munt Langford to become London office manager. It was a defining moment for the young Blackwood that October when his older brother Robert, as John was to recall years later, "with a kindness and confidence which often fills me with wonder and always with gratitude, handed over the chief conduct of The Magazine to me."[8] He set about discharging his responsibilities with enthusiasm and vigor.

The firm moved in 1850 to larger London offices in Paternoster Row, the burgeoning center of publishing activity in the city. In 1852, on the death of Robert Blackwood, John assumed full control of the firm, working in partnership with his brother Major William Blackwood II, who had returned from India in 1848 to help manage financial matters. Following William Blackwood II's death from pneumonia in 1861, the firm was reorganized, and William's son William Blackwood III, who had entered the family business in 1857, was elevated to co-partner. John also established a four-strong managerial team, with the participation of William, London Office Manager Joseph Munt Langford, and the Edinburgh Office Manager George Simpson. Between them, they strengthened the firm's lists, scouted for new publishing opportunities, and established Maga at the forefront of mid-Victorian literary production.

Under John Blackwood's energetic guidance, the firm experienced unprecedented growth and success. On the literary side, publishing successes included works by Edward Bulwer-Lytton, Charles Lever, Charles Reade, Richard D. Blackmore, Margaret Oliphant, George Henry Lewes, and all but one of George Eliot's novels. Anthony Trollope, seeking a place for experimental work, anonymously serialized *Nina Balatka* (1867) and *Linda Tressel* (1868) in *Blackwood's Magazine*, then authorized their reprints. Blackwood paid £450 for the copyright of each but failed to realize profit from either. It did not prevent Trollope's family from returning to Blackwood's in 1882 to publish Trollope's autobiography.

John Blackwood also strengthened the firm's identification with accounts of travel and exploration. James Augustus Grant's and John Hanning Speke's narratives of searching for the Nile river source in Africa, for example (the latter of which will be discussed in more detail in a later chapter), were best-sellers for the firm in 1864 and 1865. Between 1852 and 1879 the firm published both in *Blackwood's Magazine* and as separate publications work by Frederick Hardman on Africa, Richard Burton on India and East Africa, Sir Henry Brackenbury on the Ashanti Wars in South Africa, Sir Garnet Wolseley on expeditions in Canada and Egypt, and Laurence Oliphant on Japan and the Crimea.

On John Blackwood's death in 1879, the task of running the firm devolved to William Blackwood III. Over the next two decades the firm drifted, maintaining a holding pattern of print production that kept itself focused on areas of known profitability. Colonial memoirs, biographies, popular fiction, and endless reprints of George Eliot works in proven formats proved unchallenging in nature but profitable in execution. The entrance of David Storrar Meldrum as literary advisor in 1894, however, while not necessarily increasing the firm's profit margins, did go some way toward reviving the firm's literary lists. His literary judgment influenced William's decision to publish Stephen Crane, Henry Lawson, Miles Franklin, John Buchan, and Jack London. More significant, it was Meldrum who led Blackwood to encourage and publish Joseph Conrad. *Blackwood's Magazine* was to feature some of Conrad's best-known works, including *Lord Jim* and *Heart of Darkness*.

In 1903 Meldrum, as noted earlier, was made a partner of the firm, sharing responsibilities with William's nephews James Hugh and George Blackwood. By 1910 William had handed over much of the daily management to his nephews, due to ill health. Internal politics caused Meldrum to leave to become editor of *The Morning Post*. William died in 1912, leaving a diminished firm in his wake. Ironically, it would take a world war to raise the firm's fortunes once more to levels commensurate with those enjoyed under John Blackwood.

Given the richness of company documents contained within the archives of the National Library of Scotland, it is surprising how few attempts have been made to discuss the firm's general history beyond the 1880s, to view its role in early twentieth-century literature and business markets, and to establish its place in Victorian and Edwardian British cultural history. Only two works in the past century have been published regarding the firm's general publishing endeavours, Margaret Oliphant and Mary Porter's three-volume study in 1897–98, and Frank Tredrey's house history in 1954. Both suffer from the problems inherent in commissioned works: as hagiographical commemorations of the firm's activities, controversial incidents are glossed over, blame is shifted, and, in some cases, business matters and letter contents are censored and suppressed. Ultimately, both fail to present a balanced account of the sometimes rocky relationship between the firm, its published authors, and the publishing industry at large. And while both studies benefited from access to confidential papers and correspondence, they have since been superseded by the amount of information and records on the firm, unknown or lost at the time, that have accumulated and been made available as the Blackwood Papers at the National Library of Scotland.

Working through these papers makes one aware of the vast array of material that has remained overlooked or untouched regarding the firm's role in late Victorian and Edwardian publishing, political, and cultural history. This is perhaps a natural by-product of the manner in which the archives have been used; much of the work done on the Blackwood firm has centered on investigating individual relationships with authors, either as part of larger life studies or in connection with particular literary circles. Such author-centered focus is inevitable, given the sheer amount of primary material available on the firm. Seldom discussed is the manner in which such relations fit in with the firm's general underlying aesthetic and economic considerations of the literary marketplace. Likewise, little attention is paid to the history of the firm after its links with Joseph Conrad at the turn of the twentieth century, in part because of the universal understanding that by then the firm had begun its long slide into cultural obscurity.

The decay in the firm's fortunes after the successful directorship of John Blackwood can be partly ascribed to the firm's strengthened identification from 1880 onward with entrenched conservative viewpoints on literature, society, the military, and the British Empire. Viewed in such a context, the firm's rejection of unorthodox, "liberal" authors, such as George Bernard Shaw, Robert Louis Stevenson, H. G. Wells, and Thomas Hardy, can be seen as a rejection of writers who did not fit in with the firm's prevailing ideological and literary stance, a stance that was increasingly at odds with concurrent shifts and changes in British politics and literary and aesthetic concerns.

Yet these decisions that inform editorial and business policy at 45 George Street in Edinburgh and 37 Paternoster Row in London between 1860 and 1910 make little sense unless read within the context of the tumultuous and radical changes simultaneously occurring in the British literary marketplace. As Simon Eliot points out in his survey of trends in British publishing from 1800 to 1919, major technological advances occurred in the 1880s and 1890s with an expansion in paper production and the development of higher printing capacity utilizing large, web-fed rotaries and newly developed hot-metal typesetting machines.[9] Other changes included the rapid development of a wide variety of cheap publishing formats and reprints following the decline and collapse of the three-decker novel in 1894; the rapid growth of public libraries; the development of the new journalism and the mass circulation daily papers of the 1890s; the expansion of overseas syndication markets in the Empire, North America, and Europe, particularly after the passing of international copyright agreements (the Berne Convention of 1887) and less-comprehensive agreements in the United States (the Chace Act of 1891); the creation of controlled and stable book pricing through the Net Book Agreement in 1899; and the rise of new publishing firms, such as Methuen and Chatto & Windus, labeled by N. N. Feltes as "entrepreneurial" publishers, utilizing publishing practices to challenge and compete against older, more traditional "list" publishers, such as Blackwood's, Bentley, Smith & Elder, and John Murray.[10]

The establishment of associations to represent the professional interests of various sectors of the trade, such as the Society of Authors in 1884, the Booksellers Association in 1895, and the Publishers Association in 1896, also illustrated how far the business of bookselling, publishing, and literary authorship had come since the eighteenth century, when a bookseller, acting also a publisher, could "buy most Books for a Bottle and a fowl."[11] Literary production was no longer, if ever it had been, the mythologized, casual, aesthetically informed pursuit of dedicated "gentlemen" and "gentlewomen," but had become part of a highly organized and commercial system.

Thus, at the turn of the century, literary publishing was in flux, caught in the contradiction and conflict between, on the one hand, a perceived reliance on publishing "flair," aesthetic judgment ("good" literature that would nevertheless sell well), and predictable publishing patterns, prices, and book formats (exemplified by the serialized novel in literary magazines then being issued as a standard three-volume first edition followed by a cheaper 1 volume reprint), and, on the other hand, new market forces, rewarding entrepreneurial skills and emphasizing economic competitiveness, with an accompanying cross-merchandising of literary works in a variety of cheaper book formats and publication outlets (serialization in literary magazines and the popular press, syndication in colonial and overseas markets, sales to newly developing film and radio industries). The bewildering range of new outlets for marketing literary property was often beyond the average capacity of publishers used to negotiating on relatively uncomplicated publishing terms.

Whereas in the 1860s most deals negotiated by John Blackwood were fairly uncomplicated, involving first edition, reprint, and possibly serialized periodical rights, by the turn of the century matters were becoming more complicated for his successor William Blackwood III. The insertion of the literary agent as negotiator of literary property became an added factor within the publishing arena, as did the emergence of foreign markets and foreign rights as major sources of income. Such issues play their part in the evolving story of the Blackwood firm during the fifty years chronicled in this study.

Lest this book seem to be solely about facts and figures, dry-as-dust statistics, and rigid economic notations, it is important to note that one of the main themes of this survey is to place the firm, its books, and its authors within appropriate social and cultural contexts. This is not a work concerned solely with the processes of publishing and print production, but rather an attempt to follow through on the implications of studying book history in the wake of recent, dynamic methods of theoretical analysis. Robert Darnton's overworked "communication circuit," first mooted in 1984 and since modified by others, brought into Anglo-American book history circles a theoretical stance borrowed from social science models, and is one example of informed and alternative ways of discussing textual production that reach beyond mere bibliographical categorizations and statistical enumeration. It is an often unobserved point that this recent move toward more complex analyses of the modes of production, dissemination, and reception of texts is not confined to book history alone. Cultural materialism, the study of social transactions represented in the complex and interweaving connections between producers and consumers of commodities in an industrialized society, is now a common theme explored by critics in cultural studies, media studies, history, literary studies, and the social sciences, among others. It can be found in sociology in Pierre Bourdieu's articulation of literary "fields" as common social, intellectual, and ideological arenas linking producers (publishers, editors, and authors) to products (books, periodical publications, literary works), or in the anthropologist Benedict Anderson's important articulation of print as an important form through which "imagined communities" construct common national identities. Turn to literary studies and we find an allied articulation by Stanley Fish of the readers of these products, "interpretive communities" joined through common understanding and interpretations of texts, while media studies has leaned heavily on variations of Jürgen Habermas's articulation of the "public sphere" as the major arena for the construction of public opinion. The consensus is quite clear: the process of producing print for public consumption, whether books or journal, newspaper or periodical publications, can no longer be viewed simply as a linear path from producer (author) to disseminator (editor, publisher, printer, bookseller) to consumer (reader). Rather, as Stuart Hall notes in a now classic study of the popular press, such textual productions are "products of a social transaction between producers and readers," whereby "successful communication in this field depends to some degree on a process of mutual confirmation between those who produce and those who consume."[12]

The implications of such a statement for print-culture analysis has been followed through by such critics as Richard Ohmann and Matthew Schneirov, who have examined the communities of authors, editors, and readers of specific nineteenth-century U.S. journals, with the aim of illustrating how such cultural commodities can be read as "a product of human action or agency within certain structural contexts and as a cultural form or 'object.'"[13] It is all part of a healthy interdisciplinarity that seeks a closer understanding of the role of culture and society in the shaping of print. As one media studies critic suggests, urging his colleagues to pay closer attention to the intersections between cultural materialism, literary theory, and media culture, "One should not, however, stop at the borders of intertextuality, but should move from the text to its context, to the culture and society that constitutes the text and in which it should be read and interpreted."[14]

Such is the theme of several "micro-chapters" in this study, relating the manner in which social and cultural factors feed into the process of production, dissemination, and reception of individual works. In the case of Charles Reade and his novel *A Woman Hater*, for example, contemporary battles over the issue of women's rights to medical education are reflected in similar editorial battles over the novel's contents. Likewise, John Hill Burton's crucial role as unacknowledged ghostwriter of the travel diaries of the African explorer John Hanning Speke illustrates the manner in which editorial decisions and cultural assumptions and judgments inserted during the production process can substantially alter textual meanings and textual production. More important, it illustrates how a literarily inarticulate traveler, through the services of an unacknowledged "ghostwriter," was "reinvented" as an articulate, saleable commodity, with the purpose not only of safeguarding a commercial investment but also of promulgating certain views and conceptions about the role of the European explorer in the African landscape. Both these chapters illustrate the interplay of economic, social, and ideological forces in the production of texts, the process of cultural colonization and the dissemination of its conclusions in Victorian society, and the general and intentional exclusion of women from the power structures involved in these processes and productions.

At the same time, though, I offer a macroscopic view, illustrating how these individual efforts fit within larger cultural and "house" contexts, considering how the firm set about creating a distinctive identity for itself within national and international boundaries, and noting how authors and readers were subsequently invited into this invisible Blackwoodian "community" or "ecumene." To return to Stuart Hall's statement on texts as products of a social transaction between producers and readers, one sees this reflected in the firm's determination to foster unique "communities" of readers and authors at various stages in its history.

The House of Blackwood, the title of the 1954 official history of the firm, illustrates several unspoken assumptions about this issue of how the firm saw itself as a creator of unique intellectual, social, and work communities and spaces. The House functioned as a tightly run, male-dominated space, yet also suggested itself to prospective authors, both male and female, as an open, welcoming, and inclusive club of sorts. It was run on paternalistic lines, with clearly defined roles, structures of command, and subdivisions of tasks and space one might consider typical of any proper nineteenth-century bourgeois household. For example, something not often noted is how the firm's headquarters in Edinburgh was divided spatially in a manner that reflected hierarchies of value. Following the move in 1830 to premises on 45 George Street, the firm relocated its printing works to a large building on Thistle Street immediately behind its George Street premise. A small lane separated these two sections of the firm, and edited works for printing would be walked across this divide to the printing office, to be wheeled back in barrows as finished products for display and sale in the firm's imposing shop front framing the George Street entrance.

The firm's official house histories contain clear expressions of value and worth regarding these spaces: between areas of production and dissemination; between the loud, crowded, and busy spaces where print was cast, sheets printed, and folios bound, and the quiet, bay-windowed room where the finished products were displayed and sold. Although the printing office is not often glimpsed in these formulaic pronouncements of publishing reminiscence, it served as an important if unacknowledged arena where print was treated not as an individualized, aesthetic product but as part of a mechanized production process where individual texts were just one of many print runs to be completed within a workday. It is a decidedly unaesthetic aspect of publishing and literary production that runs against the grain of many declarations of the aesthetic nature and purpose of print production that are so evident in memoirs of former practitioners in the field, and most particularly in the Blackwood house histories.

But if the printing office was viewed as the equivalent of the "tradesman" or back entrance of a venerable publishing house, a needed if less-respectable part of the business, the editorial office was decidedly more esteemed: the glamorous front parlor. Indeed, at times it is *the* House itself. Admittedly, it was not common for firms to have both the printing and the publishing arms of the business within easy walking distance of each other; in fact, firms often had to subcontract the dirty business of actual print production to other specialist printing firms. Blackwood's, however, contained within its House all the necessary elements of a solid book-trading firm, including printing works, editorial offices, and sales outlets (that is, shopfronts in which to display and offer the latest wares).

Nevertheless, the editorial side of the firm was very much at the forefront of the House of Blackwood self-image. It represented a specific social space as well, an invisible arena that accommodated shifting bands of contributors and authors who were encouraged to meet and mingle, imbibe a common "culture," and share common, unspoken assumptions about their identities within this large, all-embracing Blackwoodian ecumene. And, as one finds when working through the Blackwood archives, the most fascinating details of this ecumene at work are often discovered only when one shifts focus away from the micro-details of letters between the Blackwoods and an individual author toward the range of and ranges across archival material to see how other "Blackwoodian" contributors were drawn into debating about, commenting on, and in many cases (as, for example, in the recasting of John Hanning Speke's work) actively shaping texts emerging under the firm's imprint, either as book publications or as part of the firm's monthly journal, *Blackwood's Magazine*.

How, then, does one reconcile the opposition between the assumed hierarchies of value with respect to the function and activities of a firm, and the realities encountered when analyzing the work space and patterns of such places? A particularly intriguing answer may be found by taking up points developed in Janice Radway's analysis of the workings of the U.S. Book-of-the-Month Club from the 1920s onward. Noting how the firm created a unique identity and role for itself as a mediator, arbiter, and filter of literary production by creating an internal panel of "expert" judges to read texts for subsequent recommendation and sale to club members, she makes a telling point about their evaluative methods: "The key moves in the evaluative practices of the Book-of-the-Month-Club judges," Radway notes, "was not judgment at all, but rather the activity of categorization, that of sorting onto different planes."[15] Viewing the world of print in this way, not as an organic, uniform, hierarchically organized space but as "a series of discontinuous, discrete, noncongruent worlds," or planes, Radway continues, establishes a link between producer (author) and consumer (reader) whereby the disseminator, in this case the U.S.-originated Book-of-the-Month Club, with its built-in filters of judges categorizing titles rather than providing aesthetic judgments of books, becomes less an arbiter of worth and more a literary manager of textual production.[16] And in many cases, different arenas or planes of textual production, whether it be how-to manuals, atlases, science textbooks, biographies, or novels, quite openly operate on differing planes of meaning, meeting the needs of different audiences with discrete and technically distinct codes, structures, and formats. The Book-of-the-Month Club, begun as a purely commercial proposition, established an overarching identity for itself as a nonjudgmental yet trusted provider of quality texts in a variety of subject areas, operating simultaneously on different textual planes and in various arenas.

This principle has potential for a review of the manner in which publishing houses in general, and the House of Blackwood in particular, can be seen to operate. On the one hand, one sees in perusing the entirety of the firm's lists—the manuals of zoology as well as the consciously literary novels—that contained within such publication lists are separate layers, levels, and planes of textual production and operations. Rules for engaging with such texts change and shift with each sector under consideration. Yet the fact that most analysis of publishing production has focused on the literary and aesthetic planes of textual production has resulted in obscuring the manner in which such levels coexist simultaneously with less-recognized or less-valued printed material. Thus the print works, ironically, can be seen as democratized spaces where such planes become indistinguishable, coexisting in an unhierarchized fashion.

Similarly, as they are being produced in unhierarchized yet united fashion in the print room (using the same machinery operated by the same groupings of individuals), the products of these differing planes are subsequently categorized (fiction, biography, nonfiction, reference) and then sold and marketed under a unified "house" imprint that attempts to impose an overarching identity on products emanating from this source. Publishers act as filters and managers of literary production in a complex network of activity between production, dissemination, and consumption. Criteria used and judgments made by them shift according to areas evaluated, but what is clear when one views a publishing firm like Blackwood's holistically is that the goals remain the same: to maintain a continual flow of products that on the average are commercially viable and financially successful.

One might argue that this concept of the plane could just as well mean that there would be different genres, markets, and marketing strategies for selling books. But I suggest that it extends further back, beyond target audiences and recipients of textual production, to encompass the producers and disseminators of such works, for each plane within a publishing house might have its own distinct identity and core personnel whose value is conceived in different form from other planes of operation. Thus assessments and evaluations of reference works and their authors' abilities might revolve around questions of authority and expertise (Is the author sufficiently knowledgeable to discuss the topic? Is the work authoritative in coverage?), whereas evaluations in the plane of literary fiction might revolve around questions of aesthetics and taste (Is the work "literary enough"? Does this author conform to perceived standards of "taste"?). Contained within this scenario is the editorial prerogative to mold potential material into a form that suits the codes and structures expected in these planes.

It is in these points of tension and contact that we can see most clearly the formation of a "house identity" and establish the manner in which such an identity is imposed upon texts in different arenas. Likewise, as the chapters on Reade, Speke, and Oliphant show, such moments of production have much to say about the intersection of aesthetic values and commercial interests, about the battles between authorial intention and editorial intervention. Some of the questions that are dealt with in subsequent chapters have come from looking at the troubled productions of these and other works, questions such as: What is an ideal "Blackwoodian" text within differing genres and planes? How does the firm set about ensuring complicity and acceptance of such standards? And do these individual and differing planes ultimately combine to create a unique and identifiable "house" identity? The following chapters suggest some answers to these questions.

Finding Success

Blackwood's, 1860–1879

The 1860s and 1870s marked a period of unprecedented growth for the Blackwood firm. During these decades significant works were secured whose enduring profitability was to sustain the firm for years to come. It was also a period of personal and entrepreneurial losses and rewards, publishing rivalries and poaching activity, and threats and challenges from various points in the publishing enterprise (ranging from copyright matters to distribution networks). How the firm met these challenges, what distinguished its activities during this period of rapid growth and social change, and how it prospered under the direction of John Blackwood until his death in 1879 are the main issues of this chapter.

Since 1850, following the retirement of Robert Blackwood from active partnership in the firm, the two family members charged with directing William Blackwood & Sons had been John Blackwood and his brother Major William Blackwood II. John had concerned himself with literary and editorial activities, editing *Blackwood's Magazine*, recruiting new authors and retaining old ones, publicising the firm's products, and directing the flow and direction of publications. William, on the other hand, had focused on financial matters, keeping a watchful eye over cash flow and ratios of income versus expenditure. His death in April 1861 from pneumonia caused a fundamental reappraisal and reapportioning of roles within the firm's managerial structure. William Blackwood III, the twenty-five-year-old son of Major Blackwood who had entered the firm in 1857, was elevated to co-partner in early 1862 and alternated with John in shuttling between London and Edinburgh to represent firm interests at its offices in 37 Paternoster Row and 45 George Street respectively. In London they would join Joseph Munt Langford, who five years after arriving at the firm in 1840 had become the London office manager, charged with overseeing the practical elements of the firm's activities in the capital. Langford's Edinburgh equivalent was George Simpson, who since 1842 had run the Edinburgh office. Simpson's and Langford's roles were, as Simpson put it to John Blackwood, that of "confidential clerk and overseer of your extensive business."[1]

The four of them in effect formed a quadrumvirate, participating in general discussions, directions, and decisions on what the firm accepted and published, on occasion joined by the chief proofreader John "Crumie" Brown (until his death in March 1877).[2] Over the next twenty years, almost daily letters flowed between the London and Edinburgh offices, offering exemplary chronicles of debate, consultation, and decision-making between the four. Such rich documentation of the daily thought processes behind publishing activity is unique among the archives of the nineteenth-century British publishing giants that survive to this day. And while the Blackwood correspondence has on occasion been mined for studies of individual authors, such as George Eliot, Anthony Trollope, and Joseph Conrad, it has not been examined until now for general trends and patterns, nor for what it reveals of the dynamics between the four main players behind the success of Blackwood's in the mid-century. Later chapters give specific examples of how this flow of communication informed decisions on publishing strategies and activities.

But relations among the top management were not always smooth. In 1863 John Brown, with more than thirty years of service at the firm as their chief proofreader, submitted his resignation because of disgruntlement at inadequate compensation and promotion in rank. "After these thirty-three years of service," he wrote John Blackwood, "I find myself, in a pecuniary point of view, in a much worse position than any ordinary clerk of anything like the same standing, in a House of such status as the Messrs. Blackwood's."[3] Only after John Blackwood quickly raised his salary by £25 to £250 per annum was he persuaded to stay on;

Brown eventually died "in harness," as it were, fourteen years later.[4] Similarly, letters from George Simpson at crucial points in 1850 and 1878 reveal chafing at the clear divisions in rank and value underpinning divisions of labor in the firm, undercutting Margaret Oliphant's assessment in the *Annals of a Publishing House* that the firm had chosen shrewdly in appointing two confirmed bachelors (Langford and Simpson) who, because their lives were wrapped up in servicing and supporting the aims of the firm, were thus devoid of personal ambition.[5]

While Langford and Simpson were highly rewarded for their services, they were excluded at critical moments from becoming official partners in the publishing enterprise, despite seeking such promotion. George Simpson's request to become a partner in March 1850, during turbulence and transition caused by Robert Blackwood's gradual retiring from publishing activity, was met with a response from John Blackwood that characterized the firm's strong-handed, paternalistic, and family-based approach to publishing until the end of the century. "There are difficulties in the way of any new partner being admitted to the firm," John wrote, "and I tell you at once that irrespective of these, which are for aught I know insuperable, I entertain the most decided objections to the adoption of any one not a member of my father's family into the firm which bears his name."[6]

Such strong conviction represented a standard nineteenth-century approach to family-led businesses, whereby succeeding generations were groomed for entry into the family establishment, and talented outsiders were incorporated but denied official status. That such strategies had become embedded in the operating structure of the Blackwood firm within a half-century of its founding by William Blackwood I was a direct result of the strengths, energies, and capabilities of the individuals who had led the firm to that point, subsequently represented in particular by the entrepreneurial John Blackwood. Such family independence was to prove problematic, however, when less capable and less enthusiastic family members were brought on board after John's death, a matter to be discussed in a later chapter.

Simpson was not to raise the issue of promotion again until 1878, when he had amassed enough capital to announce his retirement, making clear that his decision was due mainly to the failure to promote and confer upon him the benefits of a partnership in the firm.[7] In 1882 his close friend Joseph Langford followed suit, retiring to a life of travel and theater-going until his death in 1884. Future Blackwood family directors would be less averse to appointing non-Blackwood individuals as partners (Chapter 5). Lest we lose sight of the value of their service to the firm in the years intervening, it is important to note that Langford and Simpson, along with the two Blackwoods, formed what might be called an "ecumene"of decision makers, with the freedom to criticize, comment, and deliberate over how best to operate and profit from the production and sale of texts, both literary and nonliterary. All operated within overlapping as well as individually specialized public and private social spheres, utilizing personal contacts to acquire important political and social sources of information, and to scout out new material and cultivate relations with authors and potential suppliers of material for use in *Blackwood's Magazine* or in book form. Thus John Blackwood's personal friendship with John T. Delane, editor of *The Times*, allowed him access to a network of establishment figures sympathetic to the Conservative causes governing his choice of political material published under the firm's imprimatur[8] (for example, biographies and works by Lord John Manners, Conservative leader; W. H. Smith, M.P.; and Lord Brabourne).

Similarly there was Langford's connections with London's literary and theatrical networks: his membership in the Garrick Club helped in the cultivation and subsequent publication by Blackwood's of Charles Reade, Anthony Trollope, and R. D. Blackmore. Even Simpson, office management specialist though he was, played a role in connecting Blackwood's to external networks. His links, for example, with the Church of Scotland helped secure the contract to publish hymnals for use in church services throughout Scotland from 1864 on. (Profits from sales of hymnals between 1868 and 1896 totaled £26,895, making hymnals enduring and profitable titles in the firm's backlist.) Such intersecting networks are found throughout the firm's history, tapped and utilized with varying degrees of success for the production, dissemination, and consumption of "Blackwoodian" commodities.

Authors, Publishers, and the Literary Marketplace

It is impossible to undertake a comprehensive survey of all Blackwood author-publisher links during the twenty-year history in question in this chapter. However, the following small samplings are aimed at (1) illustrating a variety of "Blackwoodian" responses to the problematic matter of intersecting and conflicting author-publisher interests and (2) bringing to bear on these issues the concept of differing "planes" articulated by Janice Radway and discussed in the introductory chapter. How were authors and their products viewed and dealt with, and were there differing responses according to the different arenas inhabited by these texts (that is, history versus fiction, prose versus travel work)?

The Blackwood firm was no different from other major British publishers who flourished in mid-century (such as John Murray, Smith, Elder & Co., and Macmillan) in believing that the publisher, not the author, was the most appropriate individual to set the value, price, and form of a text for public consumption. John Blackwood's testimony to the 1876 Royal Commission on Copyright, chaired by Lord John Manners and including Anthony Trollope on the examining panel, is instructive in this respect. Asked whether abolishing circulating libraries might offer more rewards for author and publisher while at the same time lowering book prices and encouraging the public to purchase more books, Blackwood responded by linking author and publisher in a common business enterprise. "The business both of authors and of publishers," he argued, "is to consult and please the public and we will adapt ourselves to any case which arises to the best of our ability; but as to the price at which to sell a book the circumstances guide us, and no legislation would work any change in what is merely a business operation."[9] In saying this, Blackwood subtly conflated publisher-author interests ("We will adapt ourselves") so as to appear to represent both parties in publishing decisions that in reality were almost always made by the publisher. Equally implicit was the view that although writing texts was the province of the author, determining its value in the public marketplace was a business operation best left in Blackwood's hands and not meddled in by such committees.

Likewise, a key point made early in his testimony was an acknowledgment of the need to maximize profits through issuing texts in as many different forms as possible. On a question of whether an extension of copyright would keep book prices artificially high, Blackwood responded with the following: "My own feeling is that the extension would not reasonably affect it, because every publisher now is aware from actual experience that in order to reap the full benefit of a book, he must work it in a very cheap form as well as in an expensive one and I think that the old objection about the high price of a book is in real effect done away with."[10] "Working" a book, much like one would "work" a horse in the fields or on the roads to gain the most from it, offers an uncommonly honest view of textual production—in this case not as an aesthetic product, but as a commercial proposition requiring directing and use in as many forms as possible.

At the same time, John Blackwood and his co-respondents in the publishing enterprise took pride in affirming their dedication to the nurturing of "genius" and to establishing personal relationships with "their" authors. Often remarked upon by past critics is the sense that John Blackwood operated with a distinct code against which he measured potential authors. This code was aimed at achieving a balance of individuals to form cohesive networks, of creating interacting and linked "Blackwoodian" ecumenes. He, and his nephew William Blackwood III in turn, operated on a distinctly personal level, attempting to bind authors to the firm through personal contact and an invitation to join the invisible Blackwood community they saw themselves creating.

Whenever possible, introductions were provided and opportunities were created by John Blackwood and William Blackwood III to link individuals together. When Charles Lever's "Cornelius O'Dowd" series began its eight-year run in *Blackwood's Magazine* in late 1864, Alexander W. Kinglake requested Lever's address so that he might "take the opportunity of expressing to him his admiration for his genius and writing."[11] On his next visit to London, in May 1865, John Blackwood deliberately invited Kinglake and Lever to dine together with him at the Burlington Hotel, thus providing the beginning for what became a close friendship between the two authors. Similar introductions for Lever were made to E. B. Hamley and Laurence Oliphant, members of what F. D. Tredrey called the Blackwood's "military staff."[12] (Others in this network included two other Hamley brothers [Charles and William], Laurence Lockhart, Charles and George Chesney, G. R. Gleig, and General Sir Archibald Alison.) The Blackwood Papers contain innumerable examples of similar attempts to link authors under a common Blackwoodian bond.

Those who chose to join the House of Blackwood in turn provided conduits to new recruits. An example of the role other individuals could play on behalf of the Blackwood firm in these intangible networks of alliances is that of Laurence Oliphant (1829–88)—traveler, politician, mystic, spy, and author. Oliphant's role in linking Blackwood's to authors of literary, political, and social importance is significant.[13] It was he who steered mid-century African explorers such as John Hanning Speke, John Petherick and Samuel Baker (whose works played a major part in shaping Victorian British conceptions of "the dark continent") away from publishing rivals (such as John Murray) to Blackwood's door. (But despite a strong introduction from Oliphant, John Blackwood let slip the opportunity to publish Henry Morton Stanley's best-seller *How I Found Livingstone* in 1872.)[14] It is also Oliphant who convinced John Blackwood in August 1862 to invest in what would become one of the most enduring publishing successes of the firm—Alexander W. Kinglake's *History of the Crimea*.

The words that John Blackwood used most frequently to sum up this approach to author-publisher relations were "confidence" and "friendship." John, reflecting on a quarter-century of activity as a publisher, was recorded by the *Edinburgh Evening Courant* announcing the following at a Scott centenary dinner in 1871: "That these years had sped happily and prosperously with him he owed . . . above all, to the unlimited confidence and unfailing friendship he had been privileged to enjoy with a succession of authors second to none in this country."[15] To offer intangible assets like these was the key strategy of Blackwood's publishing relations with such authors as Charles Lever, Edward Bulwer-Lytton, Alexander W. Kinglake, and George Eliot. (But not all wanted these benefits without an attendant fair valuation of their literary worth, as will be seen shortly.)

This is not to say that material concerns did not play a part in evaluating texts for publication. John Blackwood's decisions, as noted in other sections of this book, were firmly based on gauging textual worth and literary commodity value. Blackwood made it a rule never to accept work he had not read first, whether it was an entire manuscript or a substantial portion of one. On the few occasions when he bent this rule, it was usually because of external market forces and factors, such as the author's reputation and commercial potential, that required swift action to secure, or because rival publishers were making bids that required vigorous counterresponses. This can be seen when we examine the case of Alexander W. Kinglake.

The story of Kinglake and Blackwood is instructive for several reasons, not least as a response to publishing rivalry and poaching in which major British firms engaged assiduously during the latter half of the nineteenth century. It is a story that has been misleadingly recounted in the firm's official histories, and the circumstances of Kinglake's securing for Blackwoods provides an interesting counterresponse to a more famous case of "poaching" of which the firm was victim just months before Kinglake's entrance.

Much has already been written about the firm's connection with George Eliot: of how G. H. Lewes introduced the work of the anonymous "friend" to John Blackwood in 1856; how *Blackwood's Magazine* featured the first stories by George Eliot, later published in 1858 as *Scenes of Clerical Life*; how personal relations grew; and how financial arrangements for subsequent works were negotiated over the years between the publisher, G. H. Lewes, and George Eliot.[16] Following the success of *Adam Bede* in 1859 and *The Mill on the Floss* in 1860, John Blackwood was quick to realize the importance of Eliot's work, both on an aesthetic level and as a major financial asset to the firm. He closely monitored and offered support for Eliot's next major work, which she worked on between 1860 and 1863, anticipating that she would turn to him as her publisher to issue it on its completion. On 20 May 1862, however, John Blackwood received news from George Eliot that in fact her new work, *Romola*, was to be published by someone else. Days later he learned it had been poached by George Smith of Smith, Elder & Co., who G. H. Lewes records in his diary initially offered £10,000 for the entire copyright and publication of *Romola* as a serial in the *Cornhill Magazine* and as a separate book publication.[17] In the end Eliot received £7,000 for publication in twelve monthly parts and as a separate book publication, with the copyright retained by Smith for six years.

Both London and Edinburgh members of the Blackwood quadrumvirate greeted the news of this defection with dismay. Langford, not the most sanguine of individuals in the best of times, waxed indignant over the gall of Smith in subsequently seeking to insert a handbill in *Blackwood's Magazine* advertising his prize acquisition: "They are sending a bill for Maga to which in the first flint of temper I thought you should refuse insertion, but it would certainly be more dignified to insert it."[18] He concluded, "I shall have an opportunity of talking over with you this disgusting transaction, which certainly does not surprise me on her part, but does on the part of Mr. Smith."[19]

William Blackwood "scarce thought it possible," as he wrote John on 24 May 1862, "after the confidence you had all along placed in her & the very generous treatment she had received from you and my good father."[20] He also reported that George Simpson and John Brown were so angry they were "almost incapable of any work today."[21] John Blackwood reacted more calmly to the news. For him the difficulty was not that she had chosen another publishing house but that she had not given him first refusal of the work, a right he felt was owed him as her main publisher. Hence his response to Langford: "The going over to the enemy without giving me any warning and with a story on which from what they both said I was fully entitled to calculate upon, sticks in my throat but I shall not quarrel—quarrels, especially literary ones, are vulgar."[22] More to the point, it also reflected disappointment at what he felt had been a betrayal of his confidence, a turning away from the intangible assets his House offered authors (the Blackwoodian circle) in favor of less-aesthetically motivated but more tangible assets: cash and financial security.

Kinglake's entrance must be measured against this loss, for what has remained ignored until now is the fact that John Blackwood, while couching the event in different terms, in essence gained Kinglake from John Murray, original publisher of Kinglake's best-selling work *Eothen*. Murray was to return the compliment with a bid to secure publication of the diary of the African explorer John Hanning Speke on his return to Britain in 1863. Murray's attempt to lure away a "Blackwoodian" author occasioned snorts of indignation from Paternoster Row and George Street but was responded to with a higher offer to Speke than originally contemplated (a matter discussed more fully in a later chapter).

Although the negotiating circumstances and approaches of the three publishers differed substantially, the results suggest that George Smith's crude but successful luring away of George Eliot, and John Murray's unsuccessful wooing of Speke—neatly counterpointing shifting loyalties and authorial rewards to be effected from careful negotiation—was not very unusual. Nor was Blackwood immune to picking up another publisher's author when given the chance. His approach, however, offers a distinct contrast to Smith's overtures to George Eliot.

Kinglake's links with John Murray stretched back to 1844, when Murray published the young lawyer's Gothic "Orientalist" novel *Eothen*. Kinglake and another Murray protégé A. H. Layard (author of *Nineveh and Its Remains* and later Under Secretary at the Foreign Office), were present during Lord Raglan's disastrous Crimean campaign of 1854. Along with William Howard Russell, the famous war correspondent for *The Times*, and others, "Eothen" and "Nineveh," as Murray termed them, tagged along behind Raglan's official camp, sharing "the dangers of the field, as military amateurs, or in the performance of their duty as correspondents to the Press."[23] Kinglake returned home to spend the next twenty-five years amassing documentation and information for an astonishingly detailed history of the Crimean War, which he was to work up in eight volumes by 1878.

On completion of the first two volumes in early 1862, Kinglake entered into discussions with Murray over terms of publication. Negotiations were difficult, not least because of Kinglake's oversensitive and perfectionist temperament. (As Laurence Oliphant later warned John Blackwood, he was "most particular and confoundedly fidgetty [*sic*] about what he writes.")[24] Murray's lack of immediate enthusiasm for, and his unaccountable underestimation of, its worth sent Kinglake off in a huff. George Paston records in his memoirs of life at Murray's that John offered to publish the work either on half-profit (rising to two-thirds author profits on sales of more than 2,000 copies) or to purchase the copyright outright for £1,000.[25] Despite proofs being set up in anticipation of agreement, Kinglake rejected the offer as "too gloomy," not only seeking an enhanced offer but also rejecting the idea of losing the copyright to what he correctly saw as a valuable commodity. As a result, on 20 August 1862 Murray wrote curtly to Kinglake informing him that, given the circumstances, he was now free to transfer the work and the costs so far expended in setting up type to another publisher that would be more amenable to Kinglake's demands.

The following morning Henry Drummond Wolff, a prominent Conservative politician and a close friend and contact of Kinglake, posted a private letter to John Blackwood sounding out potential interest in the work, given that, as he put it, "difficulties have arisen between Mr. Kinglake and Murray who has in writing declared the former free in the matter."[26] While all members of the Edinburgh office eagerly supported bidding for the work, John Blackwood responded cautiously, not willing to stoop to the "vulgarity" of poaching an author from another publisher. As he made clear in his response, although he was interested in discussing terms he would not "do anything which could be construed as interfering with an author while in course of negociation with Mr. Murray or any other publisher."[27] If the matter of the difficulties between Murray and Kinglake could be cleared out of the way, Blackwood continued, then he would welcome the new connection on offer.

Blackwood's hesitancy was less apparent a week later after discussing the matter with Laurence Oliphant, who had come for a casual visit. Oliphant's unreserved recommendation of Kinglake and his project caused Blackwood to respond enthusiastically to Kinglake's next missive. As he noted confidentially to George Simpson on 3 September 1862, due to Oliphant he was now convinced of Kinglake's genius and potential profitability: "There is no question that he is a most admirable writer with an immense reputation which he has not traded upon & if this is really a fine historical reading constructed with the official sanction it would sell immensely."[28] Misunderstandings and skirmishing between Kinglake and Blackwood occurred over the next few weeks, which were finally resolved in meetings with another Kinglake go-between, his aunt Mrs. Emma Woodforde, on 15–16 September 1862.

Kinglake wanted a deal that would benefit all involved but also allow him to maintain ownership of the copyright in case he felt the urge to change publishers again. As he stressed early in the proceedings, he was not proposing to sell the copyright outright, as Murray had demanded, but to offer Blackwood "an opportunity of purchasing one edition," with the right to negotiate further royalties should the edition prove successful.[29] "I could not expect you to offer me a *fixed* sum for the edition until you know more than you do at present," he added in unintended peremptory fashion a few days later. "Therefore what I could propose is that if you think fit you should at once agree to purchase the edition at a rate dependent upon the number of copies of which it may consist and that afterwards when you have read the proofs and see your way clear we should agree upon the number of copies to be printed."[30]

The matter was complex because any new publisher would also have to reimburse Murray for printing costs already incurred by William Clowes & Son, a fact that Kinglake was aware of and willing to account for in negotiations. The result was an offer from Blackwood's that matched Murray's earlier price, but with one difference: no demand was made to retain copyright from Kinglake. "We beg to offer for an edition of two thousand five hundred copies of Mr. Kinglake's History of the Invasion of the Crimea, the first two volumes [read the letter delivered to Mrs. Woodforde for countersignature], the sum of One Thousand pounds payable by Bill at 9 months after date of publication."[31] The firm also offered to pay costs of printing up to the value of £320, with the proviso that any costs above that were to be deducted from the amount paid to Kinglake.[32] The offer was accepted and signed off the following day. Kinglake had finally joined the Blackwood circle and would not leave for another thirty years.

With an offer hammered out, Blackwood and Kinglake moved swiftly to resume the stalled work, sending missives to William Clowes to restart the printing machines as soon as possible. By 6 October John Blackwood was receiving proofs of the first volume, which he found "delightful reading," and in early January 1863 the first two volumes were issued, to great controversy and even greater profit. The work quickly went through four editions, and 15,000 copies were sold within ten years. It became the most lucrative work published by the firm in the 1860s, achieving record profits of £6,454 by July 1873. Kinglake's third and fourth volumes, published in July 1868, racked up sales of almost 6,000 copies (5879) and profits of £4,107 within six years of publication, becoming the fourth most profitable work of the decade, behind Eliot's *Mill on the Floss* (£4,442), the eight-volume collection *Ancient Classics for English Readers* (£5,242), and Kinglake's first two volumes.

Kinglake continued his association with Blackwood's until his death in 1891, confounding them yearly with his writer's blocks, last-minute delays, and an almost pathological attention to detail.[33] Occasional panics marked the long, epic struggle to completion. In May 1868, while cantering through Hyde Park on his daily horse ride, and on the verge of completing corrections for the fourth volume of the *History*, Kinglake lost sensitive proofs containing attacks on Lord Cardigan. The seriousness of the matter was not to be overlooked ("He is in great fear of

being forestalled by its falling into mischievous hands," wrote William Blackwood to his uncle).[34] But the firm's managers, with the exception of Joseph Langford (who never saw the comic side of such things if he could help it), found it
difficult not to laugh at the image presented of Kinglake riding up and down Rot-
ten Row in a desperate search for scattered bits of proofs that had slipped out of
his breast pocket in a moment of overexertion. Days later, seeing that no harm
had been done, Kinglake and William amused themselves by wondering at the
amount of free publicity they might have garnered had someone, as William put
it, "made use of them to sell a newspaper."[35]

The resulting financial gains more than compensated for the travails of producing Kinglake's magnum opus. His eventual eight-volume (plus index) *History
of the Crimea* was to feature among the top twelve best sellers of the Blackwood
backlist until the turn of the century, generating more than £20,000 in profits
between 1863 and 1899. He also remained one of John Blackwood's closest
friends and was mentioned frequently in the private letters of the firm's directors
during his lifetime.

Of the women writers who were associated with the firm between 1860 and
1900, it is George Eliot and Margaret Oliphant who most consistently appear
alongside Kinglake in the confidential letters of the Blackwood firm. Margaret
Oliphant's links with Blackwood's have been well documented by others.[36] Blackwood's published her first major literary work, *Katie Stewart*, in 1852, and they
were to publish her last work, the Blackwood house history *Annals of a Publishing House*, shortly after her death in 1897. "Katie Stewart," as she was termed
in the Blackwood's private correspondence, became a major contributor to the
firm's lists and its magazine during her forty-five-year association with them, as
well as acting as editor and literary advisor when called upon to do so, forming
part of the social network of literary contacts fostered by John Blackwood during his lifetime.

Elisabeth Jay has compared Oliphant's relationship with John Blackwood to
that of factotum, a literary worker and "general utility woman" for his magazine
who depended on him for patronage and who never received the security of editorial tenure that she craved.[37] Oliphant complained to John Blackwood time and
again, "I don't think I am generally a difficult person to deal with—but perhaps
you may find it difficult to realise the difference between working steadily on a
settled plan and doing bits of work precariously, without knowing what one may
calculate upon."[38] But if Oliphant was never to be offered the sums of money and
the security she felt she deserved, there is no mistaking that in John Blackwood's

estimation she ranked with Eliot in ability. "Probably the two cleverest women in the world," he remarked after taking William's brother George to see Oliphant and Eliot one afternoon in 1866.[39]

Oliphant was never to achieve the same success or profitability as her contemporary George Eliot, a point that rankled with her. Oliphant's works were modest if consistent sellers. It is interesting that, as financial ledger details illustrate (see Appendix 3), Oliphant's literary sales peaked in the 1860s with several of the "Carlingford Chronicles" series (*Salem Chapel*, *The Perpetual Curate*, and *Miss Marjoribanks*) commanding profits of between £650 and £850.[40] Robert and Vineta Colby point out that Oliphant was paid £1,500 for the copyright of *The Perpetual Curate*.[41] The profit the firm subsequently made from the first edition (£846) meant in effect that they incurred a loss in its production, despite its being considered one of her successes. From the 1870s onward, Oliphant's fiction featured less in the firm's lists, and she was forced to turn to other publishers, such as Macmillan, to publish her literary fiction. Ultimately, the Blackwoods focused on Oliphant's nonfiction and biographical studies to generate the strong profits previously registered by her novels.[42] Most notable among these were Oliphant's 1891 *Life of Laurence Oliphant* (£2,049 profits), the 1888 *Life of Principal Tulloch* (£471), her 1872 *Memoirs of Montalembert* (£554), and her final, 1897 two-volume *Annals of a Publishing House* (£1,173). Such strong shifts in texts commissioned or accepted from Oliphant also illustrate her movement from consideration and valuation by the Blackwood firm in one literary plane (fiction) to valuation in another (biographies and historical texts). That she ends her literary career at Blackwood's writing its history, having begun it producing fiction, is quite striking.

Margaret Oliphant's reputation exemplifies one aspect of authorial identity contained within the frame of Blackwood publishing activity. Her position in the firm's list represents an assumption of worth based on intangible capital: more often than not, as Elisabeth Jay, Robert and Vineta Colby, J. A. Haythornthwaite, Dale Trela, and others have pointed out, she was viewed as the skilled laborer, solid, dependable, and gifted but not necessarily the most profitable of literary properties. John Blackwood was unable to "work" her texts (to use a phrase from his testimony to the Copyright Commission in 1876), as well as he could other better positioned authors. Her value to the firm therefore resided in her ability to participate simultaneously on different planes of textual production: from fiction, to prose and magazine contributions, to biographies and editorial work. (It is she, for example, who edits the seventeen-volume series *Foreign Classics for*

English Readers that between 1877 and 1890 sold more than 57,800 copies and generated slightly more than £706 in profits.)

George Eliot, on the other hand, represented a more tangible capital asset to the firm, combining intellectual acclaim on related literary textual planes (fiction, prose, and verse) with enormous profitability. As statistics from the financial ledgers reveal (Appendix 1), the mainstay of company profits between 1860 and 1900, aside from *Blackwood's Magazine* (Appendix 2), was unquestionably George Eliot, who was enticed back to Blackwood's in 1866 (to publish *Felix Holt*) and with whom she remained until her death in 1880. As tables 1 and 2 show, by the turn of the century Blackwood's could truthfully be described as "the house that George built," with Eliot titles forming 39 percent of those generating major profits between 1890 and 1899 yet accounting for 51.2 percent of the major income generated.

Table 1.   Titles generating profits of more than £1,000, 1860–1909

Years	Total Number of Titles	Number of Eliot Titles	Percentage of Total Titles by Eliot
1860–1869	18	4	22.2
1870–1879	23	7	30.4
1880–1889	19	5	26.3
1890–1899	18	7	39.0
1900–1909	13	3	23.0

Table 2.   Profits generated by major titles, 1860–1909 (as per Table 1)

Years	All Titles (£/s/d)	Number of Eliot Titles Sold	Eliot Sales Total (£/s/d)	Eliot as Percentage Profit of Titles
1860–1869	45,377.0.6	104,167	11,266.8.4	24.8
1870–1879	54,917.6.3	329,578	24,918.6.8	45.4
1880–1889	72,242.1.9	179,892	27,166.0.7	37.6
1890–1899	55,365.6.0	602,167	28,351.11	51.2
1900–1909	24,509.16.9	208,822	5,573.14.5	22.7

What can be learned from these statistics is that, toward the end of the nineteenth century, George Eliot was the engine that drove the Blackwood firm to profitability. What is also evident is the manner in which Eliot's titles (and in particular her collected works) were assiduously issued at an ever-increasing rate after her death in 1880, and as a result began accounting for an ever-increasing percentage

Fig. 1 Cover of sixpenny reprint of George Eliot's *Romola*, William Blackwood & Sons, 1903. The issue of such reprints rose dramatically after the adoption of new, cheap paperback formats by the Blackwood firm in the 1890s.

of Blackwood income. As one can see, sales of Eliot's work rose dramatically in the 1890s, particularly because of the move toward issuing works in cheap, one-volume, six-shilling and sixpenny formats (see Fig. 1). The unfortunate result was a dangerous overdependence upon this success, and a major collapse in profits when the market for Eliot's works dried up at the turn of the century. The reason for this collapse had only partly to do with changes in readership tastes and the decreasing popularity of Eliot's works. A more accurate assessment would be that the collapse was also a result of overproduction of Eliot texts to the point of saturation by a firm that was increasingly at sea in a changing literary marketplace.

Nonliterary Textual Production

While Eliot's works may have been the most profitable source of income for the firm during the last third of the nineteenth century, they were not the only texts in the Blackwood lists providing steady profits. Often unacknowledged in publishing studies is the importance of nonliterary textual production to company profitability: for every literary best-seller, there are a half-dozen nonliterary texts sustaining a firm's lists.

Blackwood's is no exception to this, once you eliminate Eliot's works from the equation, and it is interesting to note a shift in the types of texts being promoted and providing major income for the firm over the years. Between 1860 and 1869, for example, the eighteen texts generating more than £1,000 in profits include six within the literary plane of production by three authors (George Eliot, Samuel Warren, and Theodore Martin), four histories, travel works or other nonfiction texts by three authors (Kinglake, Speke, Hamley), three general collections (*Ancient Classics for English Readers*, *Tales from Blackwood*, *Blackwood Standard Novels*), and four general texts for other public uses (*The Book of the Farm*, *Book of the Garden*, Acts of Parliament and Scottish hymnals). Between 1870 and 1879, however, the number of major profit-generating texts had risen to twenty-three and shifted to include a new market—the educational primer and textbook. The number of profitable literary texts remained dominated by George Eliot (7 of 11), supported by Edward Bulwer-Lytton (2), Theodore Martin, and W. E. Aytoun (one each). Of more relevance is the dominance of nonliterary texts in the list, ranging from the Scottish hymnals series and General Public Statutes to textbooks and manuals on farming, zoology, geography, and metaphysics. Such practical reference, educational, and religious texts, targeted to specific communities for specific purposes, become the other dominant strand of textual production for the firm from the 1870s until the late 1890s, when sales for these texts drops due to more current texts being produced by other firms.

Operations of War is another example of an undiscussed but significant text in a nonliterary plane of operation. General Edward B. Hamley, commandant of the Military Staff College in Camberley from 1870 to 1877 (and for years previous a staff lecturer and officer there), was one of Blackwood's many military authors and a close friend of John Blackwood. In 1864, noting the lack of a textbook for preparing officers in understanding general battlefield tactics, Hamley set about writing one. It was published in May 1866 in one volume, priced at twenty-eight shillings, and over the next thirty-four years it sold 7,262 copies and generated profits of £4,212.

This may not seem that impressive, but for the firm the work represented an invaluable and intangible accretion of cultural capital; between 1866 and 1894 it was the main (and only) text used for preparation of the Military Staff College entrance examination.[43] This meant not only a guaranteed source of sales (from hopeful candidates and potential military officers) that allowed the firm to dominate the market in military texts and keep in print one of its highest priced textual productions in this area, but also a link to an important social ecumene.

Operations of War became one of the most influential texts in military training for an entire generation of British army officers. That generation, in turn, identified Blackwood's and its magazine as part of their cultural *habitus*, a main source of information in the military plane of textual production, thus becoming a group the firm began increasingly catering to in the latter part of the century. It is no surprise, then, to subsequently find in the Blackwood lists military war histories (Mercer, *Journal of the Waterloo Campaign*, 1870; Grant, *The Sepoy War, 1857–1858*, 1873; Brackenbury, *Ashanti War*, 1874; Grant, *China War*, 1875), texts on strategy (F. J. Maurice, *The Wellington Prize Essay*, 1872; Hamley, *On Outposts*, 1875; Schmidt, *Instruction for Regiments Taking Part in Manoeuvres*, 1876), and a sprinkling of military memoirs (Winn, *What I Saw of the War*, 1870; Philip Meadows Taylor, *The Story of My Life*, 1877), which increase as the century draws to an end and Blackwood's military audience grows larger. This is the market that begins to take on an important role in Blackwood print production from the 1890s on.

Production and the Shop Floor

As noted in the introductory chapter, one of the areas least explored in publishing histories is the space represented by the printing office, space that is both symbolic and a physical actuality. Where are printing offices situated in relation to the more elevated editorial and business premises? Who staffs them? What were the printers' views of the texts routinely passing through the print works and so privileged in the memoirs and recollections of bookmen and publishers? A search of conventional Victorian publishing memoirs reveals few comments from such sources.

This is equally true of the place of the printing office in the hierarchy of valued arenas in Victorian publishing. It is common to find both celebratory and evaluative texts of publishing activity that pay little attention to the significance of the print works in the business of textual production. When the shop floor does appear, it is usually in one of two contexts: (1) as part of investigations into a "great printer of letters," whereby these spaces provide the backdrop for the heroes of printing (Gutenburg, Plantin, Caxton) to develop and advance print technology; or (2) as part of studies in the *processes* of print production, whereby the mechanics of production are paramount in the discussion (typeset elaborated on, inks described, paper made, metal and manpower fused to create texts).

The official histories of the Blackwood firm offer neither of these narrative tropes, nor is there much about industrial relations or staffing levels in the print works. When the printing office does feature, it is usually in the context of a visit by a literary figure across the divide of Thistle Street Lane (the ultimate, symbolic division of men and resources in the Blackwood work hierarchy). As noted in the introduction, Blackwood's was unusual in owning both the editorial and the printing sites. The physical spaces inhabited by these two linked sectors of the Blackwood business reveal much about their symbolic positioning within the firm. While the editorial offices and front shop occupied sumptuous quarters on George Street, the printing works were housed in more cramped quarters behind the main offices and accessed via the narrow Thistle Street Lane. Manuscripts would be walked across the lane to be typeset, printed, and cut and bound in loud, mechanized workspaces. The results would be trundled back in large wheelbarrows to be displayed for sale in the quiet shop floor fronting the George Street entrance.

One of the few mentions of the printing office in the 1954 Blackwood house history is an account of a short speech made in 1898 by the head of the printing office, George Hogg, on accomplishing fifty years work with the firm, in which he recalled the visit of two eminent authors subsequently initiated as honorary members of the printing office "chapel," E. B. Hamley and John Hanning Speke. Elsewhere, Blackwood printers emerge as sources of amused journalistic commentary regarding the crabbed, handwritten, indecipherable literary texts of a number of nineteenth-century "Blackwoodian" miscreants, such as John Hill Burton. The sight of Burton's singularly unreadable manuscripts, one veteran recalled, would provoke despair among the Blackwood compositors, leading them to dub him "one of the bad hands of Blackwood."[44] John Wilson's manuscripts in "intensely bad ramstam hand" were welcomed, as "double the sum was afterwards paid for it to the compositors," while Margaret Oliphant provoked the Blackwood head compositor, Sam Kinnear, to expostulate in the *Scotsman*, "Printers ought always to be thankful for such voluminous writers as she was. The compositor got 4d extra for every page of 'Blackwood' they composed from her ms to recoup them for worry and loss of time."[45] Kinnear's conclusion harked back to the utilitarian aspect of such work. Any author afflicted with a "bad hand," he noted, should remind himself that "the deciphering of his lucubrations may cause the loss of time, money, and temper to the innocent printer."[46]

This point is particularly revealing of the manner in which all textual production was generally viewed once it entered the domain of the printing office. Throughout the nineteenth century, Edinburgh firms, including Blackwood's, operated a mixed system of payment for compositor work, whereby a few typesetters were hired to do the most expensive work and paid by time or establishment ("stab") rates, while the less-complicated typesetting work was done by piece-workers ("linesmen") who were paid by the line.[47] Thus all texts were equal in the rush to compose enough lines to earn a decent wage. Texts were evaluated on how quickly they could be turned into printed commodities, and hence any aesthetic value to be found was that extolled in the "good hand" that allowed a quick turnaround of handwritten manuscript to printed proof. Kinnear's comments made transparent the economic imperative underlying human interaction over texts in the Blackwood printing office. Here textual production was viewed not in aesthetic terms but in human labor costs. And when it came to dealing with the individuals manning the print works, the Blackwood management were quite firm in their understanding of such economic imperatives, as evinced in the events of 1872–73.

One important episode of printing office activity that is not recorded in the official Blackwood histories is in the records of the printers' strike of 1872–73. It is an incident that reveals important responses by the Blackwood management to the threat posed by the increasingly proactive British trade union movement of the mid-nineteenth century. It also offers a useful case study of the intrusion of labor struggles over the "means of production" in the general business of textual production in Edinburgh.

A London building-trades dispute in 1859 inaugurated what became known as the nine-hour-day movement, which sought to introduce shorter workweeks (51–54 hours) into the general trades workplace.[48] The success Edinburgh masons had in 1861 in establishing a nine-hour workday was soon emulated by other trades, and in 1865 the printing offices acceded to demands to reduce workweeks to fifty-seven hours. In late 1871 the Edinburgh Typographical Society, the main printing union in Edinburgh, presented a memorial to the employers seeking a further reduction to fifty-one hours. As Sian Reynolds notes in her study on Edinburgh women compositors, the events that followed involved compromises, counterbids, and further turmoil.[49]

The main Edinburgh employers who belonged to the Master Printers Association (founded in 1846 with the goal of fighting union demands) in January 1872 offered a compromise of fifty-four hours that was subsequently accepted.[50] In September 1872, however, the union returned with a claim for a fifty-one-hour week and an increase in the piecework rates. The thirty-seven firms who made up the majority of the Master Printers Association (MPA), believing that they had conceded enough in January, responded by mid-October, refusing the claim. The union called a strike beginning 15 November 1872. In the four weeks preceding the action, meetings were held on both sides, and there were compromise offers between the union and the MPA to increase overtime rates and the "stab" wages (from 27 shillings 6 pence to 30 shillings a week). The MPA, while willing to offer slightly higher wages, refused to consider decreasing work hours,[51] believing that would undermine their traditional authority in the workplace. As William Blackwood reported from an MPA meeting on 17 October 1872, echoing the general sentiment of the meeting, "Unless a bold front is now shown it will be a perpetual mill stone hanging round our necks and our office will be conducted on their will not ours."[52]

On 15 November 1872, having failed to gain further compromises from the Master Printers Association, the union went on strike. Around 800 men representing apprentices, journeymen, readers, and compositors walked out of all Edinburgh offices. In the Blackwood office, 46 compositors, 12 machine and pressmen, 3 compositor apprentices, and an undetermined number of journeymen left their places.[53] Nine of the major Edinburgh firms, however, including Blackwood's, had made plans to fill the anticipated gaps. They engaged an agent to advertise and hire nonunion, "rat" labor to be distributed among all the offices involved. Advertisements in major town newspapers brought responses from Glasgow, Hull, Manchester, and London, among other sites.[54] Their success in attracting external labor stiffened the MPA's resolve to reject further union compromises. "If the Masters hold firm today," William Blackwood predicted on 15 November, "we will break the back of the Union line at all events."[55]

Attempts by remaining Blackwood workers to support the union line were swiftly dealt with. In one case, two readers (Sam Kinnear and Andrew Wilson) who refused to "go to case" to reset type to correct a magazine proof, were threatened with dismissal if they did not undertake the task requested. Sam Kinnear gave in, and, as we have seen, remained with the firm for another twenty-five years. The younger of the two, Andrew Wilson, did not, and was promptly sacked.[56] Likewise, the firm was not above engaging in a bit of moral blackmail, sending its head of printing works (Hutchison) to the homes of the younger apprentices "to give them a few words of counsel and warning" as to the likely effect upon their careers and their families of such strike action.[57]

By 22 November, emboldened by their success in recruiting new workers, William and John Blackwood decided to declare their office nonunion: all laborers subsequently hired (or rehired) had to reject union membership in order to work there. John Blackwood reported to G. H. Lewes, "We have found it necessary to declare that we will not take a Union man into our office and we are determined to stand our ground."[58] By mid-February 1873 the strike was all but over, and union members voted 200 to 131 to return to work based on the original compromise conditions offered, of slightly better wages but no concessions on work hours.[59] Surrender was complete, and on 21 February John Blackwood was able to report that all former employees had "come back to *Blackwoods* throwing up the Union, in fact on any terms back."[60]

The printing unions emerged from the strike extremely weakened, burdened by accumulated debts and a devastating drop in membership. In December 1874 the Edinburgh Typographical Society claimed to have 900 members; by 1880 the numbers had dwindled by almost 60 percent to 342.[61] The Blackwood office saw a more drastic reduction in union representation. Between 1871 and 1881 union-registered Blackwood workers totaled 120, of whom 92 had joined between 1860 and 1873. After the 1873 strike, 56 names were dropped from the union registers. By 1881 only 13 Blackwood employees were registered union members.[62]

The Blackwood management remained strongly anti-union in years following, viewing it as interfering with their right to determine working conditions and activity. As John Blackwood saw it, union meddling merely destroyed the paternalist management style he envisaged in operation under his tenure. "We must put it to them what right have they to look to us in sickness or trouble," he wrote, "if they are to serve us in this way at a pinch."[63] Union activists, as far as John Blackwood was concerned, were merely social agitators who had "no interests in our welfare or that of those in our employment."[64] The Blackwood shop floor remained closed to such union organizers until the turn of the century, and union membership continued to be actively opposed by directors in decades following. (Such management views color Tredrey's short account of the 1896 printing works strike in his house history, on which occasion William's nephew George, who joined the firm in July 1896, "operated a machine with two non-Union men and an apprentice, and produced the November Magazine."[65]) It was not until the early 1900s that printing unions once more began to play a significant role in negotiating better working conditions for printing office workers in Scotland and Edinburgh.[66]

Distributing and Marketing Texts

As far as distribution arenas are concerned, Blackwood both adopted and diverged from established mid-century British publishing practices. One point in which Blackwood's differentiated itself from other contemporary publishing houses was its publications strategy. Blackwood's tended to space out its publications, issuing relatively large editions of a relatively small list of works, while such contemporaries as Smith, Elder & Company, Richard Bentley, and John Murray tended to publish more frequently and in smaller runs.[67] Only eight of sixty-five Smith, Elder & Company titles subscribed to by Mudie's Select Circulating Library (the main distributor of print in middle-class Victorian Britain) between 1858 and 1865, for example, were in editions of *larger* than 1,000 copies. In contrast, of the thirty-two Blackwood titles subscribed to by Mudie's on publication during the same period, only five were in editions of less than 1,000 copies.[68]

A more in-depth analysis of Blackwood publication ledgers (see Tables 3 and 4 below) reveals that the numbers of publications issued in print runs of less than 1,000 copies between 1860 and 1879 prove just as insignificant. (Such print runs were often confined to texts financed by private concerns or the authors themselves, or to first editions of texts whose success or market value John Blackwood and his team were uncertain about.) Thus, between 1860 and 1869, of 159 new or continuing publications issued or accounted for in the financial ledgers, 26 (or 16 percent) were published in runs of less than 1,000 copies. Between 1870 and 1879, some 27 out of 176 publications (or 15 percent) were issued in runs of less than 1,000 copies.

Table 3.   Blackwood publications, 1860–1869

Year	Total per Year	Print Runs Less Than 1,000
1860	10	2
1861	32	2
1862	12	2
1863	17	1
1864	13	3
1865	17	3
1866	14	3
1867	16	2
1868	15	4
1869	13	4
Total	159	26

Table 4.   Blackwood publications, 1870-1879

Year	Total per Year	Print Runs Less Than 1,000
1870	25	3
1871	22	2
1872	12	2
1873	30	3
1874	19	3
1875	18	3
1876	5	0
1877	17	4
1878	15	4
1879	13	3
Total	176	27

In his *Victorian Novelists and Publishers*, John Sutherland gives a succinct account of the standard patterns of sales and supply most British publishers adopted from the 1840s onward.[69] In most cases, texts were sold to booksellers at various discounts, either in the form of a reduction in price and/or at a prepublication rate of thirteen for the price of twelve (or even twenty-five for the price of twenty-four). Chief among trade buyers was Charles Mudie, whose circulating library, started in the 1840s, was by the early 1860s one of the biggest purchasers and distributors of texts, accounting for up to 60 percent of sales of a print run.[70] But Mudie's supposed stranglehold on the circulation and sales of texts in Britain between the 1860s and 1880s was not in fact as strong as frequently portrayed. His attempts to stave off competition from other circulating libraries in the late 1850s, for example, allied with an overextension of credit and a phenomenally high level of book purchasing, meant that by 1863 Mudie's organization faced bankruptcy, and the circulating library system, upon which many publishers depended for steady sales and income, teetered on the verge of collapse.[71]

Only the concerted efforts of a secret core group of British publishers (including Blackwood) enabled Mudie, and the circulating library system, to survive. The interesting result was a complicit intertwining of interests between producers and distributor: in 1864, Mudie's firm was turned into a public limited company and floated on the stock market, with a portion of shares being distributed (according to the sums they were owed) to the various publishers who had propped up Mudie's system. From then on, it was in the interest of many of Britain's prominent publishers to continue working with Mudie and his circulating library, if only to guarantee a decent return of 7.5 percent on their initial investments.[72]

Further sales discounts were available if the book trade "subscribed" on the day of publication and in months following initial publication, albeit at less-favorable terms. Subscription involved having each trade customer pledge to purchase a certain number of copies at preferential rates, which would then be tallied up and entered in running monthly accounts for settling at half-yearly, nine-month, or yearly intervals. This procedure, prevalent almost exclusively among the London trade, often served as an early barometer of the work's likely success or failure. As a result, much was done to drum up prepublication publicity and interest among "the trade" through advertisements, puffs, and notices in trade journals, such as the *Publishers Circular*.

As one of his major duties, either on specific days toward the beginning or end of the month, or on special days of publication, Joseph Langford (and on occasion one of his deputies or William Blackwood III, in the late 1850s and early 1860s) would trudge round the Paternoster Row area gathering subscriptions from Mudie and other retailers. Preliminary sales figures would be jotted down and attached to Langford's daily missives to Edinburgh for evaluation and decision as to whether a quick reprint was required or not. Thus the action taken on 11 December 1863, for example, the official day of publication of John Hanning

Speke's *Journal of the Discovery of the Source of the Nile*, when subscription sales were found to account for more than 45 percent of the initial 7,500 print run (3,472 copies, to be exact). "I have just sent you off telegram of Speke Subn as completed today," William Blackwood III wrote hastily, "and hope it has come up to your expectations. Langford and I think it *first rate* and by tomorrow afternoon I am sure 4,000 will be subscribed for in London alone. The appearance of the book and its get up has made a very great impression on all who have seen it and I have no doubt added much to the successful subscription. Langford says he never saw the trade so much impressed with a book and I hope they will not be losers by their liberal subscription."[73] The result was a decision to reprint another 2,500, bringing the total print run to 10,000.

But such high subscription rates were not usually the norm. Langford's December 1864 summary of the month's subscriptions for Oliphant's three-volume novel, *The Perpetual Curate*, first published in October, offers a breakdown of sales that is more in keeping with the general patterns recorded for other texts in subsequent letters and years. Seventy-five sales (which Langford describes as "going on well") are recorded as follows: 3 Kent; 10 Simpkins; 2 Caulthorn; 4 Hamilton; 2 Mitchell; 4 Smith & Sons; and 50 Mudie. "I trust we shall sell out the edition," Langford concluded.[74] They did, but it took nine years before the accounts on the publication were closed, by which time it had sold 1,351 copies of the 1,580 printed, and yielded a profit of £846 (see Appendix 3).

British publishers used other equally well tested methods to market texts outside the "golden triangle" of London, Cambridge, and Oxford. Commercial travelers were commissioned to cover specific regional areas, gathering orders from dealers, booksellers and sundry shopkeepers for remission and action. Such "commercials," as they were called, employed in other areas of British industry since the mid-eighteenth century, became extremely prevalent in the book trade industry from the first decades of the nineteenth century onward. A study on the subject dates one of the earliest recordings of such individuals in the book trade to 1811, when the Scottish firm Oliver & Boyd "sent one out to promote their interests."[75] The salesman's route is recorded as covering considerable territory, from Penrith, Lancaster, Liverpool, Oxford, and Worcester to Leicester, Nottingham, Sheffield, and York.[76]

It is not known when Blackwood's first began using such travelers, but by the 1860s these individuals had become part of a sophisticated network of sales and book-trade information. Thus we find in July 1862 William Blackwood gleefully noting to John Blackwood information from their provincial sales representative,

Mr. Roberts, who, in addition to returning with higher than expected sales accounts and orders, had reported news of poor sales for *The Cornhill Magazine*, then just beginning its serialization of the poached *Romola*.[77] "Men who used to take 7 Doz. now only take 2 [dozen] and no fresh stir from Romola," Roberts is said to have commented, prompting William, still smarting from the loss of George Eliot's work, to remark cattily, "I think they are beginning to tremble for their money. I hope the beasts will be made to pay the piper."[78]

While overseas sales were often negotiated by British publishers, these were not of necessity remunerative enough to reward the time invested in such transactions. Deals in the colonies did not offer much satisfaction, as payments were low (ranging from £25 to £150) and piracy was rife. (By the late 1880s and 1890s, however, "Colonial Editions" of Blackwood texts were being produced and marketed directly to Indian, African, and Canadian markets, reflecting the increasing use of cheap one-volume editions after the collapse of the three-decker.)

The famous German-based Tauchnitz series of reprints at least provided a guarantee against piracy in continental Europe, yet it too offered nominal sums of between £25 and £100 for the privilege of protecting continental rights for British authors.[79] The lack of comprehensive copyright protection in U.S. markets until the Chace Act of 1891, for one, often resulted in nominal sums (sometimes as low as £10) being offered to British authors and their representatives for U.S. editions. The Blackwood firm dealt with such transactions as little as possible, although it did forge a generally friendly exchange with the New York firm Harper & Sons that proved mutually supportive.[80] It also contracted with the New York printers and distributors Leonard Scott & Company to produce a U.S. reprint of *Blackwood's Magazine* from the 1850s until 1891, when Blackwood's took advantage of the protection of the Chace Act to begin producing its own American edition in conjunction with Leonard Scott. The result was a new stream of profitability from American sales of between 12,000 and 15,000 copies a year. (See Appendix 2 and Chapter 5.)

Conclusion

Under John Blackwood the firm prospered as never before. It did so by publishing authors in various literary planes (George Eliot in fiction, Alexander W. Kinglake in history, John Hanning Speke and J. A. Grant in exploration) whose works generated strong profits and meshed with literary and cultural interests of the period. It also ventured successfully into new publishing areas, tapping into the newly emerging educational markets through its primers and textbooks, expanding its agricultural lists, and securing exclusive and financially lucrative rights to print Scottish hymnals, legal statutes, and other official government texts. Blackwood's particular identification in the second half of the century as a source of military-oriented texts (an arena it had always promoted with interest) was to lay the groundwork for its later concentration on imperial and colonial histories and texts.

At the same time, the innate conservatism of its directors saw expression in its response to labor and union challenges in the 1870s; the labor strikes of 1872–73 resulted in a de-unionizing policy that was to remain in place until the turn of the century. Low labor and printing costs enabled a maximum return on textual production, contributing to the rising profitability of the firm and the establishment of the firm as one of the leaders in British publishing. That John Blackwood played a significant part in directing the firm to such success is attested by the firm's valuation on his death, which had almost doubled from £41,633 in 1845 to £80,509 in 1879. Thus in 1879 the firm could proudly declare itself one of the leading publishing firms in Britain. How all this changed, and what contributed to its subsequent decline, is the subject of another chapter.

3

Africa Rewritten:

The Case of John Hanning Speke

John Hanning Speke (Fig. 2), born in 1827, was a British military officer who in his twenties became fascinated with Africa. In 1854 he was invited to accompany the explorer and polymath Richard Burton in an expedition through what is now modern-day Somalia. The two subsequently teamed up again between 1857 and 1859 to explore unknown territory in what is now Tanzania. During this expedition, Speke struck out on his own and came upon Lake Victoria Nyanza. Based partly on instinct and partly on his perception of its immensity, Speke concluded that this was the source of the Nile River. The claim was disputed by Burton, and on their return to Britain in 1859 Speke, who had arrived ahead of Burton, announced his discovery to the Royal Geographic Society and soon secured funds for a second expedition. With a new traveling companion, James Augustus Grant (Fig. 3), Speke set sail for Africa in late April 1860, hoping to prove his theory about the lake and tracing its course down to Egypt. The expedition lasted three years, and its success led to a triumphant return in June 1863. Doubts soon began to emerge about Speke's claims, however, based on controversial

Fig. 2 Engraving from a photograph of John Hanning Speke (1827–1864), African explorer and Blackwood author, used as the frontispiece for his *Journal of the Discovery of the Source of the Nile*, William Blackwood & Sons, 1863. The complete revision of Speke's journal attempted to reshape his image and findings to suit Victorian conceptions of Africa.

Fig. 3   Engraving from a hotograph of Speke's travel companion, James Augustus Grant (1827–1892). Grant did the illustrations for Speke's *Journal.*

information Speke provided in brief and hastily presented speeches to the Royal Geographic Society. The information caused furious debate because it seemed to contradict already received geographical notions of African topography.

The controversy and interest surrounding Speke's claims ensured that a potential publishing success awaited the firm that retained Speke. The story of the resulting scramble to publish Speke, the difficulties encountered by the successful bidder in turning an explorer into an author, and the previously unknown method by which this was accomplished lie at the heart of this chapter. The results illustrate the manner in which texts could be manipulated by the Blackwood firm to suit ideological and commercial interests, as well as be contained within the textual "planes" assigned to them.

The intensity of the debate aroused by Speke's claims was due not only to Speke's imprecise speculations but also to the special fascination that the mysterious source of the Nile had exercised over European explorers (and governments) for several centuries. Speke's account appeared near the start of a period of intensive interest in Africa. With much of Asia and South America colonized, Africa was the last major geographical area untouched by European imperialism. Between the 1850s and 1890s, European powers and institutions began to intensify their involvement in "the Dark Continent," leaving their political and physical imprints on the African interior. Missionaries and explorers, such as Richard Burton, David Livingstone, Henry Baker, the Welsh-American Henry Stanley, and the Frenchman Paul du Chaillu, began filling in the maps with areas that were subsequently divided up by European powers.

But as Alan Moorehead outlines in *The White Nile*, fascination with tracing the source of the Nile dated as far back as 460 B.C., when the Greek historian Herodotus ascended the Nile as far as the first cataract at Aswan.[1] Since then, the mystery of what fed the great river, which yearly washed down to irrigate and fertilize the Egyptian plains, continued to puzzle and excite the imaginations of explorers and geographers. More important was the political and economic potential of such a source. The European power that could control and lay claim to this source would be in a strong position to control and exploit the surrounding areas dependent on the Nile for survival. The building of the Aswan Dam in Egypt at the turn of the twentieth century, generating hydroelectric power and controlling the flow of the Nile, is perhaps the best example of what such considerations could achieve.

The Edinburgh firm William Blackwood & Sons had dealt with Speke before, publishing several of his articles in their monthly journal *Blackwood's Magazine*. On hearing the news of Speke's success in late May, the firm's directors grew excited over the potential sums his account might bring. William Blackwood III, co-partner of the firm, wrote his uncle John Blackwood: "It is evident Speke has had many an adventure & it also I think indicates some plunder in store for us."[2] John Blackwood, in London during this period, seized the initiative, meeting with Speke on 20 June, three days after Speke's landing at Southampton. Speke reported that although he was eager to publish with Blackwood, who had supported his literary efforts in previous years, Blackwood had been anticipated by John Murray, who had made a substantial offer of 2,000[3] guineas plus two-thirds of the profits for the rights to Speke's account.[4] The amount staggered John Blackwood, as he wrote to William on 20 June. Considering Speke's previous difficulties in expressing himself, he could not help but consider it a hazardous offer, and "I had not thought of making any offer until we saw what we were about, & did not propose doing so now."[5]

John Blackwood nevertheless believed the situation demanded that he match Murray's offer as near as possible, and William Blackwood responded equally in favor of the proposition. John offered Speke £2,000 and a stake in the profits, and Speke accepted. Following publication in December 1863, John Blackwood conceded privately to William that the amount had in fact been too high but that, in fairness, it could not have been done otherwise. "It was too much considering what I knew of his literary powers," he wrote, "but when others offer so keenly I could not possibly let the fair fellow get less from us than he could have got elsewhere."[6]

John Blackwood, no doubt hoping to encourage Speke to complete the book in a more peaceful environment, invited Speke to stay at his home in Strathtyrum, near St. Andrews in Scotland. Blackwood also wished to prevent the poaching of his "exclusive" by London newsmen. Representatives of the *Illustrated London News* had been quick to pursue both Speke and James Augustus Grant for copy and illustrations of their expedition; Grant's diary notes their calling on 22 June, the day after Blackwood had first contacted him.[7] This and subsequent meetings resulted in a five-page spread in the 4 July 1863 issue of the *Illustrated London News*, featuring five of Grant's illustrations along with a report of Speke's address to the Royal Geographical Society in London on 30 June.

Both Blackwood's and its London and Edinburgh managers were appalled by the thought of further installments to come, and steps were quickly taken to stop their major investment from being scooped and gutted by what they considered a cheap broadsheet. George Simpson was promptly dispatched to London to impress on both Speke and Grant not only the impropriety of giving all their best material to the *Illustrated London News*, but also the financial unsoundness of issuing any of their material in installments. William Blackwood III noted to John Blackwood on 9 July that such a proposal would prove financially disastrous, as "the real buyers of his book would not care for it in that form & then we would lose all or nearly the Library demand."[8] Likewise, it was better to answer all of Speke's critics at once, rather than allow the debate to drag along over the time span of an installment series.

Simpson's discussions, in tandem with a letter from John Blackwood, forestalled any further incursions by the *Illustrated* men, and Speke agreed to complete his work in Scotland. On 10 July, William Blackwood reported eagerly that Speke, set to come up on the 20 July, "is most eager to settle to his book," adding, ironically as it turned out, "I think we will have a very busy summer of it."[9] It is important to note that no one had yet actually seen Speke's written material, relying instead on what they could glean from his verbal descriptions of the journey. As John Blackwood was to discover to his dismay, Speke, verbose and discursive, with a cigar in his hand, was an atrocious writer.

John Blackwood, scrutinizing the sample typeset from Speke's first offering—the diary account of his stay with the Ugandan king Mutesa in 1862, which was to become the central section in the subsequent revision—was appalled. Blackwood wrote frankly to his nephew William that the firm faced potential disaster. Speke's writing, it seemed, was hopeless: "He writes in such an abominable, childish, unintelligible way," Blackwood noted incredulously, "that it is impossible to say what anybody could make of them, and yet he is full of matter & when he talks and explains all is right."[10] John Blackwood could hardly believe the situation; although Speke was eager and willing to do anything to get the job done, "working away like a galley slave," as Blackwood put it, he was incapable, as far as Blackwood could ascertain, of producing the best-selling book everyone was hoping for.

Even worse, what text Speke did produce was disappointing enough to leave John Blackwood extremely disheartened. "It will be a tough job, and I almost wish at times we had let Murray have it," he wrote disconsolately, pausing only to reflect more hopefully, "but there is the material of a most curious & successful book in the excellent fellow & we must see if we cannot pull them out by hook or crook."[11] William Blackwood wrote back describing a meeting with Colonel C. P. Rigby (former consul at Zanzibar) and Speke's traveling companion James A. Grant on 22 July, in which they had acknowledged their worries about Speke's ability to produce his account. Their concerns extended also to what they saw as his need to answer accusations and criticisms stemming from his earlier expedition with Richard Burton, as well as to silence skepticism about his claims regarding the Nile source. More important, both Speke's friends and the Blackwoods recognized the need to get the work published soon, before interest in the subject died out. This was something that both Rigby and Grant suggested was already occurring. "They are both deeply concerned that Speke's book should be a success," William wrote John, "& rather sore at the feeling that has arisen in London of his having nothing very interesting to communicate, which of course they deny, & do not see how he will ever tell what the public most are for except when smoking his cigar & the moment he sits to the desk he gets into a jumble."[12]

The more Speke's jumbled notes were scrutinized, the clearer it became that something had to be done. Even the typesetters were becoming alarmed, as William noted in an effort to amuse John, quoting one of them as saying that Speke's work "never would do to go before the public; it would be the death of Mr. B. were he to attempt to correct it. The Boy that has been going over it with me has been nearly in fits with laughing."[13] What amused the typesetters ranged from mere slips in sentence construction, spelling mistakes, and slack use of punctuation, to serious lapses in grammatical and syntactical coherence. The entry for 30 April 1862, describing a boating trip on Lake Victoria Nyanza with King Mutesa, is a typical representation of the lesser faults in the manuscript:

> Then ordering the return home much to my delight, for though beautiful the N'yanza was the want of consideration for others peoples comfort, the tiring incessant boating all day long and every day, as well as Mtesa's hurry skurry about everything he undertook [to] do, without the smallest forethought, preparation or warning made me dream of the friends I left behind and look fondly forward to see what change would have been produced in those I loved though they loved not me by this forceable separation of one week.[14]

Also prevalent were grammatical contortions like those in the following entry for 3 October 1860:

> Remains to be spoken of, if the reader desires it, are the daily occupations of Captain Grant, myself and our private servants. Treating with the three obversely Rahan a very peppery little negro who had served in a British man of war at the taking of Rangoon was my valet and Baraka who had been trained much in the same manner but had seen engagements at

Lultan was Captain Grants, they both knew Hindustani but whilst Rahan's services at Sea had been short, Baraka had served nearly all his life with Englishmen, was the smartest and most intelligent negro I ever saw, was invaluable as a Slave detector to Captain Rigby and enjoyed his confidence completely.[15]

Such entries only required minor corrections, but more problematic were such entries as the following, a tangled note dated 21 February 1862: "At night when in bed M'tesa sent his Pages—boys with two cockades of hair take all the King's messages they live in the Palace constantly attending on him & with the women—to day if I desired his friendship I would lend him one musket to make up six with what I had given him for he intended visiting his relations the following morn."[16]

Faced with a flawed text of this type, John and William Blackwood realized that in order to safeguard their investment, and Speke's reputation, they needed to call in someone to "edit" or construct the book, someone who could listen to Speke and fashion what he said, and what he had written, into a commercially viable narrative. As William stated to his uncle, the material was there but the authorial presence was not. Having read some of Speke's material, he confessed to being quite bewildered about what to say about it, for "there is not a doubt of its being most interesting and full of curious and novel scenes some of which though seem most childish."[17] He suggested urgently, "Someone must be found to fashion his remarkable work."[18]

They began the process of what John Blackwood was later to call "unravelling Speke," by considering whom to enlist in the redevelopment. Several of their best and most trusted authors were suggested for the job, the first being Margaret Oliphant, who had been staying with John Blackwood the week before Speke had arrived. Although in the midst of writing her novel *The Perpetual Curate*, Oliphant reworked a typeset sample sent to her and concluded that a total revision was urgently needed. "I see nothing possible to be done with this terrible muddle of your unspeakable Captains, but to rewrite it," she noted to Blackwood. "If he doesn't mind being 'translated,' and you approve, and the gallant Captain remains at hand to explain and describe I daresay I could get through quantities of it while I am here, without injury to the Perpetual, who is the sharer of my inmost thoughts."[19]

John Blackwood, despite viewing Oliphant as a perfect choice, believed it would be unwise to utilize her talents, mainly because for certain reasons he wanted a male "editor." "I wish to goodness I could hand it over to her as nobody could do it better or so quickly," he wrote William, "but I do not think it would do to have a lady assistant, and certainly the operations on the King of Uganda's tool on page 13 would have to be obliterated first."[20] Blackwood's view was that Margaret Oliphant's involvement would somehow inhibit Speke and require shielding Oliphant from graphic material, such as the indicated passage, which described in detail the application of a blister to King Mutesa's genital area.

But Margaret Oliphant was not being excluded on grounds of incompetency, as William Blackwood made clear: "What she has rewritten reads beautifully," he noted to John, "but it is out of the question & must not be thought of further."[21] The issue revolved more around the points that not only was the material too graphic for Mrs. Oliphant to be allowed to handle, but that she did not have the required masculine "insight" into the issue, and that she had no knowledge of the politics and ideological background that surrounded the issue and also needed to be addressed. In short, she was not a "gentleman" who could bond with Speke, put him at ease, and extract the text envisaged.

Such a stance was typical of the overexaggerated concerns of both John and William Blackwood's about the suitability of the material to feminine tastes, but, more important, it provides an inkling of the form John Blackwood was hoping the work would take. It was to be in a form from which women were normally excluded, an explorer's graphic account of his struggle for survival in an inhospitable and primitive land, the detailing of which was to become almost more important than the supposed objective of the work, the geographic siting of the Nile source. Speke, and not the Nile River, was to be the hero and center of the work.

The narrative John Blackwood envisaged publishing, with its accounts of savage "native" life and harrowing adventure, thus needed, in his view, a strong, masculine hand to pull it into shape. As John Blackwood made clear to William in a letter on 30 July, Speke could be envisaged as a heroic figure, from whom "a most quaint, interesting Robinson Crusoe like narrative may be made," going on to pinpoint not only what he felt Speke's collaborator needed to do but also what he believed should be the central section of Speke's narrative, his long, enforced residence at the Ugandan court of the African king Mutesa: "The thing would be for the Editor to read it over with Speke, put questions to him & afterwards write out as nearly in his language as presentable English will permit. The rest of the narrative is not in this sort of detail at all and the centre bit of the book will be this Uganda part with the yachting on the lake & as much as can be said of the river coming out of it."[22]

So, with John Blackwood "sweating over Speke's M.S.," Simpson and William Blackwood hurriedly searched for a suitable male "ghost-writer." Several authors were suggested, including Robert H. Patterson, a Scottish journalist and frequent contributor to *Blackwood's Magazine*; the irrepressible traveler and prolific writer Laurence Oliphant; and George W. Cupples, another *Blackwood's Magazine* stalwart. All proved unavailable or unwilling to undertake the task. Eventually, John Hill Burton, a historian and a substantial contributor to the magazine, was fixed upon as a suitable figure to shepherd Speke's narrative to press.

John Hill Burton (1809–81), an Edinburgh lawyer, historian, and bibliophile, had written for the firm and its magazine since the early 1850s. An erudite scholar with a solid and sober writing style and a reputation for accuracy, he was well trusted and liked by the Blackwood family. But Burton was no mere hack. He had made his literary debut in 1846 with the erudite *Life and Correspondence of David Hume*, a well-researched work that gained him much favor. Likewise his nine-volume *History of Scotland*, published between 1853 and 1870, remained the standard work until superseded by twentieth-century research into the subject. On the basis of the latter work, he was appointed the Queen's Historiographer for Scotland in 1867, an honor he retained until his death.

As a confirmed "Blackwoodian," as John Blackwood called the coterie of authors who wrote for the firm and its magazine, Burton was well versed in the "house" style and views. He was also well skilled in completing such editorial work for the firm. In 1859, for example, he had been called in to edit and rework Dr. Alexander Carlyle's autobiography, which had been passed on in rough manuscript form by Carlyle's descendants. The result was a popular title that sold well and remained in print for several years. Knowing John Hill Burton to be a careful worker who understood the firm's needs in such situations, John Blackwood hoped Burton would accede to his request for help, for he thought him "a thorough good fellow too & we might have great confidence in him."[23] William Blackwood agreed that Burton was the right man for the job, "as you can so thoroughly trust him."[24] The implication was that with Burton in charge the firm's directors could confidently turn their attentions to other matters, secure in the knowledge that the result would be what they wanted.

Burton's previous editorial work had proven that he understood what the firm was interested in marketing and producing. He did not need to be told what to do and how to do it. On 3 August William met briefly with Burton, and Burton hinted he might be willing to undertake the work after studying a few proofs.[25] John Blackwood was glad to hear that Burton might be up to the "task of unravelling Speke."[26] He was also anxious to get Speke out of Strathtyrum, for from the tone of his letters it was obvious that Speke's welcome at Strathtyrum was beginning to wear a bit thin, in part because of his lack of progress on the manuscript: "Burton is a thorough good fellow & if we could only get Speke to comprehend the infernal absurdity & incomprehensibility of the style in which he expresses himself the two would suit each other & work well together as they are both gentlemen."[27]

Here we see Burton fulfilling one of the primary conditions John Blackwood had set for judging Speke's collaborator, that–that of being a "gentleman," a word that carries with it a wide range of cultural, ideological, and social implications. In this case the word "gentleman" meant not only someone who could be discreet about the work, but also someone who shared the value systems that, as we shall see, were to be infused into the revised text.

On 4 August, William was able to report to John that Burton had agreed to "undertake the unravelling of Speke," and that he had formed an opinion similar to that of John Blackwood regarding the correct approach, for "what is wanted as appears to him is to make Speke articulate & not in any way adorn it."[28] Burton's own views on the subject are available only through such indirect comments. Because of the secrecy of the matter, communications were oral; few notes were passed between Burton and the Blackwoods. As William Blackwood reported it, Speke, the inarticulate traveler, was likened by Burton to a small farmer who needed a good lawyer to sort out an argument but was unable to express his grievances properly. Only by endless questioning could all the information come out.

Most significant to Burton, however, was that Speke's writings were "like an endless thread and required no end of breaking."[29] Unraveling Speke was now a matter of breaking up the old narrative and constructing a new one, and William Blackwood was certain that Burton would succeed in doing this. "I think he quite understands what is required," William wrote John Blackwood.[30] Within a week Burton had no doubts about what the end result would be. As John reported on 13 August after Burton met Speke for the first time, "B[urton] thinks it will be the most complete characteristic picture of savage life that ever was."[31] This is the defining moment in the reconstruction of Speke. It illustrates exactly when the ideological framework of the text begins to be reshaped into a preconceived social model, and the work begins to be shaped along the textual plane (in this case, the travel narrative) intended for eventual marketing and selling. And once again we see the submersion of the original "scientific" purpose of the work—the detailing of the evidence for Speke's claims regarding Lake Victoria—into a narrative portraying the triumph of Speke over nature and inferior races.

Speke was installed in "Craighouse," Burton's home, and work was immediately begun on "unravelling" and reworking Speke's text. Burton's initial view of the central theme of Speke's book—the explicit portrayal of savage life, and the implicit triumph of Speke over it—began to dominate the rewriting. But first on the agenda was convincing Speke of the need for drastic changes in his text. Burton had high hopes that once Speke was brought around to accepting his views regarding the text, the work could be completed and published by October. Blackwood's Edinburgh manager George Simpson gleefully reported to J. M. Langford, "The gentleman who we have selected to assist Speke now sees that he can get into shape 2/3rds of the Book in a fortnight, and Speke were he able to do all required of him in 6 weeks and the Book may be published in *3 months*."[32] Simpson suggested that Burton would do well once he exerted his authority in due course, as "he is quite hopeful of making a respectable book if the King will only be docile under his guidance."[33] By 28 August it was obvious that Burton had managed to do so, for by then John Blackwood was reporting cheerfully to his London manager, Joseph Langford: "Speke's book will I think come out very good indeed after all."[34]

Reconciled to the fact that his writing needed polishing more than anything else, Speke buckled to Burton's authority. "Cram on, Cram on, and let us have 'Speke's discovery of the Source of the Nile and life in Africa with Captain Grant' out for Xmas reading," he announced stoically to John Blackwood, concluding, "If you like I will ginger Grant up and set him to work out the pictures."[35] We also begin to see further evidence of the planned reshaping of the work at this stage. Blackwood wrote to Langford, "It is most quaint & curious & I am in hopes we may have a real picture of barbarous life such as no traveller has ever given."[36]

While Burton was busy with Speke's narrative, James Augustus Grant, "gingered up" by Speke, was also busy working on the illustrations. As William Blackwood reported in early September, he was "most anxious that the drawings should be correct & lifelike."[37] Much attention and detail was devoted to the illustrations; indeed, that was one of the first items George Simpson and Joseph Langford concerned themselves with after meeting Speke and Grant in July. On 15 July, three days after arriving back in Edinburgh, Simpson was writing to Langford about the matter of the size and subject matter of the proposed illustrations.

It is significant that Simpson's letter demonstrates even at this early stage a deliberate process of careful restructuring and redefinition that foreshadowed the similar reshaping of Speke's written material. Earlier, Langford had relayed to Simpson Grant's initial insecurity about completing the illustrations and Grant's fears that his draftsmanship was not up to the task.[38] Simpson was firmly of the opinion that Speke should and must overrule Grant's objections, for "any man can be got to put a thing into Drawing after the Travellers have laid down incident, costume, landscape & Ethnographical features."[39] That Grant had been on the expedition meant, as far as Simpson was concerned, a more accurate rendition of the events from him.

Equally important was the size of the engravings made from the illustrations. Simpson wanted large illustrations, which "*tell* far better than the number of small ones," and a careful detailing of African scenery.[40] Describing the plates made for a recent work by Livingstone on Africa, Simpson noted they contained conventional, unrealistic items that were not in Grant's African drawings, something he believed that the engraver, who had also worked on the previous book, should be aware of, so as not to repeat his earlier mistakes. "I looked over the plates done by him for Livingstone," Simpson wrote, "and was struck with the appearance of the old conventional Eastern *Tree* which we all know so so well, but which did not I am certain once show itself in the Drawings you and I looked over last week. His Blacks too, in Livingstone's are just the old things."[41] Such blunders, Simpson emphasized, needed to be avoided, and the work on the illustrations done judiciously, for "all the world will have their eyes upon us in this affair."[42] By August, with Burton taking charge of the writing, Simpson and Langford were proceeding to drop illustrations that did not fit into the newly defined scope of the work. "Mr. Blackwood," Simpson advised Langford, "is confining it entirely to the last expedition . . . his view is therefore keep out of the Illustrations all that refer to anything but the Nile Journey and those cuts should be at once in the Engraver's hands"[43] (Fig. 4).

By the beginning of October, the textual and the illustrative work had been completed. The process of change from original manuscript to final product can be recovered because the National Library of Scotland holds the manuscripts and proofs covering all three stages of revision. The initial manuscript contains sections from Speke's original African journal interspersed with manuscript written by him on his return to Britain, as well as material "rewritten" by Burton. This material was subsequently typeset in its entirety, and the first proofs were extensively revised and written over by Burton, forming the basis for a second proof, which underwent further corrections and deletions before the final printing.

Fig. 4 Illustration by James A. Grant for Speke's *Journal of the Discovery of the Source of the Nile* (1863). Such illustrations were carefully produced to match the revisionist themes introduced into Speke's work.

Speke's original journal presented a journey that was frustrated not only by African cupidity and hostility to foreign intruders, but also by Speke's naivete in dealing with Arab traders and African porters and villagers. It demonstrated his overwhelming ambition and drive to become the first white explorer to reach Lake Victoria at all costs, an ambition that precipitated the abandonment of the temporarily incapacitated Grant at crucial moments in his push forward. It also detailed quite frank discussions of sexual matters between Speke and his African hosts, and hinted at sexual liaisons with African women during his travels. Burton's additions to and revisions of the journal not only changed spelling, punctuation, and grammar but also recast and suppressed passages that would be potentially damaging to the image envisaged for Speke. Speke was to be viewed as a standard bearer for British values, the stern imperialist, paternal, and patient yet firm in coping with adverse circumstances and unruly porters. The presentation of Africa and its people was accordingly manipulated to further highlight Speke's qualities and achievements.

One immediate result of the smoothing of Speke's text into such a form was the loss of the spontaneity and sharp humor punctuating the original manuscript.

After his first audience with King Mutesa, for example, Speke took special note of the king's retreat to his palace hut:

> The Kings gait in retiring was very Majestic but truly ridiculous so much so that I was induced to enquire whether he had been injured in the region of the pelvis: this however was the studied step of all his forefathers in immitation [*sic*] of the Noble Lion.[44]

The final, revised version, by comparison, lacks the crispness of the original and is more ponderous and lumbering in its language:

> The king's gait in retiring was intended to be very majestic, but did not succeed in conveying to me that impression. It was the traditional walk of his race, founded on the step of the lion; but the outward sweep of the legs, intended to represent the stride of the noble beast, appeared to me only to realise a very ludicrous kind of waddle, which made me ask Bombay if anything serious was the matter with the royal person.[45]

Likewise, in an incident where Speke mediated in a local dispute, there is a humorous if caustic note of the source of the problem—a villager insulting a group of Arab traders by threatening to complete the circumcisions they had received as children:

> The Arabs added, and all they found fault with was an expression that in his wrath Manua Sera had given utterance to which was that he vaunted their fathers and mothers had made them Mussulman but he would improve their appearance by cutting the whole of their concerns off. Now however as Manua Sera wished to make friends they would abide by anything that I might propose.[46]

In the interests of propriety, Burton deliberately and long-windedly paraphrased the pithy remark into obscurity and humorlessness:

> To which the Arabs made a suitable answer, adding, that all they found fault with was an insolent remark which, in his wrath, Manua Sera had given utterance to, that their quarrel with him was owing chiefly to a scurvy jest which he had passed on them, and on the characteristic personal

ceremony of initiation to their Mussulman faith. Now, however, as Manua Sera wished to make friends, they would abide by anything that I might propose.[47]

If the ideal explorer was meant to maintain a certain gravitas in his trek through Africa, he was equally meant to maintain a discreet silence regarding sexual matters. Burton eliminated passages dealing with Speke's treatment of King Mutesa and his courtiers for venereal disease, as well as long discussions between Speke and members of Mutesa's royal family regarding pregnancy and sexual practices. More important, the ideological context of the work was changed and manipulated to suit the defined purpose of the work. Speke's original introduction began as follows:

> Our motto being "Evil to him who evil thinks," the reader of these pages must be prepared to see and understand the negroes of Africa in their natural, primitive or naked state; a state in which our forefathers lived before the forced state of civilisation subvented it.[48]

What is notable regarding this introduction is the link it establishes between Africa and Europe. The link is inevitably one designed to illustrate the superiority of European civilization, a civilization that has "progressed" beyond the "primitive" state of African civilization. Also implicit in this beginning, however, is an invitation to the reader to view the African people in light of an almost Rousseauian view of the "Noble Savage" existing in a state of nature once common to all humankind. This view of Africa and its peoples was rejected during the revision process. In the revised first proofs, the passage was struck out and substituted with the following statement in John Hill Burton's handwriting:

> In the following pages I have endeavoured to describe all that appeared to me most important and interesting among the events and the scenes that came under my notice during my sojourn in the interior of Africa. If my account should not entirely harmonise with preconceived notions as to primitive races, I cannot help it. I profess accurately to describe naked Africa—Africa in those places where it has not received the slightest impulse, whether for good or for evil, from European civilisation.[49]

As can be seen, the revision is more overtly hostile and categorical in its definition of Africa. The narration is more authoritarian: it is no longer the reader but Speke who is allowed to "understand" Africa, presenting only what he thinks important about the subcontinent. Even more crucial, all links between Europe and Africa have been erased. This is a naked, dark Africa disconnected from and untouched by European impulses and civilization.

In similar manner, passages were rewritten to turn what had originally been noted as supposition and rumor into verified fact. At one stage, passing through the land of the Wazaramo, a tribe of "expert slave hunters," Speke wrote in his journal that travelers seldom saw traces of them but "Albinos however have been seen and the traces of burnt witches are of frequent occurrence [sic]."[50] The published version presents it differently: "We sometimes noticed Albinos, with greyish-blue eyes and light straw-coloured hair. Not unfrequently we would pass on the track-side small heaps of white ashes, with a calcined bone or two among them. These, we were told, were the relics of burnt witches."[51] The change is subtle yet significant: authority has been added in revision. In the original version, Speke relates something obviously gained secondhand. He has not seen Albinos or burnt witches but has merely heard of them, from whom he does not say. In the revised version, however, Speke the African expert is now a personal witness to these sights. With a few brief changes we have moved from speculation and vagueness to an authoritative statement detailing African otherness and unchristian practices.

Other passages further emphasize an implied moral judgment of Africans. African society, in contrast to European civilization, is depicted as of nomadic nature, dominated by superstitious beliefs (encouraging polygamy and self-interest), lacking an effective government and a structured agricultural base, and gripped by intertribal rivalries exarcerbated by the slave trade. The result, the revised text unequivocally states, is an African man who "works his wife, sells his children, enslaves all he can lay hands upon, and, unless when fighting for the property of others, contents himself with drinking, singing, and dancing like a baboon, to drive dull care away."[52] Even when Africans come in contact with the outer world, the revised text suggests that few seem to profit. Freed slaves, for example, are described as retaining "all the superstitious notions of the true aborigines, though somewhat modified, and even corrupted, by that acquaintance with the outer world which sharpens their wits."[53] They become individuals caught between two worlds, lacking the moral, religious, or social ties necessary for being useful workers. "Having no God, in the Christian sense of the term, to fear or worship, they have no love for truth, honour or honesty. Controlled by no government, nor yet by home ties, they have no reason to think of or look to the future. Any venture attracts them when hard-up for food; and the more roving it is, the better they like it."[54]

This is not to suggest that Speke objected strenuously to such an interpretation of African civilization. That Speke believed to a certain extent in such evangelical views can be seen in the similar conclusions reached in the introductory paragraphs of both manuscript and published texts. Both stress and echo a view common to the period, that Africa had been historically cursed since biblical times by an absence of Christianity in its midst: "Whilst the people of Europe and Asia were blessed by communion with God through the medium of His prophets, and obtained divine laws to regulate their ways and keep them in mind of Him who made them, the Africans were excluded from this dispensation, and consequently have no idea of an overruling Providence or a future state."[55]

Such rhetoric, as Christine Bolt has pointed out in *Victorian Attitudes to Race*, reflected the increasing and dominant use of religious and political generalizations to justify nineteenth-century colonial activity in Africa.[56] "Opening" Africa, to use a phrase often quoted in Speke's journal, was deemed necessary on the grounds that a continent without a proper religion and civilization needed enlightening and rigorous management. Speke's triumph over the inhospitable "Dark Continent" could thus be seen as conforming to a standard view that success in Africa called for a type of "muscular Christianity" coupled with a vigorous "management" of the indigenous population.

The finished product pleased the publishers. As William Blackwood contentedly noted to his uncle John toward the end of October, Burton "'had put a great deal into the book that he got from conversations with Speke,' just the very thing you wished & I told him so."[57] The printing and binding proceeded apace, and on 11 December 1863 the book was formally launched in London. On and before its publication, John Blackwood did what he could to encourage interest in the work, sending news of it to friends, and advance copies to reviewers likely to be able to help in its promotion. In his letters Blackwood developed and actively promoted the theme that had underpinned John Hill Burton's revision of the work. He presented the journal as an accurate picture by Speke of "savage life," made all the more interesting by the quaint, and thus, in his interpretation, more genuine, narration.

Although acknowledging the need for outside help in setting down Speke's story, Blackwood was careful to present the work as almost entirely Speke's own, thus glossing over its complete revision and reconstruction by John Hill Burton. Writing to John Delane, editor of *The Times*, on 7 December, Blackwood described how Speke's "ideas of grammar are of the most original description," continuing: "However, we have done nothing to his text except by questioning him, and correcting him where he was likely to prove unintelligible. So the book is entirely in his own quaint language, and a more genuine one never was published."[58] He went on to say, "To me it realises savages and savage life in a way that nothing else ever did; but I daresay I am not a fair judge, as I seem to see and hear my modest good-natured dare-devil friend in the midst of these brutes, as quiet as if he were smoking his cigar in the woods at Strathtyrum."[59] Likewise, in describing Speke's writing difficulties to another correspondent, Blackwood stressed Speke's simple nature, repeating a metaphor seen in previous correspondence with William: "He certainly has not the pen of De Foe but he has the heart of Robinson Crusoe with a dash of Friday about him."[60] While tacitly acknowledging Speke's literary failings, John Blackwood was quick to point out that the work, while implicitly written up by someone else, was still authentic, told as it was in Speke's unusual and plain manner. "Speke," Blackwood stressed, "as you may have heard or at all events will speedily perceive is anything but a literary man & has the vaguest possible notions as to composition. The difficulty therefore was to let him tell his own story in his own way & yet prevent him from being unintelligible. With what success this has been done I cannot well tell. At all events the book is genuine."[61]

At the same time as Blackwood was promoting the work as "genuine," he was also privately thanking and remunerating Burton with £250 for having "made" it so. Acknowledging the debt to Burton in a letter on 21 December, he wrote: "I cannot however sufficiently thank you for the skill and good feeling with which you entered upon the cause & have carried it through," for "had you not so kindly taken the 'Bana' to your home I do not know how the thing could have been done."[62] He also commented on an aspect of Speke's character that had been carefully hidden from prospective readers of the journal: Speke's lack of literary understanding of what had been achieved. "That he should rightly understand," Blackwood wryly noted, "the literary merit of what has been done to his work is not, as you know, in the nature of things, but he warmly appreciates the merits and kindness of 'Old B.'"[63]

Anxious as Blackwood was to project Speke as being cast from a heroic mold, there was no disguising the fact that Speke did not quite measure up. While Blackwood had no doubt about Speke's courage and determination, the characteristics he stressed most in his descriptions of Speke were simplicity and energy—specifically, a childlike simplicity and an impetuous energy. Implicit in Blackwood's comments was the realization that these traits made for an often ungracious self-centeredness that did not give proper credit to those to whom it was due. But in public Blackwood sought to turn these characteristics into advantages by suggesting that it was these specific traits that had made it possible for Speke to survive and conquer in Africa. As he wrote to John Delane, "I never met with such a mixture of simplicity and almost childish ignorance, combined with the most indefatigable energy and the most wonderful shrewdness in his own particular way. It must have been this strange mixture of character that carried him through, and gave him such power over these creatures."[64]

The issues raised by Speke's claims regarding his discovery were not conclusively settled for another eleven years. In 1875 Henry Stanley successfully proved Lake Victoria's role as the source of the Nile river during his circumnavigation of the lake. But for John Blackwood, the scientific and geographical questions and criticisms raised by Speke's claims were merely side issues. What mattered most was that Speke had achieved what others had failed to do: he had found the true source of the Nile. As he wrote to John Hill Burton shortly after Speke's death in 1864, the most important point about Speke's journal had been its record of his unique role in history as the first to uncover the Nile source: "The[y] may cavail [sic] as they like about the Discovery, & he must of course be wrong on some points, but in the main he has done it & the man who first forced his way through those regions, where the Nile unquestionably does rise, will live to the end of time as the Discoverer."[65]

As we have seen, this had not been the sole motivation for the firm working so hard to reconstruct Speke. Blackwood's profession that Speke's discovery of Lake Victoria was what set him apart from all others formed only a small part of his willing reconstruction of Speke's work, yet it was to prove important in the successful marketing of Speke's account. By emphasizing Speke's unique role as a successful explorer and Imperial adventurer, rather than as a scientist or geographer, Speke the inarticulate traveler was transformed into an articulate, saleable commodity. Filtered through the literary and editorial reconstructions of John Hill Burton and the Blackwoods, Speke's account provided the firm with a product that was successful with the reading public. It did so by reiterating standard views of Africa that fitted generalized, European notions of the area. Its appeal in and beyond the borders of Great Britain was confined by the sales figures. Within a year of initial publication, the work had sold 7,600 copies and gone through three editions, and foreign rights to the work had been negotiated in France, Germany, and the United States. Speke's successful reinvention as author, and the process of his transformation, can thus be seen as a classic example of how the Blackwood firm manipulated both text and author to serve ideological purposes, as well as to safeguard a commercial investment.

Reade Revised

A *Woman Hater* and the
Women's Medical Movement

In 1876 the struggle over the right of British women to medical education was at its height. The movement, which had been gathering momentum for more than a decade, now took more forceful action to institute change through existing legal and institutional frameworks. Bills were introduced in Parliament to amend the British Medical Act of 1858 to give women the right to serve as physicians, and there was intense lobbying of university and medical committees to gain women the right to be admitted to their medical programs. In the summer of 1876 Charles Reade (1814–80) threw his literary weight behind the movement, addressing the issue of women physicians in his novel *A Woman Hater*. The work, serialized in *Blackwood's Magazine* between June 1876 and June 1877, and subsequently issued as a three-volume novel, depicted the struggle of women to qualify in the British medical field. Although described by one critic as "an amatory novel of manners" in which the misogynist main character is moved by the charms and tribulations of a female physician, the work was also a thinly disguised polemical plea on behalf of the movement for medical reform.[1]

Reade's work was one of the first to dramatize the pioneering efforts of Elizabeth Blackwell and Sophia Jex-Blake to breach social and medical antagonism and prejudices and to redefine women's roles in British society. Reade's publisher, Blackwood's, however, was not sympathetic to the cause espoused, resulting in troublesome ideological clashes. The objections of the firm's managers, reflecting in microcosm the contemporary responses of conservative social forces to the women's medical movement, made the process of composition and publication troubled and uneasy.

Previously unpublished letters between the firm's managers and Reade suggest that Reade's work was initially accepted only with the idea of "taming," or containing the author to conform with the firm's preconceived notions of literature and intended audiences. But, as in the case of the medical movement the text spoke for, initial attempts at containment soon proved unsustainable, and the firm, much like the entrenched social elements threatened by the proposed reforms, began a rearguard action to retrieve and rein in this new and potentially disruptive force. The manner in which both social and literary challenges to entrenched ideological positions were met, and the end result of these clashes, provides us with a fascinating perspective on contemporary reactions to women healers, as well as on the infiltration of social agendas into the business of publishing.

The Medical Reform Act of 1858 was passed by the British Parliament in response to growing public concern over the lack of codified standards regulating the medical profession in Britain. The standards and regulation of medical licensing and practice enshrined in the 1858 act also marked a movement toward an increased professionalization of medical practices. Needless to say, the Act implicitly addressed itself to regulating male medical practitioners, as women had been excluded from medical study and practice. Until the second half of the nineteenth century, except in the unlicensed and unregarded area of midwifery, women in Britain were not allowed access to any medical training whatsoever. This was in direct contrast to other European countries, such as Italy, where women had played a central role in the study and practice of medicine in universities for several centuries.[2] As Ann Oakley has suggested, British attitudes on this subject were part of a larger socialized process of limitations imposed on women before and during the Victorian era.[3] The middle-class ideology of domesticity, and the implication that women were incompatible with occupational roles outside that defined sphere, was a central factor in the widespread nineteenth- and early-twentieth-century social and institutional opposition to women's education and to women practicing as physicians. One of the most ferocious and powerful opponents of the women's medical movement during this early period, Sir Robert Christison (1797–1882), president of the British Medical Association and personal physician to Queen Victoria from 1848 to 1882, voiced the general, mid-century institutionalized view when he suggested that "female practitioners were not wanted in this country . . . that [they] would be injurious to medicine as a scientific profession and that, in the nature of things, the constitution of the female mind and frame is, with rare exceptions, quite unsuited to the exigencies of medical and surgical practices."[4] Such intransigent beliefs ignored even contemporary examples of dedicated and eminently suited female practitioners, such as Elizabeth Blackwell and Elizabeth Garrett-Anderson, who had managed to evade the restrictions placed in their way and carve out successful medical careers.

In fact, it was precisely the ability of Blackwell and Anderson to qualify under the new regulations of 1858 that first focused male medical attention on the thorny issue of women physicians. Elizabeth Blackwell (1821–1910), an American though born in Bristol, was the first woman to qualify as a physician in the United States, graduating from Geneva University in Upstate New York in 1849. After further training in Paris and London, Blackwell returned to New York, where she practiced for seven years before coming back to Britain in 1858, the year the Medical Act took effect. One of the Act's aims was to establish a register of all legally qualified medical practitioners in Britain. Those currently practicing who had received medical qualifications from foreign universities were allowed to register. All those applying for registration subsequent to 1858 were required to hold certified qualifications from one of nineteen approved British medical examining boards.[5] As a foreign qualified medical practitioner, Blackwell was licensed, and thus able to establish a precedent by becoming the first woman registered under the Medical Act. She returned to the United States soon after, however, declaring that the obstacles to successful work were too great for her to overcome on her own. "I shall therefore endeavour to prepare others for English work by receiving and educating students in America," she wrote her sister in 1859.[6] Blackwell was an inspiration for future pioneers, one of the first of whom was Elizabeth Garrett-Anderson.

Elizabeth Garrett (1836–1917), later Elizabeth Garrett-Anderson, decided to become a doctor after attending a series of Dr. Blackwell's lectures in London in early 1859. Unlike Blackwell, she faced more substantial difficulties under the newly enacted laws. In order to qualify in Britain, she was required to undertake a medical program approved by one of the nineteen organizations listed in the Medical Act. Several organizations refused her application for examination, before the Hall of Apothecaries, under threat of legal action by Garrett's father, reluctantly agreed in 1861 to examine her once she fulfilled the required conditions of study. Despite many setbacks, including being forced to seek private tuition when refused access to classes and medical wards in Edinburgh, St. Andrews, and London, Garrett-Anderson completed her studies and passed the required exams in 1865. She was duly registered the following year.

Garrett-Anderson's registration provoked an immediate reaction among leaders of the medical community. Elizabeth Blackwell's registration could be ignored as an exception that impinged little on the accepted state of things. Garrett-Anderson's success, however, was seen not only as a challenge to cherished perceptions regarding women's limitations and role in society, but also as a professional and economic threat to male hegemony in licensed medical practice. One leading medical journal declared, "For ourselves, we hold that the admission of women in the ranks of medicine is an egregious blunder, derogatory to the status and character of the female sex, and likely to be injurious to the highest degree to the interests and public estimation of the profession they seek to invade."[7] Such rhetoric suggests that underpinning the virulent opposition to women's medical practice was the fear of losing control. Garrett-Anderson, and those who followed her, were in effect challenging the norms of society, which demanded a compliant, subordinate role for middle-class women, and the medical organization that upheld and reinforced such norms in theoretical, scientific language.

In striking contrast, such objections were less in evidence regarding women's participation in nursing. Florence Nightingale's small volunteer group of dedicated female nurses had done much during the Crimean War of 1854–56 to illustrate the capabilities of middle-class women to operate beyond the domestic confines of the home. But Florence Nightingale's success in transforming nursing from a menial, untrained occupation to a highly skilled, honorable profession suitable for educated women was grounded in socially acceptable ideological terms. Nightingale's "women in white" were invested "with the sanctity of a religious vocation,"[8] with official prefixes of "Sister" and uniforms modeled on nuns' habits, emphasizing the pious and sanctified creed underlying their work. Similarly, this profession was presented as a natural corollary to a woman's supposed domestic nature, a natural extension of the ministering "angel in the house" role that male society accorded her. Nursing was also less threatening professionally, subordinate as it was taken to be to the qualified medical practitioner. Nurses could be allowed to tend and clean the sick and wounded but were not allowed to make important medical decisions. Furthermore, the long work hours and low wages for those who chose it as a vocation ensured that there was little economic threat to established medical practice.

Thus, while Florence Nightingale's crusade to open the first nursing school for women was successful in 1860, Garrett-Anderson's struggles to open up medical education to women a few years later resulted in setback. After Garrett-Anderson's successful registration, the board of the Hall of the Apothecaries changed the regulations to prohibit medical students from substituting private instruction for class instruction.[9] In so doing, the board in effect made sure no woman could emulate her. With few medical institutions willing at the time to allow women to attend courses in such "indelicate" subjects as anatomy, and no concessions allowed for private tuition to make up for the deficit, the issue of women healers seemed successfully controlled.

Four years later, Sophia Jex-Blake (1840–1912) led the next major challenge to the medical system. Born in Hastings and educated at Queen's College for Women in London, where she briefly taught mathematics, Sophia Jex-Blake committed herself to battling for women's rights to medical qualification and practice after a period of study under Elizabeth Blackwell in New York. In 1869, after gaining support from professors sympathetic to the cause, Jex-Blake and five other women were allowed to matriculate in the medical program of the University of Edinburgh. Their battle to complete their studies, in the face of general medical and university opposition, lasted four years. The arguments used against their admission ranged from the belief that mixed classes would impair class discipline and inhibit lectures on such "sensitive" subjects as anatomy, to the suggestions that biological and religious grounds made women unfit for medical work. One correspondent summarized it in the medical journal *The Lancet:* "I believe most conscientiously and thoroughly that women as a body are sexually, constitutionally and mentally unfitted for the hard and incessant toil, and for the heavy responsibilities of general medical and surgical practice."[10] More to the point, declaimed a member of Parliament in a contemporary debate on the subject, "God sent women to be ministering angels, to soothe the pillow, administer the palliative, whisper words of comfort to the tossing sufferer. Let that continue to be a woman's work. Leave the physician's function, the scientific lore, the iron wrist and iron will to men."[11] In all cases, it was seen as imperative that this movement be stopped, interfering as it did with the established status quo. The issue seemed contained in 1873 when, after lengthy proceedings, the university council nullified the original admission of Jex-Blake and her female colleagues, declaring it illegal under university regulations. The wide coverage accorded their struggle, however, converted influential allies to the cause. Over the next three years, the movement to force the issue of women's education and women's rights to be physicians onto the political agenda gathered pace, with much help in Parliament from Sir William Cowper-Temple, James Stansfeld, and Russell Gurney. Their efforts culminated in various proposals presented to Parliament between May and June 1876 calling for the explicit removal of restrictions on granting medical qualifications on the basis of sex.[12]

It was at this juncture that Charles Reade's novel began its serialized run in *Blackwood's Magazine*. Reade was one of the most successful writers of his time, judged by his contemporaries as the equal of Charles Dickens and George Eliot and able to command extraordinarily high sums for his work.[13] Best known now, if at all, as the author of the massive historical romance *The Cloister and the Hearth*, during his lifetime Reade had often courted controversy with his depiction of sexually frank material and his espousal of radical issues. *Griffith Gaunt*, with its candid treatment of sexual jealousy, infidelity, and bigamy, caused an uproar on its publication in 1866 and was bitterly attacked for its "immorality." Other works, such as *Hard Cash* (1863), which tackled the issue of mental asylum reforms, and the sensational and extremely popular work *It Is Never Too Late to Mend* (1856), which urged the reform of prison conditions and treatment of prisoners, were among the many he wrote as a result of "being inspired by a moral purpose."[14]

In the case of *A Woman Hater*, the justice of women's claims to medical education, and the renewed efforts to secure Parliamentary reform on this issue, gave Reade the themes he needed. In early February 1876 he approached Joseph Langford, Blackwood's London manager and a fellow Garrick Club member, regarding publishing his new novel, "a story of strong sexual interest but no improprieties," in *Blackwood's Magazine*.[15] For years Langford had been urging John Blackwood, head of the firm, to offer for Reade's work, suggesting that his literary reputation and sales potential were worth paying for.[16] Langford had frequently stressed his belief, in the light of Reade's controversial reputation and writing, that controlling and managing Reade was the key to successfully introducing the author's material into the magazine's pages. In 1865, for example, when Reade had approached Langford regarding the possibilities of serializing *Griffith Gaunt* in *Blackwood's Magazine*, Langford urged John Blackwood to consider the idea of guiding Reade in an appropriate manner. "He is a queer temper but has never yet met his match in a publisher," he noted, "and I think would be plastic enough under your treatment."[17] Blackwood was impressed by the initial material submitted, but he rejected the work because Reade sought too a high price for it.[18]

After Reade's approach in 1876 regarding *A Woman Hater*, Langford reiterated his views concerning Reade's pliability, telling Blackwood: "You know that I have always believed that C.R. would prove much more practicable and amenable to management under your direction than in the hands of any publisher with whom he has hitherto been connected. . . . There is no doubt I think that if he could be controlled his work would suit Maga, and you could approach him in a way that would bring him into harmony."[19] Such advice fitted in with the role John Blackwood accorded himself. It could not be denied that publishing was first and foremost a business, designed to produce a profitable commodity. But a central concept promoted by most leading Victorian publishers, of whom John Blackwood was one, was that their products were issued primarily for aesthetic, not commercial, reasons.[20] Lip service was paid to their desire to produce high-quality literature, meant to educate and entertain but never to raise a blush to the cheeks of middle-class maidens. Thus the marketplace was further stratified by the concept of intended audiences. In Charles Reade's case, it was believed that his potential audience might need to be protected from any deviations from the established aesthetic norm.

Reade's works, however, published by less aesthetically involved but more commercially astute houses, had proven quite successful despite the occasional ban by Mudie's Select Library, the primary distributor of most mid-century publications.[21] John Blackwood faced a difficult decision. On the one hand, there was Blackwood's defined, aesthetic views of what he believed his intended audience expected of a "Blackwood" product. The novels John Blackwood had serialized in *Blackwood's Magazine* were aimed at a mainstream, essentially middle-class reading public. It was an audience thought likely to vote Conservative, an audience that was viewed as suspicious of change and unwilling to tolerate challenges to the literary and social status quo. With such an audience in mind, John Blackwood could not help but approach Reade's controversial output with suspicion. On the other hand, the commercial success that other publishers had gained with Reade's work suggested an economic benefit that the Blackwood firm could not ignore. The solution was to combine both aesthetic and commercial aims by "taming" Reade, restraining, channeling, and directing him to produce a text fitting the editors' conceived notions of appropriate fiction and satisfying the magazine's intended audience. Thus Blackwood, in his self-appointed role as arbiter of literary taste, consciously planned to subordinate and make compliant this potentially troublesome author, much like the male physicians—who considered themselves the sole arbiters of disease and its treatment—consciously sought to defuse the perceived threat of the women's medical movement.

At this stage Reade had given little away regarding the possible subject of the work, but his suggestion that it would be one of "strong sexual interest" slightly worried John Blackwood. In a note meant to be shown to Reade, Blackwood indicated to Langford his interest in securing the work, "as I have a very high opinion of his Genius and I am very much inclined to entertain the proposition if we can arrange matters." He insisted, however, on seeing a considerable portion of the work before committing himself, for Reade's genius often strayed into areas of which Blackwood did not approve. As Blackwood tactfully expressed it, Reade's sometimes "eccentric" tastes had in the past produced material "that would be unsuitable in the Magazine." In light of this, John Blackwood asked for a portion of the manuscript and an outline of the general scope of the work before proceeding, "as I should be in a very serious scrape if I found myself constrained to publish what could neither please my readers nor myself."

It is clear that Blackwood intended from the beginning to assert his right to manipulate the material should it overstep his view of appropriate fiction. In a subtle aside meant simultaneously to flatter and warn Reade, Blackwood noted: "I have always found the biggest fish the most ready to listen to any little bit of advice or remonstrance and happily . . . such advice or remonstrance are very rarely called for." But, he added he did not foresee any such problems, for "I know well that a man of power must have his swing or he cannot do his work well and in my 30 years experience as an Editor I have never had any serious difficulty in that way."[22]

Reade responded vigorously to this initial salvo in a long letter dated 19 February 1876. He interpreted Blackwood's description of his general "eccentricities" as a veiled attack on the supposedly salacious nature of his work, and suggested that his writing, although franker in tone than some of his contemporaries, was nevertheless ideologically sound. "What I have revelled in and dwelt upon has been virtuous love," he announced. This, he suggested chauvinistically, was a theme far superior to those developed by some of his contemporaries, for "the frailties our female writers dwell upon I skim, when I do not entirely avoid them."[23] Having said this, though, he was willing to let Blackwood read part of the manuscript before making a decision, telling Langford in private, "Mr. Blackwood has his opinions and has a right to judge."[24] He even expressed a willingness to allow Blackwood editorial privileges over his story at this early stage. "If at any part of the tale Mr. Blackwood finds lines in the ms. which would give him pain to publish," he wrote, "they will be pointed out to me, and I shall excise them before the copy goes to the printer."[25]

An intriguing point is why Reade chose to publish with Blackwood, whom he must have known would prove antagonistic to his subject matter. It certainly wasn't for the money. Reade surprised Langford by mentioning he had turned down a higher offer from Chatto & Windus, casually confiding, "I do not care for that."[26] One biographer has suggested that Reade's vanity stirred him to publish in a monthly journal that had accepted Anthony Trollope and George Eliot, authors he admired but thought himself the equal of.[27] Reade's nephew hinted at subterfuge, coyly suggesting that the work appeared anonymously in the magazine for specific reasons "never revealed, even to Messrs. Blackwood."[28] A possible explanation may lie in a comment Reade made early in the negotiation process. From the beginning, Reade had hinted that his work would prove revolutionary in theme. A week into the negotiations, he slyly announced to John Blackwood, "This story will contain nine characters; one of them is entirely new in fiction, yet is a character of the day, and will I think lead to profitable discussion." He went on to say, "In dealing with this character Mr. Blackwood can, I think, be of great service to me."[29]

Such a statement suggests that Reade had an ulterior motive in placing *A Woman Hater* with Blackwood. Running the story through *Blackwood's Magazine*, a bastion of conservative opinion, published in Edinburgh, the city that had seen the bitterest opposition to women physicians to date, was a way of striking at the heart of the enemy. Edinburgh was also, in Reade's opinion, a major intellectual capital, "the only centre of British literature, except London."[30] And having judged John Blackwood as among those opposing the reforms espoused, Reade might have seen this as an opportunity to test the power and passion of his argument, before publication, on an influential leader of the Edinburgh community. Guided by Blackwood's objections, he could then refine the argument to penetrate, as one commentator suggested, "within the very gates, so to speak, of the enemy's citadel."[31]

This indeed seems to be the implication of many of Reade's subsequent responses to Blackwood's objections. "You can expect in me certain powerful convictions, which unfortunately do not accord with your own at present," Reade sternly warned Blackwood at one point, concluding, in a lighthearted but provoking manner, that converting Blackwood to the cause was partly his aim: "I warn you, your prejudices will be sore shaken by this tale. Yet we shall worm our-selves into your reason, we shall rouse your manhood, and your sense of fair play, and we may even touch your heart, and, if we do that, 'you are done for.'"[32]

Thus we see two conflicting, ideological agendas being drawn up between pub-lisher and author. On the one hand, the publisher, seeking to appropriate Reade's text to fit into a predefined periodical discourse, and on the other hand, the author, seeking to espouse change by working within, while yet escaping, the ideologi-cal and literary boundaries assigned him.

The initial chapters sent for Blackwood's approval had little that seemed rev-olutionary, centering as they did on the amorous intrigues of several members of the British landed gentry in the glamorous surroundings of Hamburg. Black-wood's first impressions were that it was "unquestionably good." As he told Lang-ford, "it is strong meat & if it does not get too high there is no mistake about it."[33] After reading further installments, Blackwood felt confirmed in his original view. "There is no doubt as to its great merit and powerful interest," he wrote Lang-ford on March 13, continuing, "There is great fun too. They are a very amorous lot and the bad man & bad girl are perhaps too transparently bad." What Reade intended to do with this amorous and bad lot, though, gave Blackwood some qualms, for as yet there was no sign of the revolutionary character Reade had warned Blackwood to expect. "I think he must mean to send more today," Black-wood noted, for "there is no introduction yet of the other character in the drama on which you said he so much relied." Nevertheless, Blackwood concluded, he felt it was a strong beginning, "altho I wish the tone were a shade more agree-able & like the Magazine."[34]

Langford agreed that Reade's work seemed up to the mark, for "there is real power beyond a doubt and the story starts in a way that may lead to very inter-esting complications, and of course he is workman enough and artist enough to be allowed to lay out his canvas in his own way." He also assured Blackwood that Reade seemed quite amenable to editorial suggestions and only required gentle handling to be moved in the right direction. "You may do what you like with him with a little humouring," Langford suggested.[35]

On March 21 Charles Reade sent Blackwood a large section of the new work, announcing dramatically that it was "a great chapter of human nature and of infant civilisation."[36] Blackwood was finally introduced to the new character and theme Reade had hinted at but not revealed earlier: "Aesculapia, or the Doctress and her struggles."[37] Having transported his main characters back to Britain, Reade in this section clumsily contrives an encounter between the self-confessed misogynist Harrington Vizard and the starving female physician Rhoda Gale. Vizard buys lunch for the forlorn, hungry woman and is promptly rewarded with an uninterrupted, fact-ridden account of her struggles against social and medical prejudice. This account would eventually encompass two monthly installments and take up more than twenty-eight double-column magazine pages. Reade, making much issue of the originality and topical relevance of this section and of his new character, pressed Blackwood to keep it a secret, for "new ideas of any magnitude are now very rare in fiction" and others were bound to take it up and bungle it before Reade's work was ready.[38]

Reade also used the supposed originality of the work as a lever to force Blackwood to a decision, urging him to set a date soon for the start of its run in the magazine, while public opinion was focused on the novel issue of women physicians and there was still a chance of profitably introducing such new material. To do so, Reade suggested, would also significantly aid the women's cause, "for if we strike while the iron is hot, that is to say, while the ladies are still struggling, we shall serve a good cause and perhaps make a big hit; but we shall fall comparatively flat, if we hang fire till Cowper Temple and others have righted the wrong without our aid."[39] In noting this, Reade cleverly balanced ideological and material concerns. On the one hand, he meant his story to serve a cause that he knew John Blackwood did not agree with. On the other hand, there was the suggestion that speedy publication of such controversial material could materially enhance Blackwood's pocket. There was nothing like public controversy to improve sales. Reade was careful to emphasize that the controversy would be confined solely to the question of principle. Bearing in mind John Blackwood's views of Reade's previous "eccentricities," a phrase Reade knew masked a distaste for his often controversial subject matter, Reade assured Blackwood: "There is to be no bigamy, concubinage, seduction, nor anything the most prudish person may not read."[40]

With the true purpose of Reade's work now revealed, Blackwood was left to ponder his options. After reading through the new batch of manuscript, he wrote on March 27 indicating his willingness to begin the work in the May number of the magazine, "if you think you are far enough advanced to keep up the Numbers continuously from that time." As far as Reade's style was concerned, Blackwood thought it powerful and vivid enough to make him confident that Reade would produce "a capital Novel." He was even prepared to accept the disruptive novelty of a woman physician, while making clear his opposition to the cause. "I am no believer in lady doctors and do not think the movement can ever come to much," he told Reade, "but your idea is novel and delicately handled may be very popular."[41] Blackwood's only immediate reservations concerned Reade's "love of plain speaking and warm flesh tints," which Blackwood insisted needed to be toned down.

Blackwood took great alarm, however, at Reade's next letter, in which Reade intimated he would be addressing the issue of male doctors whose consultation caused some women "to lose some of that delicate bloom which adorned their modesty before." It is doubtful whether Reade meant to suggest, as Blackwood supposed, that rape by unscrupulous physicians was an ever-present threat in the profession and yet a further reason for allowing women into medical practice. But, for John Blackwood, the danger of such potentially libelous accusations being made threatened the integrity both of Reade's work and of the magazine's reputation. "The above subject carried out fully and forcibly would compromise both you and me and defeat the object you have in view at the first start," Blackwood angrily warned Reade. It was one thing to suggest that there were some bad apples within the profession, but to generalize this into an assault on male doctors was something Blackwood would not allow.

In fact, Blackwood argued, taking his cue from his medical acquaintances, Reade would be better off arguing the opposite, for "as a body medical men are justly esteemed, and I suspect young girls would be better in their hands than in those of strong minded women." He concluded: "I would shrink and advise you to shrink from anything like a general accusation of the Doctors as impairers of female modesty."[42] Reade realized he had overstepped the mark, and immediately wrote to placate Blackwood, carefully distancing himself from the libelous imputations and assuring Blackwood that the statement had been misunderstood. In fact, he would now drop any hint of the subject, for "such a matter as this must not enter into the narrative." Reade stressed, furthermore, that in the interest of balance he would include in the dialogue statements that represented the opinions of those in favor of women physicians and of those against. Thus one character would be seen to state that "women should mind their own business and not meddle with men's." Rhoda Gale, of course, would be seen to object to this. "You must not however, be shocked if she should say 'why should not the female intellect be tried in a science where the male intellect has blundered for centuries,' and so give a little sting of the mindless errors, which at various epochs have had the unanimous assent of physicians, 'not one of them female.'"[43] Blackwood, satisfied with this, proceeded to send the manuscript to be prepared for printing.

Thus the first major clash over the substance of Reade's "new" material resulted in concessions modifying the theme and language of key points in the "Doctress" section. Blackwood felt he was succeeding in containing Reade in such a "ticklish" area. Reade, however, viewed it as providing a useful gauge of the reactions of the Edinburgh establishment. "Old Christison is alive and they are frightened in Edinburgh," he told Langford with a laugh after dealing with Blackwood's criticisms.[44]

Over the next two months Blackwood continued demanding that Reade make changes to the text, mostly insignificant substitutions of words and phrases deemed vulgar or inappropriate, such as "left" instead of "sacked" or "lover" instead of "fancy man." Blackwood's defense was that "a chance word or expression that may grate often does mischief drawing more attention than it deserves."[45] In fact, there was little in the opening sections to disturb the parochial feathers of the magazine's readers, a point that was reflected in the favorable comments reported to John Blackwood after its commencement in the June issue. "All I heard of part one of *Woman Hater* in London was in its favour,"[46] he reported to Reade at the end of June, including a tribute from Margaret Oliphant, who found "a swing of easy power about him [Reade] which is beyond praise."[47]

The first four installments of the work, appearing between June and September 1876, had little to indicate any links with the concurrent struggles for medical reform. If Reade's initial purpose had been to influence public opinion regarding women's roles in society, the initial installments were a signal failure in this direction. Four women (an opera singer, two bored socialites and their protective aunt) and four men were shuffled around Hamburg and England in a plot filled with matchmaking, social banter, mistaken identities, and worries about observing social proprieties. The female characters were little more than iconic representations of women as Victorian patriarchal society wanted to see them, their lives dominated by romantic and material concerns, their days taken up with an endless succession of outings, entertainment, and eagerly awaited romantic encounters. Therefore Reade's introduction and subsequent development of Rhoda Gale, the struggling physician, in the October and November installments of the magazine marked a radical break in style and characterization. Rhoda Gale, much like the new political force she represents, acts as a disruptive force, breaking not only the social patterns and social norms established by the female characters in earlier chapters, but also the approved narrative flow of the work. "It is a novelty in Novels and gives occasion to think," was the noncommittal view of John Blackwood on first seeing the proofs in late June.[48]

Reade's novel act was to tip a tract into the middle of the work. The introduction of Rhoda Gale serves as an opportunity for Reade to recapitulate the struggle to open medical training to women at the University of Edinburgh between 1869 and 1873. "You will hear a story the public is deeply interested in and does not know it," the reader is warned, "a story that will certainly be referred to with wonder and shame whenever civilisation shall become a reality, and law cease to be a tool of injustice and monopoly" (October 1876, 381). Reade had based his remarks on information gained during the summer of 1876 from Sophia Jex-Blake, the leader of the ill-fated assault of the educational barriers at Edinburgh.[49] As a polemical plea, the section stands out for its power and persuasive argument, so well supplied with facts and figures that, as one critic noted sarcastically, "it is necessary to confer on the narrator a phenomenal memory acutely cultivated by art to render its delivery credible."[50] Even Sophia Jex-Blake was impressed by Reade's devoted recapitulation of the events, concluding in a review of the work that "the chapter thus occupied may take and keep its place in contemporary history in virtue of its great general accuracy."[51]

Reade's editors, though, had their doubts about its efficacy and interest, and throughout the summer these "ticklish" middle parts occupied much of their attention. At first Langford was impressed by the powerful writing and, confident that Blackwood was succeeding in "redirecting" Reade in the proper direction, suggested that Reade now be allowed more freedom with reference to "the lady doctor." "A good deal of licence may be allowed to the writer of a really powerful work of fiction without breaking in upon the Editorial responsibility," he suggested to John's nephew and co-business partner, William Blackwood III.[52]

By October, however, Langford had changed tack and now wrote objecting to the polemics on aesthetic grounds. Unlike Jex-Blake, Langford saw no merit in hammering the reader with facts. "I am not inclined to make a periodical too closely responsible for any matter in a long story by a known or popular author," he wrote William Blackwood III, "but I do not think readers of a story want a pamphlet in the middle of it."[53] Doing so merely showed a lack of skill, a lack of artistic merit. "It is *bad art* in fiction to give these details which are in fact the statistics of a controversy."[54] In Langford's view, Reade needed to stop lecturing and instead work harder on gaining the reader's empathy and support. "The object would be better gained by making the lady act and speak so as to gain the respect of readers, not by making her scold, and abuse people who though they *may* be in the wrong are entitled to some consideration at least and of whom the world in general are friends."[55]

John Blackwood's objections were less aesthetically motivated. While also findng the work unconvincing, he remained opposed to Reade's arguments and told Reade so in forceful terms in mid-July:

> To begin with, I do not believe in the movement being wise or likely to be useful to any material extent, and I would have advised any young lady whom I took interest in against taking part in it. Also, I do not believe in the old Doctors foozles or otherwise taking the vulgar Trades Union view of the Women becoming dangerous competitors, and it is giving the rowdy medical students too much credit or foresight that they thought of it in that light.[56]

But his conclusion harks back to aesthetics. In spite of everything, he found the section "temperately told" and said: "I know from the interest I (an unbeliever in lady doctors) take in it that it is thoroughly well done, so do not let any remarks of mine dishearten you in the slightest degree."[57] Blackwood insisted only in restraining Reade from issuing any potentially slanderous remarks about the male medical profession, and ordered him to back up all controversial statements with proof. "Take care that nothing is said which can possibly be construed as unfair or in any degree libellous as the Doctors will be very furious and would give us no end of trouble on the slightest pretext," he warned Reade. Moreover, Blackwood took the view that credibility required that Reade insert more queries and doubts concerning Rhoda Gale's statements, for he was allowing the self-professed misogynist Harrington Vizard to be too partial to Gale. "I am not sure that the Woman hater should have taken a Womans Tale so absolutely as Gospel," he noted, for "impulsive as he is it does not seem natural that with his shrewdness he should have occasional doubts."[58]

Reade saved his response for a personal visit a week later, but in a letter to William Blackwood he suggested that the polemics were coming to an end. "By the way, don't let him [John Blackwood] get flustered about the medical woman," he exclaimed, for "the controversy is pretty well disposed of. She will offend no more except by superior skill and insight into the sources of disease."[59] Reade by this stage was wanting to move on and complete the final sections of the work. John Blackwood, however, was now grappling with the all-important fifth and sixth sections and remained "the reverse of happy" about them, unable to deal with material so alien to his own beliefs and value systems. "The *Woman Hater* exercises me much & is not so pleasant a subject for waking thoughts as G. Eliots works," he confessed to William Blackwood.[60]

After reviewing the sections in conjunction with Reade's new material, the editor set out once more to redirect the recalcitrant author to safer ground, demanding elimination of passages and changes in wording. The demands included deleting sentences intimating close physical contact between the sexes ("Pray let me strike out 'Zoe and Fanny screaming and pinching Ned Severne right and left.' It has a very disagreeable effect"), words like "seduction," and denunciations of Edinburgh doctors as trade unionists and "scum of the Medical profession."[61] All such requests were made in the interests of avoiding controversy. "You have no idea how far I am stretching a point in this medical business," Blackwood fretted to Reade. "It will raise a storm and my old Medical friends here will be frantic with me."[62] Underlying all this was the fear that what the fictional characters said would be interpreted as reflecting the official view of the magazine itself. Thus Reade was told to make it clearer that these radical statements were those of a biased partisan, and to insert notes disclaiming any strong identification with these views.

Reade bowed once more to Blackwood's demands and in an obsequious fashion declared, "Believe me, I make this sort of alteration for you with great pleasure, and as to the doctors I feel that on the whole your excisions have been improvements and that you deal with me in that liberal and friendly spirit, which has made the leading authors of the country your friends."[63] The result was that short disclaimers were inserted at crucial stages: "She is now going into a controverted matter," the reader is told as Gale launches into the details of the 1869–73 Edinburgh campaign, "and though she is sincere and truthful she is of necessity a *partisan*. Do not take her for a judge" (October 1876, 447). Likewise, Vizard concludes to his sister after recapitulating Gale's story, "That is *her* chat, you understand, not mine. We are not obliged to swallow all that" (November 1876, 572).

By now, Reade had all but given up fighting such matters, exhausted as he was by personal and public stresses. He also slackened in his opposition once he had achieved his main goal, that of inching the main portions of his polemical plea for women doctors past Blackwood's censorious hand. "I am happy to say that I now feel the story safe from *failure*," he wrote. "At early periods I have had my doubts; for one thing it has been written under extraordinary disadvantages—Ill-health—Litigation—Controversy—besides family misfortunes and dissensions and cares."[64] Blackwood interpreted the capitulation as a victory for the firm, a tribute to his skill in handling authors. "Our wild horse seems tamed & he is a gentleman," declared John to his nephew William.[65] "The fact is that he sees that he is in good hands," Langford exclaimed on reading about Reade's concessions.[66]

Having forced Rhoda Gale past Blackwood into the novel, Reade began the task of integrating her into the text. Reade based his description of Gale's past on the recorded experiences of both Elizabeth Blackwell and Sophia Jex-Blake. Much of the fictional character's childhood life and family relationships mirror Blackwell's American upbringing, while Gale's experiences as a medical student in Edinburgh were directly drawn from Jex-Blake's descriptions. All this was added as a means of authenticating Reade's handiwork, part of a "system" of documentation Reade implemented in writing many of his novels. Reade approached his works by applying his energies to collecting all the relevant facts needed to develop fully his major "themes." "I propose never to guess where I can know," he wrote in 1853.[67] This "Great Systems" of documentation, as Wayne Burns has pointed out, led Reade to equate truth with facts. "If facts equalled truth," Burns noted, "then, the more facts the better, and the way to achieve ultimate truth, in literature as in other matters, was through a systematic application of the Baconian method."[68] The results were to be found in such works as *Hard Cash*, in which facts were regurgitated for the reader in great quantities. Ultimate truth in *A Woman Hater* was to be found in the twenty-eight pages detailing the injustices suffered up to that point by female medical aspirants.

Lesser but equally valid truths were also supposedly to be found in Rhoda's achievements subsequent to her encounter with Harrington Vizard. Gale visits, prescribes, and laughs at the law in her role as chief medical overseer of a small English village. Despite antagonism from suspicious villagers and hostile medical authorities, Gale forthwith proves herself an ideal practitioner, banishing disease, poor living conditions, and social prejudice in her district. The details of her attempts to perform her job are uneasily grafted onto the main storyline, but they reflect an idealized situation in which Gale's medical skills are recognized and eventually accepted. Not only is this socially disruptive element enclosed within a stereotypical study of social manners, it is also eventually absorbed and usefully harnessed.

Yet in suggesting Rhoda as an ideal medical role model, Reade also turns her into a sexually ambiguous individual, whose statements on love ("It disturbs the judgment and perverts the conscience"), while meant to illustrate her total commitment to the "science" of medical healing, are later undercut by lesbian tendencies (October 1876, 446). Reade's answer to contemporary opinion that medicine would somehow "desex" or defeminize women proves rather problematic in implementation. On the one hand, Gale's dedication and pursuit of learning is meant to contrast favorably with the frivolous-natured women whose romantic concerns are disrupted by Gale's appearance. Gale is seen to be a paragon of virtue, wedded to medicine like other women are to men. "I love science as other women love men," Gale declares to Vizard (December 1876, 657). But it is precisely this dichotomy that compromises Reade in his development of Gale's character. Contemporary social ideology suggested that a woman's main role in life was to be found within the boundaries of marriage and the home.

While John Blackwood expressed no objections to the sexual ambiguities of Gale's character, he nevertheless declared himself relieved to read in the manuscript that Gale's fellow medical student was giving up medicine to marry and settle down: "I confess I was glad when I came to the point where the 'wretch' Cornelia had gone and married a Professor," he told Reade.[69] If Jex-Blake and others with her zeal did the same thing, Blackwood implied, channeling their energies into socially acceptable areas such as marriage, everyone would be better off. Thus Reade's attempted "neutering" of Gale can be read as a reaction to this view, an illustration of the manner in which such energies could be harnessed in other ways to greater social benefit. As a result of such suppression, though, Reade fails to work out an adequate method for conveying Gale's emotional and sexual needs. The result is that Gale, "not of an amorous temperament," is seen to be all the more open to female attachment, first following Vizard's sister Zoe, then attaching herself to the opera singer Ina Klosking, to whom she writes "love-letters twice-a-week" (February 1877, 274; June 1877, 656). "I am very unfortunate in my attachments," Gale is made to state. "If I fall in love with a woman, she is sure to hate me, or else die, or else fly away" (April 1877, 417).

If Gale's character seems ambiguous, the polemical conclusions to the work are less so, and leave the reader in no doubt as to Reade's belief in the justice of the women's cause. More to the point, as Reade had feared would happen, political change had overtaken his arguments. In August 1876, two months before the serialized introduction of Reade's "revolutionary" character, amendments to the Medical Act were passed explicitly removing gender restrictions in the examination procedure. In late 1876, Sophia Jex-Blake and Edith Pechey matriculated at the Irish College of Physicians, the first institution to make use of the new regulations, and by early 1877 had passed their examinations and become the first women to be noted in the Medical Register since Elizabeth Garrett-Anderson eleven years earlier. In 1878 the University of London opened its doors to women, and other institutions soon followed. By 1887 more than fifty women had passed onto the Medical Register, and by 1891 the number had risen to one hundred.[70]

Thus in his concluding remarks, serialized in the June 1877 issue of *Blackwood's Magazine*, Reade repositioned his text to reflect the concurrent changes in the law. "Even while her narrative was in the press," he asserts, "our Government declared it would do something for the relief of medical women, but would sleep upon it" (June 1877, 677). By this he meant that while reforms may have been enacted in Parliament, there was as yet no real commitment from them to support or enforce these new laws. Reade warned that the reform movement could not afford to rest on their recent achievements, for vigilance and further pressure was needed "so that no temporary, pettifogging half-measure may slip into a thin house—like a weasel into an empty barn—and so obstruct for many years legislation upon durable principle" (677). The reform movement's momentum needed to be retained, he argued, to fully ensure that these gains were not lost.

Even more important for him was the continued need for social change. In his conclusion, Reade reiterated contemporary feminist views by suggesting that social attitudes, and the values and views of women themselves, needed to be addressed and changed before the women's movement could claim total success. In a polemical passage decrying the confinement and oppression of women through physical, mental, and economic methods, he drew on the physical restrictions of the corset, crippling lungs and ribs, as a metaphor for how society treated women. "Her life, too," Reade declared, "is in stays—cabined, cribbed, confined: unless she can paint, or act, or write novels, every path of honourable ambition is closed to her" (June 1877, 679). Opening medical schools to women, then, represented one of the first steps in freeing women from these restrictions, and from the intellectual shackles of the "three 'C's'—croquet, crochet, and coquetry" (678). Reade's conclusions were unequivocal. Medical education for women was in society's interests, for the results would be role models who would lead women to expect more from life, who "would leaven the whole sex with higher views of life than enter their heads at present; would raise their self-respect, and set thousands of them to study the great and noble things that are in Medicine, and connected with it, instead of childish things" (678–79).

Surprisingly enough, there was little opposition to such strong statements from John Blackwood. Blackwood still remained unconvinced by Reade's arguments, but that did not concern him, because the literary exposure of this issue no longer posed an economic or legal threat to the firm or its magazine. Blackwood had not lost readers, his medical acquaintances had not sued him for libel, and his fears had proven unfounded regarding the expected negative reaction to the subject. "I hear distant mutterings of wrath or surprise and sorrow among the

Doctors," he confessed to Reade after the crucial middle section had run its course in November, "but none of them have ventured to address me on the much vexed Lady Question, and altogether it has passed off much more quietly than I expected."[71] On receiving the concluding part in February 1877, he reiterated to Reade: "The public have said less either pro or con Rhoda than I expected."[72]

More to the point, the initial struggle to open educational and medical opportunities for women through political reform had succeeded and was rapidly becoming less of an issue. Blackwood had done his best to contain the issue within what he felt were acceptable literary parameters. And while Reade had been "tamed" to Blackwood's satisfaction, Reade had succeeded in his goal of forcing the issue of women's medical education onto the pages of *Blackwood's Magazine*, and thus into the homes of an audience normally hostile to such social and literary challenges. Although Reade's work ultimately had little effect on the political resolution of the issue of women physicians, the editorial battle over *A Woman Hater*'s contents provides us with an important perspective on the effects of conflicting aesthetic judgments and cultural agendas on the production of "Blackwoodian" texts.

5

Shifting Ground

Blackwood's, 1880–1912

On John Blackwood's death in October 1879, William Blackwood III became head of the firm. Age forty-three at the time of transition, William was to face personal and business difficulties and turbulence in the aftermath of John's demise. There was the bitter battle for succession and partnership fought between two sides of the Blackwood family, and there was also the disintegration of the decision-making network fostered under John's direction, which left William bereft of capable and trusted associates within a few years of his ascendancy. How William sought to overcome these obstacles, and what the results were, are the topics of this chapter.

As noted in Chapter 1, the firm underwent an extensive evaluation of worth not long after John Blackwood's burial. Every piece of equipment was counted and valued, every text measured and investigated. The task of assessment was an important one, and Joseph Langford, the long-serving London office manager, was appointed to oversee the final valuation. The firm's legal representative, David Lyell, writing to Langford to confirm his appointment, made it clear that objectivity and a fair assessment were called for and that consequent and clear rules of conduct must be observed: "This being a friendly family valuation," he wrote, "we thought it right in the interests of both parties that, while acting in the capacity of an arbitrator, you should not be the guest of either of the families while it lasts. There can however be no objection to your visiting and accepting the hospitality of either of them, it being of course understood that the business on which you are engaging does not form the subject of discussion."[1]

The two parties in question were William Blackwood and John Blackwood's heirs. Underpinning this message, the wording of which had been approved by both William and John's widow, Julia, was a simmering family feud further fueled by changes earlier imposed by William on the firm's management structure. Julia, severe yet protective of her husband's reputation and his children's legacy, held a grievance against William. The grievance came in part from the manner in which she believed her side of the family had been dispossessed of their rightful place in shaping the future of the firm—in particular, John's young son John Alexander (Jack) had not been taken into the firm as a partner on his father's death, as William had been on the death of *his* father in 1861.

The reason Jack had not been included had much to do with William's perceptions of Jack's abilities. Jack, born on 12 January 1857, was a charming individual with indifferent working habits. During his years at Eton College, for example, he did not shine academically, as evinced in letters sent back to his uncle William in the Blackwood archives. His apprenticeship in the Edinburgh office of the firm did not inspire those who supervised him either. "What he has done all his life I cannot understand," wrote William to Langford in May 1878, "but he has certainly never learned to write or keep his mind fixed on what he is doing."[2] Jack's lack of a work ethic did not disappear with age. "Is he likely to ever settle down and be useful in the business?" inquired a family relation a few years later, continuing, "He seemed to feel his father's death so much that I hoped it would be his turning point in life."[3] William did not think Jack would ever "settle down," and in the aftermath of John's death he made his view that Jack was not fit to join the firm clear, to the fury of Julia. She never forgave him this offense, and in 1882, when Jack fell terminally ill (he died of undisclosed causes in early May), she caused a permanent break in family relations by publicly accusing William of contributing to Jack's decline by not providing him with an opportunity to apply himself on behalf of the firm. This, coming on top of the death of his mother in January 1882, deeply affected William. As he confessed to the family's longtime friend William Lucas Collins, the matter had "made me almost useless for work."[4] The result was a complete cessation of contact until the mid-1890s.

Unlike the period that marked the transition from Robert and Alexander to John and William Blackwood II, when family loyalties and individual skill were sufficient in quantity and quality to guarantee a smooth transition from one generation to the next, the 1880s provided no such option for the Blackwood family. Aside from Jack, the only other potential Blackwood inheritor deemed capable of joining William was William's brother George, who at the time of John's death was serving as a military officer in India. It had been hoped that George, like his father, Major William Blackwood II, would eventually return to take up a place in the firm as financial advisor. However, his death in October 1880 in the Battle of Maiwand, one of the many British-Afghan skirmishes marking the Afghan border wars of the period, was a blow to family hopes. Instead, William was forced to look elsewhere for help, in this case settling on his cousin Archibald McCall Smith, who had begun working for the firm shortly after John's death. Following Langford's retirement as London office manager in 1882, McCall Smith was seconded to London to take over this role.

The loss of Langford as literary advisor marked the end of the strong quadrumvirate that had ruled Blackwood's for almost thirty years. Langford's departure followed that of George Simpson, who retired as Edinburgh office manager in 1878. A new set of individuals took on their responsibilities. Thomas Henderson, who served as Edinburgh office manager until his death in 1893, replaced Simpson. Likewise, McCall Smith acted as London office manager until his removal from the post in 1896. And a successor to John "Crumie" Brown, chief Maga proofreader until 1877, was found in Alexander Allardyce, a native of Aberdeen whose career before joining the firm included stints as a newspaper editor in India and Sri Lanka. Until his death in April 1896 from pneumonia, Allardyce was to act as an erratic literary advisor to William.

Although these new recruits were enthusiastic, they lacked the single-minded drive that had marked Simpson's and Langford's careers. But even more, their commitment was subject to the vagaries of ill health, alcoholism, and mental instability. Allardyce's letters throughout his twenty-year association with Blackwood's, for example, are punctuated by frequent breakdowns (and alcoholic binges) requiring extended recuperative treatment in Edinburgh's Craiglockhart Hospital (later famous as the meeting place of Siegfried Sassoon and Wilfrid Owen during the First World War), or in the sulphurous waters of the northern

Scottish spa-town of Strathpeffer. McCall Smith's penchant for hefty drams in the gentlemen's clubs of London was serious enough at one point for the firm's legal representative in the capital, R. J. Haldane, to recommend shipping him off to a remote Scottish island where he would be free of the evil influence of alcohol. "The only place I can suggest," he advised William, "where he would be away from drink would be Shetland—I fish there every year and might find some island where he could board. But it is useless a man flying from drink unless he has the moral courage to drive drink from him."[5] Similarly frank comments and receipts of doctor's bills paid by William Blackwood to treat Thomas Henderson for alcohol abuse near the end of his life in 1893 can be found in the firm's papers.

Evaluating Textual Worth

The result of this weakened support structure was a problematic lack of critical expertise in evaluating literary and textual worth. William, naturally conservative in nature, and less likely to take risks on unknown talent than John, felt greatly the loss of Joseph Langford after 1882. For all of Langford's dourness of opinion, he at least had been connected to the literary world in London, via the Garrick Club and his interest and activity in the theater world. (During his free time he translated and produced several plays for the London theater.[6]) Blackwood's circle did not extend greatly in these directions, nor did those of his new staff. One can see this in the well-established set of authors William continued to turn to for new works (such as Charles and Edward Bruce Hamley, Laurence Oliphant, Margaret Oliphant, and Archibald Alison) and in the number of authors whose worth William frequently underestimated and rejected over the next two decades. The young George Bernard Shaw was an early casualty; his first work, *Immaturity*, recommended by Langford in 1880, was barely read before being turned down by William, in part because he had difficulty concentrating on work while uncertainties remained over his brother George's fate in Afghanistan.[7] Thomas Hardy[8], Arthur Conan Doyle,[9] and H. G. Wells[10] also failed to place their work with the firm, as did Robert Louis Stevenson. The latter case is telling for the manner in which the firm clung to set views about purchasing and marketing texts throughout the 1880s and early 1890s.

In 1892 Stevenson, through his longtime friend and legal advisor Charles Baxter, offered Blackwood's the initial serialization rights for what was to become the *Weir of Hermiston*. "But it has occurred to me that there is one quarter in which the very Scotchness of the thing would be found a recommendation and where the queerness might possibly be stomached. I mean Blackwood," Stevenson wrote to Baxter in December 1892. Charles Baxter's response highlighted William's hesitation at the asking price, which was higher than anything Blackwood had expected: "I've seen Bill Blackwood, who is staggered at what I've asked him: £2,000 for the serial rights. You see, an old humdrum house has no machinery for selling these all over the world. But here is the sort of idea that he settles at: to pay £2,000 for the *Magazine* rights *and* an edition of say 3 or 5,000. I say, not good enough, and I'll see what better can be done."[11] (The work was published elsewhere two years after Stevenson's death in 1894.)

William's response provides insight into the firm's general publication strategies, which over the final decades of the nineteenth century explicitly sought to link serial publication rights in *Blackwood's Magazine* with subsequent hardcover publication options. Works secured for the firm in this way included, among many, F. Marion Crawford's *Saracinesca* (serialized May 1886–April 1887 and issued in three volumes in March 1887), Margaret Oliphant's *Who Was Lost and Is Found* (serialized June–November 1894 and issued in one volume in October 1894), Neil Munro's *Children of the Tempest* (serialized November 1902–August 1903 and issued in one volume in July 1903), and Katherine Cecil Thurston's sensationalist best-seller *John Chilcote, M.P.* (serialized January–October 1904 and published in September 1904). William was extremely skeptical of seeking "names" for the sake of a literary coup—sensible prices for long-term prospects was part and parcel of his approach to commissioning work (in particular for the magazine). "Experience of past years goes to show that no special article from some popular idol of the day or hour repays the extra premium that has to be paid," he noted in a memorandum on this issue.[12]

But such attitudes could not hold in face of competition from new, "entrepreneurial" publishers, such as Chatto & Windus, Methuen, William Heinemann, John Lane, and Elkin Mathews (who were not afraid to take on and publish controversial works and new authors), the rise of professionalization within the industry (such as the insertion of the literary agent into the negotiation of literary worth, discussed in Chapter 7), and other changes simultaneously taking place across British publishing. The development of higher printing capacity utilizing large, web-fed rotaries and newly developed hot-metal typesetting machines meant cheaper production costs and faster delivery of print runs. Experiments with cheap publishing formats and reprints following the decline and collapse of the three-decker novel in 1894, rapidly combined with the creative use of new arenas for syndication (such as silent films and theatrical performances) and overseas markets in the Empire, North America, and Europe to offer greater challenges for such traditional "list" publishers as Blackwood's, John Murray, or Richard Bentley & Sons.[13]

Blackwood's continuing emphasis on the traditional pattern of initial serialization in *Blackwood's Magazine*, followed by publication in book format (which continued through to the end of the First World War), is in retrospect not surprising. For a firm steeped in the patterns of mid-nineteenth-century publishing activity, it was a reassuring format that served as a means of positioning the firm's products within the literary marketplace. It offered the maintenance of a stable "house identity" through the works championed and issues discussed in the magazine's pages, a method of promoting forthcoming works, and a profitable enterprise in its own right.

The Blackwood firm was not the only one to see the benefits of utilizing an eponymously named literary periodical to promote its works and earn intangible literary capital in the process. *Bentley's Miscellany* (founded in 1837), *Macmillan's Magazine* (founded in 1859), and *Longman's Magazine* (founded in 1882) were just some of the journals created like Blackwood's to keep their firm's names in front of the reading public. Reasons for so doing, as William Tinsley declared on finding his losses for *Tinsley's Magazine* (launched in 1867), running at around £25 a month, were quite plain: "What cheaper advertisement can I have for twenty-five pounds a month? It advertises my name and publications; and it keeps my authors together."[14]

Keeping one's "authors together" recalls the point raised in Chapter 1 about creating house identities and literary networks (a theme discussed further in Chapter 6). The editors of *Blackwood's Magazine* offered a literary network that was shaped deliberately by editorial policy to produce maximum returns on their investments in authors, while at the same time concerning themselves with holding aloft "the twin banners of sound criticism and Tory politics."[15] This policy generated substantial profits throughout the magazine's history, making it second only to George Eliot's works as a major source of income for the firm. This point must be tempered, though, by the fact that the magazine's substantial profit margins subsequently declined by almost 40 percent between 1860 and 1900, as seen in Table 5.

While general profits and sales in the United Kingdom toward the end and turn of the century register a steady drop, the rate of decline slowed after a drastic dip in the 1880s (reasons for which will be covered later in this chapter). One

Table 5.   *Blackwood's Magazine* sales and profits, 1860–1915

Magazine Sales by Decade	Total Magazine Sales	Total Profits by Decade
July 1860–June 1870	763,299	£45,137.19.7
July 1870–June 1880	666,036	£37,702.1.6
July 1880–June 1890	596,260	£31,467.12.5
July 1890–June 1900	632,677[a]	£26,532.12.9
July 1900–June 1910	613,276[b]	£31,007.12.6
July 1910–June 1915	362,658[c]	£19,289.11.11

[a]The total includes 131,950 in U.S. sales for 1891–1900.
[b]The total includes 120,225 in U.S. sales for 1901–10.
[c]The total includes 60,000 in U.S. sales for 1911–15. The Blackwood financial ledgers in the National Library of Scotland do not go beyond 1915, hence the partial returns here. Sales figures beyond 1915, however, are available from memorandum notes in MS 30680 and MS 30866, Blackwood Papers, National Library of Scotland.

factor accounting for this slowing in decline is that from 1891 U.S. sales were included in the annual financial returns. In order to subvert U.S. copyright restrictions set by the Chace Act of 1891, Blackwood's began producing simultaneously two versions of the magazine, in Edinburgh and in New York, for distribution in the United Kingdom and the United States (the latter via its New York-based agent, Leonard Scott & Co.).[16] Whereas previously it had entered into agreement with Leonard Scott to publish and distribute the magazine in the U.S. market independent of Edinburgh control, after 1891 the firm began to monitor production more closely, as well as enter into clearer agreements about sales territories and markets. Thus in 1894, a series of cautionary letters were sent to Leonard Scott when it was discovered that they had advertised for sale in British colonies the American edition of *Blackwood's Magazine.* "When we arranged with you for an American edition of the Magazine," William Blackwood stated emphatically, "It was on the understanding that the exclusive sale and agency of the Magazine was to be on the American Continent alone; and your now entering into competition with our edition in the Colonies is quite against the agreement then come to. We trust therefore you will at once take steps to countermand the instructions under which your agents are endeavouring to push the sale of the American Magazine in the Colonies."[17] Leonard Scott representatives retreated, and sales borders were quickly reestablished for future reference. Profits and sales started to lift only in the second decade of the twentieth century, primarily because of the journal's participation in government-sponsored propagandistic cultural formations during the First World War, when mass wartime audiences were targeted with texts aimed at consolidating support for the war effort.[18]

Threats and Challenges

Despite clear signs that the magazine was losing in readership between 1880 and 1890, its solid profitability initially assured the editor that little needed changing. "Maga was never going stronger or better than at present," William noted with an odd sense of complacency in the early 1880s, "this is the general opinion I have heard in many different quarters."[19] Even so, he admitted that careful monitoring was needed to maintain its position as a leading journal: "A careful study of Maga sales for past few years shows that, as I stated years ago, best to be hoped for with the severe competition is to keep up circulation."[20] This complacency was rudely disturbed by the emergence in March 1883 of the *National Review*, a monthly journal founded by Alfred Austin, co-edited with the conservative journalist William J. Courthope, and published by the London firm W. H. Allen that was to be "devoted to political and literary matters . . . [and] to be unashamedly committed to Tory principles."[21]

The idea for the *National Review* took shape in a conversation between Alfred Austin and Benjamin Disraeli shortly before the latter's death in 1881. The suggestion was for a philosophically consistent journal that would, in the words of Austin, promote Conservatism "by the demonstration that Conservatives have capacity, and not only political capacity, but capacity of the large and generous sort," and in so doing, "to go a long way towards converting people to Conservatism."[22] While not officially affiliated with the Conservative Party, it drew major support from the Carlton Club, a bastion of conservatism in London and one in particular seen as a Blackwoodian space. From the start, Austin secured a sponsorship pledge from the club of 1,000 paid subscriptions, which contributed substantially to the estimated sales during its first ten years of just under 5,000 copies a month. (Sales rose to an average 10,000 copies per issue after Leopold J. Maxse took over the editorship in 1893.)[23] Over the seventy-seven years of its existence, the *National Review* gained a reputation for consistency and standing as a "long-lived, eloquent, and self-confident Tory spokesman."[24] It also drew heavily on Blackwood's pool of contributors and political sources, including critic and academic George Saintsbury, essayist Sir Herbert Cowell, and Sir Stafford Henry Northcote (leader of the Conservative opposition in the House of Commons).

The arrival of the *National Review* represented a threat to Maga's self-perceived role in leading and reflecting nineteenth-century conservative and High Tory political and social agendas, and helps partially to explain the downturn in sales experienced by *Blackwood's Magazine* during the 1880s. Throughout its early his-tory, the Blackwood firm's political stance as evinced in its nonfiction publications and its magazine, as one historian of the Conservative Party has observed, repre-sented a specific High Tory Radical paternalist strand of the Conservative move-ment, one that ran both "too far ahead and too far behind their times; ahead, in that their shadowy prevision of the welfare state and a planned economy would not be generally accepted even a hundred years later; behind, in that their views on such subjects as the church were as reactionary as those of the Ultras."[25] While John Wilson and his Edinburgh cohorts in the 1820s and 1830s launched conservative attacks on radical literary movements (hitting out at targets as diverse as Wordsworth, Coleridge, and the "Spasmodic" school of poetry), others, such as the economist David Robinson, produced powerful economic treatises that were taken up by John Maynard Keynes and others a century later.[26]

In the 1880s and 1890s William Blackwood III continued this tradition of conservative formations, publishing polemical material from military, colonial, aristocratic, and opposition Tory figures, such as Sir Theodore Martin, Sir Archibald Alison, Gathorne Hardy (secretary of state for India, 1878–80), Lord Wolseley, Frederick Lugard (soldier and African administrator), Sir Edward Braddon (pre-mier of Tasmania, 1894–1904), and Sir Henry Stafford Northcote (Conservative MP for Exeter, 1880–99, governor-general of Australia 1903–7, and son of Sir Stafford Henry Northcote). Lord John Manners and Lord Brabourne (member of the Tory opposition in the House of Lords, 1880–85) were also mainstays of the firm's magazine and book lists (their importance to Blackwood's is reaf-firmed by the commissioning of biographies of Manners and Brabourne from trusted Blackwoodian authors after their deaths).

From mid-century onward, consensus within the firm, reinforced by a delib-erate targeting of audiences after William Blackwood III took over in 1879, viewed its textual productions as speaking to and for a specific network of read-ers and opinion-makers in upper-middle-class, military, colonial, and political circles. The arrival of the *National Review* threatened the monopoly Blackwood's believed it enjoyed in this area, encroaching on its target markets and audiences and poaching a significant proportion of the firm's established coterie of authors. Given the internal turmoil from which the firm had just emerged, to find an upstart publication intruding into the textual space that William Blackwood III considered to be uniquely his, was something he could not ignore.

Upon hearing of plans for the *National Review*, William Blackwood III began an immediate counterattack, writing to trusted confidants for further information, cajoling potential defectors into remaining away from the new publication, and attempting to downplay the potential impact on sales and readership for his flagship journal. Seeking a strong political piece to counter the potential impact of the rival magazine, William made an urgent request for a contribution from Sir Henry Stafford Northcote (son of opposition leader Stafford Henry) in February 1883, noting:

> Maga must do her best to have a strong political paper which will challenge comparison with the utterances of her rival the "National," which will be primed with all the secrets that Lord Carnarvon & Lytton and Mr. Balfour can give it, but I hope you will stand by the old ship that has been so true to the party from her birth, and never touted for subscribers from its ranks to give it a floating hand. I see from advertised contents of the first number that nearly all the writers of the articles have at one time or another had articles rejected by my late Uncle and I do not believe Malloch or Mr. Pollock contribute without a payment.[27]

William secured "The Opening of Parliament," a polemical view of current parliamentary debates and issues by stalwart contributor Lord John Manners. The article, William later wrote Lord Manners (not forgetting to point out early signs of negative reactions to the newly launched competitor), was sure to "Pull over our new Conservative rival on which the Pall Mall Gazette and today's Scotsman are jubilant at its weaknesses. I feel sure our Article will bear most favourable comparison with its political paper as well as my whole number which I hope you and Lady John will like."[28]

William kept a nervous eye on what this new voice of the conservative establishment was producing, and by whom, and took careful note of defectors who had been enticed away to the *Review's* pages. Even in retirement, the faithful Langford could not resist sending his views on the matter, exclaiming in December 1883: "I was greatly disgusted to find Sir Stafford writing in that little wretch Austin's Magazine. He ought to know better than to support a rival to faithful old Maga."[29] After a few issues, though, William grudgingly accepted that it was not badly written, but he continued to downplay its effect on Maga. "The more you examine Maga's new rival," he commented to John Skelton, "the less you will fear it although it has one or two by no means bad papers. . . . I give it a year to live."[30]

The *National Review* continued to prosper beyond William's predicted one year, its popularity adding to the decline in Maga's circulation. As William was to confess, "It may nevertheless have cost Maga a good few subscribers," concluding forlornly, "I trust they will ere long come back to their first love."[31] Such was not to be the case until the First World War. Maga's sales continued a downward trend dating back to 1860 (when sales averaged 7,537 copies a month), to decline even further in face of Austin's competition, moving from annual sales of 63,000 (or 5,270 copies a month) in 1883 to 55,831 (or 4,652 a month) by 1890.

Targeting Audiences

Among the effects of such competition was a decided hardening and shifting in tone in the magazine to maintain a bedrock of loyal colonial and military audiences through essays and tales focused on Britain's overseas possessions and activities. Similarly, as noted in Chapter 1, the firm's book publications concentrated on complementary niche markets. That is not to suggest that the firm's policies remained static as time went on, in particular following David S. Meldrum's entrance as London office manager in 1896 (a matter explored later in this chapter), but in the face of challenges, such as Austin's journal, William quite consciously ventured into literary production that catered to markets he understood well—hence the reliance on popular women's and Scottish fiction, military works, and colonial tales, as well as on tried and tested nonliterary textual production such as textbooks, medical handbooks, atlases, and catechisms that had served the firm handsomely in the decades previous to John Blackwood's death.

One 1930s critic, discussing the history of upstart John Lane in the 1890s, has suggested that the fin-de-siècle could be seen as dominated by what N. N. Feltes has since called "list publishers": "The great fixed stars in the publishing firmament, Macmillans, Longmans, John Murray, Blackwoods, Smith Elder, had each a sort of magnetic or gravitational attraction and drew all the clients they needed into their respective orbits."[32] This has been disputed by N. N. Feltes, among others who see this period as one marked by a shift in favor of new, "entrepreneurial" firms operating in less-traditional modes and offering new approaches to marketing texts.[33] It is perhaps true to say that Blackwood's, realizing it was starting to lose "clients," began aiming more directly at its steadiest customer base: the colonial audience.

The colonial market was a market that other publishers had sought to enter since the early 1840s, when John Murray had begun Murray's Colonial and Home Library, which was aimed at selling cheap reprints both at home and abroad.[34]

While the Blackwood firm had connections with retailers and publishers in Australia, India, Canada, and South Africa, it had made little concerted effort to market aggressively in these areas, in part because of difficulties in establishing transport and distribution networks. Early discussions in 1858 with Smith, Elder & Company about joining forces to sell complementary texts in India, for example, were unsuccessful,[35] and little was done to follow through on this idea until the 1890s. It was Macmillan's successful establishment of the Macmillan's Colonial Library in 1886 that prompted Blackwood's and other firms, such as Oliver & Boyd (who began marketing textbooks in India in the 1890s), to reconsider the potential of such markets. And the potential, as publishers soon realized, was huge. Sir Walter Besant noted at the time, "Largely as a result of British colonial policies, the readership of the English speaking world had expanded from 50,000 in 1830 to 120 million by the late 1890s."[36]

While the Blackwood firm had dabbled in exports of its titles in the past, it began producing texts for the colonial market in earnest following the demise of "three-decker," or three-volume, format in 1894. The decision by circulating libraries not to stock three-volume works after 1894 caused profound changes in the distribution system that for almost fifty years had provided guaranteed profits to British publishers. Experiments in cheaper formats, and establishments of new imprints, followed in short order, as did decisions to implement a system for regulating prices throughout the entire publishing sector. (Hence the formalization in late 1899 of the Net Book Agreement, whereby publishers set a fixed price for books that all booksellers were required to adhere to, once trade discounts had been accounted for.)[37]

Until 1894, Blackwood's had generally retailed their three-volume novels at twenty-five shillings and six pence for a first edition, following it a year later with a one-volume reprint at six shillings. Cloth-bound nonfiction texts ranged anywhere from twenty-five shillings to seven shilllings and six pence in price. From 1894 onward, the firm began issuing novels in six-shilling, cloth-covered editions. It also created a Colonial Library series, taking sheets from the same print runs and producing separate cloth- and paper-bound editions to be sold in British colonies overseas at two shillings (cloth) and 1/6 (paper). The series continued through to the 1920s. As the sample cover of the 1905 colonial edition of South African Douglas Blackburn's *Richard Hartley, Prospector* indicates (Fig. 5), these editions were rather plain in appearance and distinctly branded as part of Blackwood's Colonial Library. At the same time, distinctive copyright statements were also clearly positioned on the front to ward off improper sales of such texts.

Richard Hartley

Prospector

BY

DOUGLAS BLACKBURN

Author of 'A Burgher Quixote'

EDINBURGH AND LONDON

WILLIAM BLACKWOOD AND SONS

This Edition is for circulation in India and the British Colonies only

Fig. 5 Cover of Colonial Library edition of Douglas Blackburn's *Richard Hartley, Prospector*, William Blackwood & Sons, 1905. Such editions were produced solely for sale overseas in India and other British colonies. (The apostrophe in "Blackwood's Colonial Library" is misplaced on the Blackwood cover, demonstrating that Blackwood proofreaders were not infallible.)

"This Edition is for circulation in India and the British Colonies only," warns the italicized note at the bottom of the cover.

As sales to colonial markets grew, so too did their importance in contract negotiations. Authors who negotiated without adequate representation often did not get the most from colonial rights. In 1894, as we shall see in Chapter 7, Sophia Jex-Blake could negotiate a royalty of only one shilling and sixpence per copy for English sales, and a five pence royalty per copy for colonial sales of Margaret Todd's *Mona MacLean*. In contrast, when the literary agent James Brand Pinker negotiated in 1899 for *Capetown to Ladysmith*, George Steevens's follow up to his best-seller *With Kitchener to Khartum*, he forced Blackwood's from an initial offer of a £1,000 advance and 24 percent royalties on all sales to a final offer of a £3,000 advance, 25 percent royalties on the first 10,000 copies sold, and 30 percent royalties on all sales subsequent, covering both English and Colonial rights.[38]

E. M. Forster's discontent in 1907 over Colonial royalties offered for *The Longest Journey* caused him to seek another publisher for his next novel, *A Room with a View*. Blackwood's initial offer was based on the lukewarm sales and reception of Forster's first work, *Where Angels Fear to Tread*, published by the firm in August 1905. (Out of two impressions of 1,500 copies, 1,172 were sold within the first year, yielding a small profit of thirty-eight pounds and five shillings.) For *The Longest Journey*, Blackwood's offered a 10 percent royalty on the first 500 copies sold, 12.5 percent on the second 500, 15 percent on the second 1,000 sold, one shilling a copy on all sold beyond 2,000, and 10 percent royalties on colonial sales. This did not please Forster, who felt shortchanged by the low returns on overseas sales and wrote to say so. "The royalty on the Colonial edition," replied William Blackwood III, "has no bearing on what may be arranged for the Home edition, and as we cannot expect, judging by the sale of 'Where Angels Fear to Tread' more than the ordinary small demand from the Colonies, we do not see our way to increasing the rate of royalty, which we would point out is, at 10 percent, a very fair rate, and one which is only exceeded by authors whose books have a large demand in the Colonies."[39]

"Am quarrelling with Blackwood," Forster subsequently reported to R. C. Trevelyan, "and I think I shall have to go elsewhere. We broke over the Colonies, and we aren't the last people who will break over them."[40] After much debate, the offer was amended to 12 percent royalties on first 500 sales, 15 percent on sales between 500 and 2,000 copies, one shilling on sales between 2,000 and 5,000, 25 percent on all sales beyond 5,000, and 12 percent royalties on colonial sales (as demanded by Forster).[41] Sales were not encouraging for this work either, nor were they aided by a low-key promotional campaign. Having classed Forster as one of their less-successful popular novelists, the firm spent just under £70 in advertising, half of what they spent promoting their best-selling novelist Katherine Cecil Thurston's *The Mystics* one month earlier. (Thurston's work went on to sell 19,000 copies between 1907 and 1913, generating £714 in profits.) Forster's work, published in two impressions totaling 2,112 copies, could only manage sales of 1,771 between April 1907 and December 1912, producing a total profit of eighty-four pounds and four pence. Forster, disillusioned by the lack of income and by the firm's lackadaisical approach to his work, then turned to Edward Arnold, who served as a more supportive and generous publisher of Forster's subsequent successes *A Room with a View*, *Howard's End*, and *A Passage to India*.

New Staff, New Networks

While the firm contemplated new marketing strategies and slowly began turning to colonial markets for sales (albeit at as low a cost to themselves as possible), for most of the 1880s and early 1890s its lists featured few successes, apart from isolated examples, such as Anthony Trollope's posthumously released *Autobiography* (1882) or Laurence Oliphant's two-volume novel *Altiora Petio* (1883). Much of the firm's income during this period was generated from reprints and collected editions of such old Blackwood stalwarts as George Eliot, John Hill Burton, Alexander W. Kinglake, and E. B. Hamley, as well as from the diminishing but still substantial profits of *Blackwood's Magazine*. The firm was not to score a major publishing success until it issued journalist George Steevens' sensational account *With Kitchener to Khartum* in June 1898 (which in little more than a year generated profits of just over £5,550, second only to profits gained from the magazine and the 1890s reprints of George Eliot's works) (Appendices 1 and 2).

In the late 1890s, William's circle of advisors was to change, and with this change came a new lease on life and development. William's nephews George William Blackwood and James Hugh Blackwood joined the firm in 1896 and 1898 respectively; J. H. Lobban, a "hard headed, highly educated and well read Aberdonian," much like Allardyce in many ways, took on the position of chief proofreader after Allardyce's death in 1896; and chief among the newcomers was David Storrar Meldrum, who in late 1893 approached the firm about publishing his novel *The Story of Margredel*. Meldrum's novel was accepted for serialization in *Blackwood's Magazine* (running from December 1893 to March 1894) and was subsequently published in February 1894 in a six-shilling-volume edition.[42] William liked Meldrum's work, and, more to the point, he liked Meldrum's critical commentaries on contemporary writers, which Meldrum did not hesitate in conveying in subsequent correspondence and which seemed to match William's own views. "I thank you for your kindness in writing and telling me of your detestation of the pushing and vulgar way of some of these modern writers," Blackwood noted with feeling late December 1893, "and I am pleased to hear you endeavour to keep clear of their cliques."[43]

Over the next two years, Blackwood came to rely heavily on Meldrum for advice, evaluation, and editing of manuscripts; for commissioning of writers for the magazine; and for details of literary gossip from the capital. In May 1896, because of the internal crisis caused by McCall Smith's continuing unfitness for duty in the London Office, William offered Meldrum the post of London office manager, which Meldrum accepted and undertook until James Hugh Blackwood was of age and sufficiently trained to take over the financial and technical aspects of this role in 1901.[44]

Meldrum's valuable role in convincing William Blackwood to publish Joseph Conrad's early work, such as *Heart of Darkness* (1899) and *Lord Jim* (1902), is discussed later in Chapter 7. Conrad was one of the many literary talents Meldrum was to champion for the firm's lists; others included Stephen Crane, John Galsworthy, Henry Lawson, Miles Franklin, and John Buchan. Meldrum was astute in gauging that the firm needed to recover its position as a leading publisher of the day by actively seeking out and developing new talent, rather than waiting for individuals to come to the firm. As early as May 1896, almost a full year before Edward Garnett is reputed to have suggested to Conrad that he submit material (in this case his short story "Karain: A Memory") for publication in *Blackwood's Magazine*,[45] Meldrum urged William Blackwood to consider Conrad's work as a potentially lucrative commodity. "What you write me about getting hold of a paying novelist," William responded, "is very much what we know, and have felt ourselves, and the difficulty is to spot the men who are just rising into a reputation, and whose work would be likely to carry large sales with it. . . . If you hear anything good about Joseph Conrad, will you kindly let me know. I have read none of his things. Is he not a Yankee author?"[46]

Like Langford before him, Meldrum was a member of the Garrick Club, the literary gentleman's club of London. He made contacts there and used it often as a base for social and business occasions. Thus we find Meldrum arranging lunches at the Garrick for prospective authors he hoped to entice into the circle of contributors to the firm's magazine and lists, or organizing dining parties for groups of "Blackwoodian" writers, either potential or actual, for whom he served as a social go-between. The "network" of writers that John Blackwood had encouraged in his time (and that William Blackwood could only shyly attempt to emulate) was continued through Meldrum's contacts in appropriate literary circles.

We can see this at work in Meldrum's bringing Conrad together with a wide variety of authors linked to the firm in one form or other, and the invisible network through which these contacts led to other friendships, links, and potential publications. Conrad was invited to lunch with Blackwood's "colonial" writers, such as the South African Douglas Blackburn (author of *Richard Hartley, Prospector*, a best-selling parodic riposte to H. Rider-Haggard's overblown visions of Africa, such as *She*), as well as invited to attend late-night dinners at the Garrick, such as the one in October 1900 where Conrad met Stephen Gwynn, a leading Irish novelist (and later nationalist member of Parliament for Galway City 1906–18). Gwynn, an avid but oddly placed contributor to *Blackwood's Magazine* (a nationalist producing work for a conservative journal whose politics he did not agree with), returned later with an introduction for Roger Casement, a fellow Irish nationalist with colonial credentials and a link to Conrad.

Roger Casement (1864–1916), British consular officer, reformer, and Irish nationalist leader, was knighted in 1911 for his efforts in exposing Belgian colonial excesses in the Congo at the turn of the century (but was subsequently executed in controversial circumstances by the British in 1916 for war-time treason). Conrad and Casement first met in 1890, when Conrad arrived in the Matadi Station in the Congo to take command of a steamer for a Belgium commercial firm whose transport service Casement was responsible at the time for coordinating.[47] Conrad's impressions of Casement, as recorded in his Congo diary, were extremely positive. "Made the acquaintance of Mr. Roger Casement," he wrote soon after arrival in Matadi in mid-June 1890, "which I should consider a great pleasure under any circumstances and now it becomes a positive piece of luck. Thinks, speaks well, most intelligent and very sympathetic."[48] Conrad resided with Casement during the three weeks he was based at Matadi and accompanied him on expeditions to neighboring villages to organize porters for the company's caravans into the interior, and it was from these incidents that Conrad drew heavily in *Heart of Darkness* nine years later.

Their friendship was renewed in late 1903, when Casement wrote Conrad in connection with gaining support on behalf of the Congo Reform Association, subsequently launched in March 1904 to combat the excesses of commercial and human exploitation in the Congo instigated under the rule of King Leopold of Belgium. Casement subsequently stayed as a guest of Conrad at his home at Pent Farm in early January 1904. Jessie Conrad recalled of this visit, "He was a very handsome man with a thick dark beard and piercing, restless eyes. His personality impressed me greatly."[49]

Casement's introduction to the editors who had supported Conrad's earlier literary endeavors came the following year, when Stephen Gwynn contacted William Blackwood III regarding a potential contributor he felt sure would fit in well with past interests and published work (such as Conrad's *Heart of Darkness* and Hugh Clifford's Malay tales). "It just occurs to me that I don't believe Roger Casement, the Congo man, has ever written about his African experiences, and he can write well," Gwynn remarked in July 1905.[50] William responded enthusiastically, and after Gwynn confirmed in mid-August that Casement "will write for you with pleasure avoiding simple expressions on subjects of diplomatic controversy,"[51] Blackwood sent a formal letter of invitation to the new prospect, outlining possible approaches.

> My good friend and contributor, Mr. Stephen Gwynn, when writing me last month very kindly suggested to me that you might be willing to contribute to my Magazine on subjects connected with the Congo, and I shall be happy to hear from you that such is the case. I daresay you know very well the kind of article which suits Blackwood, but I may mention that even where political matters are under discussion, that the method I prefer is one dealing with matters from a first hand picturesque point of view combined with interest for the general reader. . . . I always think that anything which tends to make an article supremely readable, even to those not specially interested in the subject, goes far to guarantee its success.[52]

Casement responded by sending him "The Careless Ethiopian," a sketch "avoiding the political aspects altogether of the existing Congo controversy, while seeking to throw some light on the actual conditions of native life in the interior."[53] Blackwood subsequently reviewed and returned the piece, concluding that, although he enjoyed his writing, "I have a feeling that you could do better and I am reluctant for you to make your debut in Maga with this paper."[54] Casement concurred, and while promising to produce other work, never did, thus leaving unrealized this potential link.

There has been some speculation as to whether Casement was Conrad's inspiration for Kurtz in *Heart of Darkness*.[55] More certain is Casement's appearance in Stephen Gwynn's writing, where he crops up as a minor character in a sketch published in the September 1905 issue of *Blackwood's Magazine*. "I see he refers to me," Casement informed Blackwood apropos Gwynn's "An Irish Festival," "for I am the 'British Official' who told the tale of the Dublin waiter in the Hotel and the Gaelic League."[56]

Gwynn's presence as mentor and mediator can also be glimpsed behind another Irish link with Blackwood's—in this case Violet Martin, who with her cousin Edith Somerville formed the literary team of Somerville and Ross, which was responsible for such works as *The Real Charlotte* (1894) and the comic masterpiece *Some Experiences of an Irish RM* (1908). Throughout their joint writing career (which began with the publication of *An Irish Cousin* in 1889 and ended with Martin's death in 1915), they corresponded with and enjoyed the support of Stephen Gwynn.[57] As a result of his encouragement and at his suggestion, when Violet visited Scotland in 1895 she made a point of visiting the George Street headquarters of Blackwood's (in the company of Andrew Lang), to discuss publishing the just completed *Beggars on Horseback: A Tour in North Wales* (the pair's follow-up to the critically acclaimed *The Real Charlotte*). Martin found a shy and quiet but friendly William Blackwood in his editorial office, a man not only with a "pronounced Scotch accent" but also "tall, sandy fair, rather bald, with a moustache, very plain, receding forehead and long shoehorn nose, but has a nice and kindly face, and is quite uneditorial"[58] (Fig. 6). The visit was a success: the book was accepted and published by Blackwood's in June 1895, as were short stories and Irish tales in subsequent years, and Somerville and Ross joined the growing number of women promoted in the firm's lists over the next two decades.

Casement's near association with the firm, and Ross and Somerville's successful connection, is illustrative of the manner in which the Blackwood policy of personal contact continued to work, even in the face of changes in methods of conducting business in British publishing. Likewise, we see here complex negotiations of roles and positions by authors in relation to the firm. Gwynn, the ultranationalist, placed himself unusually in the role of mediator for both Anglo-Irish and colonial submissions to Blackwood's while Casement emerged from a nationalist Irish community to contextualize himself within the colonial framework offered and supported by Blackwood's.

Such positioning of authors within interlinked literary networks or spaces allows us entry once more into Jan Radway's concept of literary planes, as well

Fig. 6   Photograph of William Blackwood III (1834–1912), taken in the 1890s. The photograph reflects his perceived conscientious and dutiful attitude to his work as director of the Blackwood firm from 1879 to 1912.

as, to a certain extent, Pierre Bourdieu's articulation of the "literary field." Conrad is one author who has been caught up in recent attempts to utilize such theoretical articulations to establish his role and place in British literary production at the turn of the century. It has been argued by Peter McDonald in *British Literary Culture and Publishing Practice, 1880–1914*, that Conrad specifically and carefully constructed early works, such as *Nigger of the Narcissus*, to secure himself recognition in the "literary field" occupied and guarded by the powerful critic W. H. Henley (and represented by the material published in the *New Review*).[59] This particular arena, a mixture of avant-garde impressionism and muscular aestheticism, may well have offered a home for Conrad. But as far as the Blackwood firm (and David Storrar Meldrum) was concerned, the literary network with which they most identified him was a different one, occupied by the likes of literary and legal historian J. H. Millar, popular Scots novelist Neil Munro, colonial chronicler Hugh Clifford, reformer and colonial agent Roger Casement, journalist and adventure and romance novelist Bernard Capes, and the conservative politician and historian Sir Herbert Maxwell. "Millar, Munro, Conrad, Capes, Sir Herbert in his way—that's a cluster difficult to beat among the young men. And they write in a way to please the old *Maga* readers, I fancy," Meldrum noted in November 1897.[60]

Thanks to Meldrum's prescience and to William Blackwood's subsequent attention to Meldrum's advice, authors like Conrad were attracted for a time to join the firm's lists. What other suggestions and critical steers Meldrum was to give Blackwood during his tenure in the London office can be only partially reconstructed and guessed at, because crucial letters from Meldrum dispatched daily to William in Edinburgh are now lost. What remain are tantalizing fragments and comments regarding Conrad, Crane, and a few others collected by William Blackburn in 1958, which reaffirm Meldrum as a supportive, active commentator and an effective literary commissioner for the firm. During his fourteen years at Blackwood's (from 1896 to 1910), Meldrum did his best to develop the firm's lists beyond the range apparent during the 1880s and early 1890s. His efforts were recognized in 1903, when he became the first non-Blackwood individual to join the firm as a director, co-leading with William, George William, and James Hugh until 1910.

In 1911, reminiscing about his connection with the firm and its magazine, Conrad wrote to his literary agent Pinker: "One was in decent company there and had a good sort of public. There isn't a single club and messroom and man-of-war in the British Seas and Dominions which hasn't its copy of Maga."[61] Stephen

Gwynn wrote similarly about the intangible network Blackwood's and its magazine represented to him in terms of audience and contributors, consumers and producers, noting,

> But certain publications have an atmosphere of their own, a personality which is not entirely the editor's, nor is it made by the readers, nor by the combined influence of all the customary writers. It results from all of these, and when I write, say for *Blackwood's Magazine*, I feel myself part of a society; I am affected by its tone, knowing in a general way what will interest it, what it will like and dislike. It does not get rid of me as the first audience; nothing by which I cannot interest myself thoroughly is going to interest this circle; but one writes there with a certain pleasure as one goes to a hospitable house.[62]

It was both Blackwood's strength and weakness that its name, its lists, and its journal could evoke such specific identity among its contributors and readers. Such "branding" was not unique or unusual. In setting up the Bodley Head imprint in the 1890s, for example, John Lane and Elkin Mathews worked hard to promote their lists as offering readers gentility and sophistication through inexpensive aesthetic products. "To buy a Bodley book, in other words, was to obtain 'culture'—in the social, as well as the intellectual, sense—at rock-bottom prices . . . and to feel part of a 'choice' and 'rare' population oneself."[63] Similarly, Blackwood's offered readers a list based on their vision of quality works at reasonable prices but enclosed within a conservative framework and approach to textual production that for the most part coasted on profits generated by the reprinting of Kinglake and George Eliot. As noted in Chapter 2, in spite of the efforts of advisors like Meldrum, at the turn of the century Blackwood's undoubtedly remained "the house that George built." Not until the First World War, when demand rose for the type of patriotic, militaristic reading material that had become the speciality of Blackwood's, did the firm's fortunes improve.

Creating House Identities

Nineteenth-Century Publishing Memoirs

and the

Annals of a Publishing House

The year 1894 was difficult for Margaret Oliphant. Having sustained an extended family since the death of her husband in 1860 solely on her writing income, at the age of sixty-six she was beginning to tire of the burden. And as was frequently the case throughout her life, her income was not meeting her expenditures. The costs of the wedding of her adopted niece, Madge Wilson, in late 1893, met by Mrs. Oliphant, were subsequently added to by costs of house repairs and expenses incurred on trips to the Riviera (undertaken in a vain attempt to improve the health of her son Cecco, who was to die 1 October 1894 after a long illness). In July 1894, she turned once more to the Blackwood publishers for help, requesting an advance of £200 on future work for the magazine and seeking a way to create a permanent source of income working as an advisor for the firm. "I wish very much I could make myself practically useful about manuscript reading or any other actual business work, such as a great establishment like yours must require—I wonder if you could advise me as to the possibility of getting something of the kind to do, as a sort of permanent thread of income."[1]

William Blackwood's response came the following month. Having mulled over the issue, he wrote to Mrs. Oliphant offering her the opportunity to write a three-volume celebration of the firm's history and the magazine's relations with the great authors of the nineteenth century. "I have long wished to have a history of the House of Blackwood and the Magazine written to do full justice to those who have gone before me in the management of its affairs," he stated, "and to let the present and rising generation realise the class of men they were, and how close and friendly their relations were with the leading authors of their time, and the loyalty that subsisted between them and their publisher."[2] He offered Oliphant a yearly stipend of £500 until the work was complete, and concluded, "You have been so long and intimately connected with the House and the Magazine, and moreover you are so thoroughly in touch with Maga's past, that you would I think and hope find the task a congenial one."[3] Oliphant accepted the opportunity, telling William: "I began my married life by my first story in Maga—the proof of which (Katie Stewart) I received on my wedding day. I should like to wind up the long laborious record (which seems to me now to have been so vain, so vain, my life all coming to nothing) with this."[4] Oliphant completed two volumes of the work shortly before her death in 1897. The third was written by Mary Porter, daughter of the previous director John Blackwood.

The finished product—the three-volume memorial to the Blackwood firm—reveals nothing of the turmoil generated during its production. But turmoil there was, caused by conflicting demands of a firm intent on honoring its editorial acumen in discovering and steering illustrious literary figures and careers, an author intent on celebrating individualistic authorial power, and a family focused on enhancing the reputation of its illustrious family members. The result was a complex negotiation between parties intent on imposing differing interpretations on the final "house" image offered for public consumption. It is also another pertinent example of clashing views on and assumptions of literary worth and value as contained within the production process.

To trace the roots of such literary memorialization, one must go back several decades to another publishing memoir, in this case one of the first to celebrate Scottish publishing "flair" and entrepreneurship. The story begins with a fifteen-year-old bookseller's apprentice hurrying through the streets of Edinburgh in early 1816. It is five o'clock in the morning, and with great purpose he strides toward his destination, a bakery on the north side of town, "a cellar of confined dimensions, reached by a flight of steps descending from the street, and possessing a small back window immediately beyond the baker's kneading-board."[5] Seated on an empty sack in the windowsill, book in one hand and a reading candle stuck in a bottle in the other, our young apprentice will spend the next two and a half hours reading to the baker and his two sons as they prepare the day's baked goods. "The baker was not particular as to subject," we are informed in this individual's memoirs. "All he stipulated for was something comic and laughable. Aware of his tastes, I tried him first with the jocularities of *Roderick Random*, which was a great success, and produced shouts of laughter. I followed this up with other works of Smollett, also with the novels of Fielding, and with *Gil Blas*; the tricks and grotesque rogueries in this last mentioned work of fiction giving the baker and his two sons unqualified satisfaction."[6]

Don Quixote, Robert Burns, and picaresque novels are the mental fodder of the morning, as are news and information from local papers and journals. In return, our young hero receives a breakfast of penny rolls hot from the oven. The apprentice is the Peebles born and bred William Chambers, who with his brother Robert will go on to become one of Scotland's and Edinburgh's foremost publishers and printers and founder of *Chambers' Edinburgh Journal*. This famous anecdote forms one of the most telling moments in the *Memoir of Robert Chambers with Autobiographic Reminiscences of William Chambers*, which William wrote and published in 1872. Embedded in it are several themes that Chambers uses to celebrate and justify his fifty years in the bookselling and publishing trade, themes I would argue are recycled in subsequent publishing memoirs, including not least the Blackwood memorial.

Chambers's modest one-volume memoir is one of the first of a series of works issued over the last quarter of the nineteenth century by major Scottish publishing houses, chronicling their contributions to Scotland's literary and cultural heritage. These include Thomas Constable's 1873 magisterial three-volume celebration of his father, Archibald Constable (founder of the *Edinburgh Review* and celebrated "handmaiden" to Walter Scott, a giant figure in the early nineteenth-century Scottish literary world), Thomas Hughes's 1882 paean to his friend the Scots-born Daniel Macmillan, and Mrs. Oliphant's and Mary Porter's three-volume chronicle of the Edinburgh firm William Blackwood & Sons published in 1897–98.

What, then, are the themes to be dug out of Chambers's anecdote, and how are they subsequently expressed in other publishing memoirs that litter the latter quarter of the century? In Chambers's case, one finds four major issues present in his narrative: (1) self-improvement/self-help (lad of pairts); (2) curiosity, love of inquiry, and love of reasoning; (3) faith (both personal and religious); and, underpinning all these, (4) civic nationalism. Civic nationalism is a term often used to describe the manner in which Scottish cultural and national identity has asserted itself over the last few centuries. The political yoking of Scotland to England, begun with the union of Scottish and English parliaments in 1707 and completed after the quelling of brief Jacobite uprisings in 1747, is often said to have resulted in a complacent, depoliticized Scotland in the nineteenth century, a period during which there existed, as one critic has neatly summarized, "an ideology of noisy inaction."[7] More to the point, however, is that it was not an identity forged through constant violent upheaval, as has often characterized Irish political history, for example, but rather a cultural identity drawing on "a well behaved, enlightened appeal to pluralist democracy."[8]

Chambers's narrative of his and his brother's life is an exemplar of this view of civic responsibility and cultural interplay, emphasizing the ability to raise oneself from humble circumstances through faith, self-reliance, and self-education—in Chambers's case from farming stock reduced to insolvent, petty business concerns (his father was at different junctures of his life a draper and a manager of salt-mining works), to respectability and high social position, and subsequently to act in service of one's community. (As well as major philanthropic work, such as establishing a free library, reading room, and meeting house for the Peebles community, late in life William Chambers served in the distinguished position of Lord Provost of Edinburgh from 1865 to 1868.) As the preface makes clear, this memoir is meant to serve as moral instruction, and Chambers urges that "if a perusal of the narrative serves in any degree to inspire youth with notions of self-reliance, along with a hopeful dependence on providence when pressed by adverse circumstances, I shall be more than recompensed."[9] In the anecdote of the baker, we see all these issues at play: the young, disciplined apprentice, whose faith in self and in Providence, allied with self-initiative and self-reliance, leads to dispensing and encouraging inquiry and literary knowledge in a manner that reflects service to the social "ecumene," even as it also results in personal gain (breakfast).

Much of the brothers Chambers's lives were spent in work that reflected these set values. Robert Chambers, for example, made his name quite early through collecting and publishing important collections of Scottish social and cultural history, such as *Traditions of Edinburgh* (1824), *Walks in Edinburgh* (1825), and *The Popular Rhymes of Scotland* (1826). Both brothers subsequently embarked on experiments in publishing inexpensive, self-improving works for the masses, including founding *Chambers' Edinburgh Journal* in 1832 and writing, editing, and publishing

Chambers' Encyclopedia (1859–68). William's closing statement regarding his brother reemphasizes the cultural values and commitments underlying this rags-to-riches narrative: "His whole writing had for their aim the good of society—the advancement in some shape or other of the true and beautiful. . . . In the long list of literary compositions of Robert Chambers, we see the zealous and successful student, the sagacious and benevolent citizen, and the devoted lover of his country."[10]

A similar commitment to cultural interplay and civic values underpins Thomas Hughes's panegyric to the life of Daniel Macmillan (1813–57). Thomas Hughes (1822–96), better known as author of *Tom Brown's Schooldays* (1857, first published by Macmillan), was an author, lawyer, and devout follower (as was Daniel Macmillan) of Frederick Denison Maurice (1805–72), cleric, academic, religious thinker, and founder of the Christian Socialist movement. Hughes's memoir of the Arran-born founder of the Macmillan publishing empire follows in the narrative rags-to-riches footsteps of Chambers's text. As the preface states: "The following memoir tells the story of a young Scotchman born in a peasant home, who, with no schooling but what he could get in a small provincial town, before he was 12, and in spite of a want of means and wretched health, won his way to the front rank in a difficult business, and died at forty-four, the founder and head of a well known firm of publishers."[11] And as in Chambers's case, Macmillan's life is offered as an object lesson in one's rise through (1) self-improvement/self-help; (2) curiosity, love of inquiry, and love of reasoning; (3) Faith (in this case, religious); and (4) civic nationalism (in Macmillan's case through active participation in the Christian Socialist movement, uniting religious faith with socialist beliefs). But whereas Chambers spent his life working for and within the Scottish community, Macmillan was one of the increasing breed of entrepreneurs who took the high road to London to seek their fortunes or, in Macmillan's case, Cambridge, where in 1843, after several years in the London trade, he set up as a bookseller, printer, and publisher.

In Hughes's text, Macmillan's subsequent successes are due in part to family and community traits ingrained at an early age, in particular by his Calvinist-bred, churchgoing grandfathers. "From his earliest years," we are reminded, "he seems to have combined in a striking manner the characteristics of his two grandfathers; of Elder Malcolm, the man of order and duty, of Elder William, the man of progress."[12] The work ethic of such individuals as Chambers and Macmillan are held up for admiration in these texts. They are specific products of Scottish cultural values and heritage, something quietly acknowledged and supported by the morality tales these memoirs become. But in Macmillan's case, Hughes's memorial explicitly rejected aspects of his cultural identity because of the religious agenda underpinning the work.

What we have in effect is a text that sets out not only to celebrate Macmillan's life but also to commemorate the role Christian Socialism, and the teachings of F. D. Maurice in particular, played in guiding Macmillan in his later years. For all the good Calvinism may play in fostering a healthy work ethic, the Arran version of religious activity is also seen as having been a narrowing force in Macmillan's life, one from which he quickly and gladly escaped:

> Daniel Macmillan was before all things a devout Christian, one whose faith informed and coloured his whole life, and who was not ashamed of letting this be plainly known. This of itself is perhaps not yet so rare even in these days as to excite any special interest, but it does, I think, become so when we compare the narrow religious atmosphere in which he was reared with the Catholic freedom and breadth of that into which he rose. Examples are common enough of those who, bred like him in the strait Calvinism of the Scotch church, have shaken off the whole system of theology grafted onto the central truth which gives all its strength and vitality to that system.[13]

Thus unlike William and Robert Chambers, whose emphasis on faith in self-improvement and self-help drove them into exploring and publishing literature and work for the benefit of the workers, Macmillan is portrayed as an individual whose faith in Christianity (Baptist) and socialism drove him to specialize in publishing important religious texts and moral literature (Charles Kingsley's *Westward Ho!*, Thomas Hughes's *Tom Brown's Schooldays*, F. D. Maurice's influential *The Kingdom of Christ*). We have moved from a memoir that places the publisher within a specifically Scottish context, to a memorial text that illustrates how Scottish roots and background shape the religious faith and subsequent success of a publisher on a wider, national stage. This is a necessary move that is dictated by shifting centers of influence in the nineteenth century. The Scottish and Edinburgh publishing challenges to London in the late eighteenth- and early nineteenth-century (when the pen of Scott and the publishing of Constable reigned supreme)—collapse after the crash in the British bookselling market in 1826. Publishing power and expertise subsequently ebbed southward. The inevitable exodus of publishers, editors, and writers to London from Scotland in general, and Edinburgh in particular, from the 1820s onward, reflected this shifting balance of literary and cultural power between the two rival capitals.

Such acknowledgment of the shifting patterns of cultural power, and the role of Scottish cultural identity within the larger framework of a British identity, are also chronicled in the three-volume publishing history of the Edinburgh firm William Blackwood & Sons, published in 1897–98 to celebrate the centenary of the firm's founding. William Blackwood III and Margaret Oliphant negotiated the undertaking of the Blackwood publishing memoir over the months of July to December 1894.

For William Blackwood, the significance of this work was plain. It was to be a record of his firm's achievements in fostering literary genius, done in the manner of past publishing memoirs. As useful matrixes to follow in developing the work, he recommended to Oliphant that she study the structure of Samuel Smiles's *Life of John Murray* and the three-volume history of Archibald Constable, as well as William Chambers's work. From the very beginning, he stressed that the Blackwood volumes were to be not so much a history of a family as a story of publishing flair and a celebration of the cultural significance of the firm's showcase magazine. "There is every prospect I think of your making a splendid work," he remarked to Oliphant in December 1894. "The materials are so vast and varied when one looks into the history of the Magazine and it is her Memories & the results therefrom more than our own family that will be the interest to the public I expect."[14] Margaret Oliphant approached the project from a slightly different angle, viewing it more as her artistic swansong, a concluding statement on literary life. She noted, "I can think of nothing better if I must go on with this weary life so long, as to conclude everything with this book."[15] If this was to be literary hackwork, the implication was that it was to be hackwork celebrating literary individuality and artistic merit. While both visions for the most part seemed complementary, on occasion they were to diverge during the production of the text, with consequent results.

Matters seemed to be settled by the end of 1894. William Blackwood began sending Oliphant large containers of house documents and private correspondence culled from the firm's archives. He also made plans to announce the project in the *Athenaeum* as a precursor to gathering letters and other material from outside sources. On New Year's Eve 1894, however, a third key player with a radically different agenda came on the scene, someone whose demands were to complicate and vex project development for years to follow. The intruder was Mary Porter, who with her mother, widow of John Blackwood, had begun to gather material for a proposed epistolary memoir of her father John Blackwood, just after Oliphant had concluded negotiations for the house history with William. One can only speculate as to the uncanny timing of the Porter project, coming as it did so soon after the matter was decided between Oliphant and Blackwood. Oliphant was one of several to receive a letter on 31 December 1894 requesting John's letters for inclusion in this proposed volume. Dismayed by this turn of events, she immediately contacted William for advice on how to respond. Satisfying such a request was tricky, for her position as official chronicler, as yet not publicly announced, made the situation extremely uncomfortable. "It vexes me and seems to make it almost impossible to keep from betraying some one, either you or her," she wailed.[16] Something had to be done to stop the John Blackwood memoir from proceeding, for two such parallel volumes would, as Oliphant put it, "be very inconvenient to our design would it not?"[17]

William had also received a letter from Mary announcing her intention to write a memorial about her father. He responded immediately, asking Mary to drop plans for the memorial volume, interfering as it did with "the great work I have already arranged for" and "for which I have for many years past been collecting and getting into shape for whoever might be entrusted with it."[18] Affirming that he had begun arrangements with Mrs. Oliphant early that summer to undertake this work, he took great pains to stress that Oliphant's work would necessarily be more in depth because she had exclusive access to the firm's documents, access Mary Porter would be denied if she persisted in working on her competing volume. He concluded that it would be in the best interests of the family if Mary and her mother allowed the story of John Blackwood's life to be dealt with by Margaret Oliphant, for he had every hope that her complete attention to the compiling of the firm's history would produce a literary masterpiece. "The work is intended by Mrs. Oliphant to be a very important landmark in the literary history of this century," he exclaimed.[19]

Blackwood had strong reasons for heading off this bid for the right to recount family history, reasons that grew out of internecine family conflicts dating back more than fifteen years. Julia Blandford, widow of John Blackwood, reserved where her husband had been expansive, quiet yet sharp in manner, had never forgiven William for the manner in which he had taken control of the family firm following John's death in 1879. His assumption of total control of the firm had denied a role and a stake in the business for her young son Jack. In her view, the firm's success in the mid-nineteenth century had been due entirely to John's genius. Family pride had been dented when his heir had been denied his rightful role in the family business. In her eyes, that young Jack's perennial poor health left him often incapable of work did not matter, and she did not acknowledge the effect of his lack of ambition on his chances of gainful employment. (He was to die tragically young in 1881 in his early twenties.) Nor had she been happy with the manner in which J.B.'s life had been described as "uneventful" in the obituary printed in *Blackwood's Magazine* at the time. An underlying current of resentment at such family slights, and the view that the time was now ripe for a work extolling John's genius and "eventful" participation in the great events of his day, perhaps even to the detriment of other individuals involved in the firm's activities, manifested itself in this struggle to control family history. She steered her young daughter Mary toward taking part in the family project.

But Porter's abilities to recount this tale of genius were doubted by the other participants in the drama. Oliphant and William Blackwood feared that Porter and Mrs. Blackwood's planned memoir, depending as it would almost entirely on John's private correspondence gathered from friends and acquaintances, would in fact end up being a testimonial to his social life rather than a study of his business and editorial acumen. The effect would thus prove detrimental to the picture they envisaged presenting to the world of the Blackwoodian publishing flair. As a result, negotiations between the three parties concerned progressed slowly over the next few months. A compromise was eventually offered by Margaret Oliphant, who suggested that she was willing to accept material written by Mary for incorporation into the third volume of the history, which was to deal with John Blackwood's editorial and business activity. At this stage Oliphant was sure this would not add significantly to the work's length. "It is not likely I should think that she should write very much, for unaccustomed persons soon get tired of literary composition," she wrote dismissively.[20]

But it was made clear at the start that Oliphant, the writer, was to be firmly in control of whatever material Porter produced. There would be an acknowledgment of the contribution, but no right to a veto or final decision on the trajectory and drive of the narrative. Thus the stiff response when Oliphant subsequently learned that Mary Porter was passing herself off as joint author of the memoir. In a curt letter to Porter, she wrote: "The scheme of a double biography is the worst that could be conceived and indeed I don't see how it could be carried out at all." There was no room for such dual efforts in this project. If this was to work, it was to be on the agreement that Porter's efforts were to be subsumed into Oliphant's larger narrative. Porter's task was to produce personal reminiscences, not attempt to piece together a complete life and letters. The latter was

Oliphant's province alone. "When I said that I should be happy to add to my book, a critical notice from you under your name," Oliphant emphasized, "what I meant was your own narrative, your own recollections, what is entirely individual to yourself & the family, indeed anything that is your own bearing on Mr. Blackwood's life and character—which of course is in its way much more valuable than any hodge podge of extracts from letters which are very difficult things to manipulate, and require an experienced hand."[21]

To forestall any further confusion, Oliphant arranged to meet Mary to discuss matters. In mid-March, over tea and crumpets in Oliphant's drawing room in Windsor, the two sat down and worked through the issues to everyone's satisfaction, although Mary Porter and her mother still felt touchy about who should be allowed to vet and handle John's correspondence. In the end, Oliphant won them over to her view that it would be best if she handled the sorting and arrangements of relevant correspondence extracts. "We shall manage both ladies quite comfortably I feel sure," she wrote soothingly to William after concluding the tête-à-tête.[22] Word spread through the Blackwood clan that all had been resolved. "Glad to hear you think all will be plain sailing with our great book," wrote William's cousin and aide Archibald McCall Smith, enclosing some article proofs for Mrs. Oliphant. "From some remarks dropped by my aunt Mrs. John B. the other day I gathered such was likely to be the case as she spoke very nicely about the literary part being in your hands."[23]

With roles now carefully demarcated, Oliphant and Porter set about carrying out their respective duties. Oliphant spent the summer months working through boxes of material sent to her by Alexander Allardyce (chief *Blackwood's Magazine* copy editor and literary advisor) and Archibald McCall Smith. Occasional reports returned of strange and unusual items encountered in these packages—the entire manuscript of John Gibson Lockhart's *Some Passages in the Life of Adam Blair* from 1822, edited proofs of James Hogg's poetry, old prints. As Oliphant described it, it was like turning over a huge literary dust heap, "all giving some valuable scrap."[24] In early autumn she produced and read out a draft introductory chapter for William, who declared it an excellent opening. September 1895 brought another visit from Mary Porter, who read Oliphant her précis of her father's life. Oliphant deemed it better than she expected. "She has given her sketch of your uncle's early life very nicely I think," Oliphant reported, "and I see my way to form an effective background to the more individual sketch, which I think will be great advantage to the book."[25] Porter's contribution was not going to hinder the work after all. "I think it should be a very successful volume," Oliphant concluded.[26] By the end of the year, Oliphant had drafted the first seven chapters of the first volume.

Over the next year and a half, and until a few days before her death in June 1897, sections for the first two volumes arrived with regularity, written in Oliphant's miniature script. Her work pleased William Blackwood and his editorial advisors, conforming as it did for the most part to the conception they shared of publishing flair and family abilities. One small spat, however, illustrates how approaches to publishing details could diverge between author and publisher.

In early May 1897, proofs of Oliphant's chapter on John Gibson Lockhart, one of Blackwood's early editorial advisors and contributors, were gone over by William and his press reader, J. H. Lobban. Oliphant had drawn extensively on Lockhart and John Wilson's letters of 1817–22 to sketch out the relationships between the firm's founder and his magazine's early team of advisors and contributors. What fascinated her about these letters was the immediacy, emotional power, and lack of inhibition found in them. The contents of these letters, she confessed early on to Archie McCall Smith, "betray their characters and their dealings with your grandfather so very clearly and graphically that the traditional reticence of your house may feel implicated."[27] Deciding that the dramatic effect, interest, and emotional content of these letters were safe enough to reveal at this late stage in the century, seventy-five years on, she used them to craft a chapter charting strong clashes between Lockhart and Blackwood over authorial activities and editorial content. It is even more revealing that she included extracts from Lockhart revealing his discontent over low payments for work done for the firm.

But in reflecting on the contemporary realities of the literary marketplace, making transparent the role that money played in literary activity, Oliphant ran afoul of the "house image" that William Blackwood wanted to project. As Blackwood wrote anxiously on reading the proofs, revealing personal clashes over material was one thing, but exposing the economic realities of publishing was another matter entirely. "In going over the Lockhart chapter," he explained, "I have been a good deal exercised about the passages in Lockhart's letters relating to the scale of remuneration for his Maga contributions, and the advisability of taking the public as much into our confidence about these purely private details, which only caused a brief rupture between him and my grandfather."[28] More important, Blackwood felt, was that Lockhart's epistolary complaints about low payment were couched in a tone that implied less than fair behavior on the part of his grandfather. Casting the publisher as a villain and an uncharitable employer would not do. He blue-penciled sections to be eliminated and cautioned Oliphant,

"It is my desire to do equal justice to my grandfather, which is also I am sure your own, and I think by omitting what I have marked, nothing of importance is lost, and everything objectionable removed."[29]

Oliphant's response was more sanguine about the potential damage to reputations from these comments. As she noted, enough time had passed to soften the effects of these old disputes. More to the point, such information provided gossipy details that were sure to appeal to readers. "I am not quite sure that I agree with you about the money passages in the Lockhart letters," she wrote, "for the public loves such scraps of information and the period is so far back that it can have very little bearing upon today."[30] Nevertheless, she bowed to Blackwood's wishes, cutting and shifting material to provide a kinder spin to the incidents. Blackwood was relieved. "I thank you for meeting my wishes and suggestions about the alterations," he responded, "and though I know that the public like reading about such private concerns, yet I feel it is not a taste to gratify when we have ample more good materials, and equally interesting and attractive."[31] Another crisis had been averted, and the firm's image remained intact.

On 16 June 1897, Oliphant finished final corrections of the first volume of the memoirs. She died nine days later. The two volumes she had completed were subsequently proofed by J. H. Lobban, Blackwood's new editorial assistant, and issued in early September 1897. In these two volumes, one finds a detailing of the past national and international successes of the Blackwood family of publishers that at the same time emphasizes their inheritance of Scottish cultural values, their link in the chain of cultural heritage stretching back to the Scottish Enlightenment. Yet the difficulty lay in developing these themes within the straitjacket of contemporary contexts, in having also to suggest that the firm's directors enfolded their Scottish heritage within a wider national identity. The result is a text that identifies and revels in a marked Scottish heritage that is safely labeled as part of an exciting but lost past, commented on from the perspective of a current, united British national identity. This is done through emphasizing the romance of past Scottish publishing history and focusing on the peculiarly Scottish personal characteristics, sound judgment, and publishing flair of the Blackwoods.

The two volumes of the Blackwood memorial are constructed linearly, charting the rise of the firm, and in the first volume the rise of its founder William Blackwood (1776–1834) from humble beginnings as an Edinburgh-based bookseller to the heights of dominance in London, and so by implication British literary circles and culture. Crucial to this romantic enterprise is the cautious figure of the editor and publisher. Oliphant conjures up the figure of William Blackwood, founder of the firm, not as a grasping businessman but as a daring adventurer seeking nuggets of gold in the mines of Literature. She notes at one stage:

> It is a common belief in the literary world that publishers are the most grasping of middlemen, eager only to have the lion's share of the profits. But in those days there was a certain spirit of daring and romance in "the Trade." The Revival of Literature was like the opening of a new mine: it was more than that, a sort of manufactory out of nothing, to which there seemed no limit. You had but to set a man of genius spinning at that shining thread which came from nowhere, which required no purchase of materials or "plant" of machinery, and your fortune was made.[32]

The founder William Blackwood (1776–1834) is represented as the canny Scot who is able to set the men of genius at their task of spinning golden threads of literature, befriending, encouraging, and gathering together a coterie of authors to form an engaged and directed unit. Throughout the heady early days of the firm's development, from the founding of the famous *Blackwood's Magazine* and its publication of the infamous Chaldee Manuscript in 1817, to its published attacks on Coleridge, Wordsworth, and the Cockney School of Poetry, William Blackwood is cast as a bedrock of levelheadedness in the face of a whirlwind of literary production and intellectual high jinks. He is the guardian in rough times, behind whom shelter such contributors as John Gibson Lockhart, William Maginn, Thomas DeQuincey, and John Wilson ("Christopher North"). Present here are the themes we have traced in the memoirs of Chambers and Macmillan: (1) self-improvement, or rise from humble beginnings to publishing prominence; (2) faith in literary talent and literary genius; (3) inquiry and love of reasoning (the merry band of Blackwood's early authors and contributors are ever present and ever vocal in the celebrated round reading room of the firm's headquarters); and (4) civic nationalism. In this case, though, William Blackwood's activities are seen as contributing to the cultural heritage of his native land, Scotland, but also remain contained within a larger national identity that is British. A contrasting portrait is evident in Porter's third-volume summary of the firm's history.

Porter's assuming of the writing duties for the third volume was inevitable in light of Oliphant's death in June 1897. Even before then, Mary had begun chafing at the restrictions originally imposed, particularly as throughout early 1897, with Oliphant beginning to fail in health, Mary began taking on further responsibilities for sorting and organizing potential material for the third volume. March 1897 saw matters reaching a crisis point, after William rebuffed an attempt by Mary not only to gain compensation for the work she had done up to that point, but also to demand total control in drafting the forthcoming volume. Margaret Oliphant, consulted on the matter, wrote William sanguinely: "She seems to wish to have the third volume to herself, concerning which I have no objection, if it pleases you." In fact, contemplating the prospect, she rather hoped the issue would be resolved in a way that would absolve her from further literary work. If this were the case, "I should be quite pleased," she wrote relievedly, "to confine myself to revising, or putting in a scrap here and there, as indeed your uncle John's brightest years are already fully represented in the second volume."[33]

Despite Oliphant's assent, William was not so quick to agree. "I am sure Mrs. Oliphant will be grateful for any help you can give her but you must not overlook the fact that she has undertaken to write the life," he wrote stiffly to Mary, "and I could not sanction any plan of co-operation between you, further than what we originally came to, in which you offered to render her every assistance in your power in the arranging of the correspondence."[34] Weeks later, Mary confronted William, demanding £200 in payment for her work on the manuscript, raising once more the issue of control over the third volume, and threatening (rather idly) to take the volume to a rival publisher if a compromise was not forthcoming. William resisted briefly, but he gave in after a letter from Oliphant intimated her acceptance of Mary's increased role in the enterprise. "I think Mary Porter should have what she asks," Oliphant wrote peremptorily. "Better to lose a little money than make any sort of trouble additional."[35] Furthermore, she was now of the opinion that Porter was capable of the task ahead, if perhaps a bit unsure about her abilities to tackle any in-depth analysis of the magazine's content. "Her work you know is really very good," she concluded.[36] Blackwood assented to give Porter £150, but he made no official commitment to have Porter undertake the final volume on her own until September 1897, three months after Oliphant's death, whereupon he offered her a further £100 on completion of the work, thus raising her gains to £250.

Once arrangements had been finalized, Blackwood did his best to contain Porter's eagerness to focus on the social and domestic spheres of John Blackwood's life to the detriment of his literary and editorial activity. A first draft of the manuscript, submitted in November 1897, prompted great consternation and a detailed letter from Blackwood laying out the areas Porter was specifically not to attempt. Domestic details and excessive hero worship was to be eliminated, he thundered, for "the book will stand or fall by the way in which the history of your father's connection with Lever, Aytoun, Thackeray, Delane, Laurence Oliphant, Mrs. Oliphant, the Hamleys, Kinglake, James White & George Eliot, etc. is told."[37] Authors and books, Porter was reminded, should be the key elements in the history of John's life, *not* his home and social life. "In your present narrative," Blackwood warned, "the characters are seen only in passing glimpses as they enter into the history of your father's household." He went on to emphasize, "It is above all things essential that the whole atmosphere of the book should be a literary and not a social one."[38]

The struggle between family vision and publishing history continued right through until the volume's publication in late 1898. It is not surprising, compared with Oliphant's memorial volumes, that it was not as well received as an uneasy combination of celebratory announcements of editorial achievement interspersed with lengthy domestic description. Despite the best editorial efforts of William Blackwood and J. H. Lobban, traces of Porter's original agenda seeped through to the final published text. Substantial descriptive sections and extracts from J.B.'s personal letters reaffirmed the domestic happiness to be encountered in his private life, as exemplified in the extended chapter detailing life at Strathtyrum, John's main residence in St. Andrews. Here, we are reminded, John's household was open to all, for "there was much pleasant visiting and dining all round amongst the little coterie, who all knew each other." Indeed, "without any difficulty a dinner-party could be got up at short notice. There was always some one anxious to meet some one else, and my father was very happy when he could arrange a dinner under those circumstances. . . . He invited people because he wished them to come, or for what might be thought the even more unusual reason that he thought they wished to come themselves!"[39]

Long sections on John's fondness for cigars, his passion for golf, and his social grace (a man who seemed never to be without a kind word for strangers and friends alike), often narrated in the form of personal reminiscence on the part of Mary Porter, shift abruptly into disquisitions on authorial relations between benevolent publisher and grateful author. For example, the effectiveness of the description of John Blackwood's last encounter with his friend Charles Lever in Trieste, meant as a poignant conclusion to the author's connection with the firm, is undercut by the domestic-centered framing of the event as well as by an undertone of anti-Semitic commentary. We are told at one point:

After dinner we adjourned to the garden for coffee and cigarettes, and
Mr. Lever sat up till very late. The second evening the same pleasant party,
with the addition of the clergyman, Mr. Callaghan; the same amount of
laughing and talking, perhaps rather more. Many were the jokes about
their neighbours, the society being mainly composed of wealthy Jewish
merchants and their families; but the impression was that the jokes were
all kindly, the wit without sting, and that the Jews had been made the best
of in that cheery happy-go-lucky household. Indeed he mentioned that on
some festive occasion, Lord Dalling, in an amiable whisper, had remarked
at last, "Lever, I like your Jews," and this, of course, made everybody feel
quite happy.[40]

Despite this, and as result of the passage of time, the volume has come to stand
as an official representation of the firm's self-image, taking in and completing the
house image sketched out in Oliphant's memorial text.

As we have seen, the overall result of this three-volume celebration of literary relations is a complex and sometimes uneasy textual construction, weaving
together a jostling variety of editorial, authorial, and cultural identities. Attempts
to grapple with the paradox of containing and at the same time emphasizing a
unique Scottish national identity within a larger British context and past publishing history is ever present in Oliphant's work, published at the end of the century (while not present at all in Porter's text). In the end, these attempts to place
the role of the publisher in a central position in the cultural life of Scotland and
Britain demonstrates how Scottish cultural identity wove indelibly through representations of the lives and work of the Blackwood publishers in the nineteenth
century, and how the hitherto unknown production of the firm's "house" image
became a battleground for competing textual representations.

7

"A Grocer's Business"

William Blackwood III and the
Literary Agents

"A mistake,"[1] "A parasite living on our vital forces,"[2] and "Middlemen . . . to be avoided"[3] were some of the comments that irate publishers directed at literary agents, who had just become part of the publishing process at the turn of the century. William Heinemann, one of the most virulent critics of literary agents of this period, had this to say about their usefulness: "My theory is that when once an author gets into the claws of a typical agent, he is lost to decency. He generally adopts the moral outlook of the trickster, which the agent inoculates with all rapidity, and the virus is so poisonous that the publisher had better disinfect himself and avoid contagion."[4] By 1917, however, the year of this outburst, literary agents were a significant part of the publishing process, a "necessary evil," according to William Blackwood III, because of "the increasing desire of authors to be saved all personal trouble of negotiations."[5] In 1894 there were six agents registered in the London *Post Office Directory*.[6] By 1914 there were more than thirty agencies and syndicates advertising literary services in trade journals.[7]

The historical role of the professional literary agent as mediator in the publishing process has been described in detail in several works, including James Hepburn's short but groundbreaking study *The Author's Empty Purse and the Rise of the Literary Agent*. The act of individuals negotiating literary worth on behalf of authors was not a phenomenon new to the twentieth-century, and indeed had been in evidence throughout much of the nineteenth century. The century saw famous examples of informed friends or unpaid connections negotiating book rights, royalties, and copyright issues with publishers on behalf of authors. John Forster, for example, described by one commentator as a man who "bridged the gulf between the patron of the eighteenth century and the literary agent of the twentieth," acted as mediator and counselor for, among others, Charles Dickens, Tennyson, Thomas Carlyle, and Robert Browning from the 1830s to the 1860s.[8] Forster was instrumental in counseling Dickens toward retaining tight financial control over his literary property; in negotiations with Richard Bentley in 1838 for *Oliver Twist* and *Barnaby Rudge*, for example, Dickens's successful attempts to retain control of his copyrights, as opposed to selling copyright outright, caused Bentley's chief clerk, Edward S. Morgan, to proclaim exasperatedly about Forster that Dickens's "feeling of discontent so pertinaciously exhibited was to be attributed to the meddling agency of some person by whose advice Mr. Dickens allowed himself to be swayed."[9] Thackeray paid tribute to Forster's negotiating skills when he wrote, "Whenever anybody is in a scrape we all fly to him for refuge—he is ominiscient and works miracles."[10] Others who performed similar functions for authors included George Henry Lewes for George Eliot from the 1850s to 1870s, Theodore Watts-Dunton for Algernon Swinburne in the 1880s and 1890s, and the North American Thomas Aspinwall, who while U.S. consul in London from 1827 to 1854 acted as transatlantic agent for Washington Irving, James Fenimore Cooper, and the historian William Hickley (author of *Ferdinand and Isabella* and *The History of the Conquest of Mexico and Peru*).[11]

By the latter quarter of the nineteenth century, matters had begun shifting from such unorganized, casual activity by individuals to organized, commercial negotiation by dedicated professionals. One of the first such agents to establish himself was the Scots-born Alexander Pollock Watt, who opened an agency in London in 1875. Little is known about Watt's early life. Born in Glasgow in 1834, he worked in the Edinburgh book trade before marrying the publisher Alexander Strahan's sister and moving to London in 1871 to help in Strahan's London operations. By 1878 he had branched out into other areas, including representing the author George MacDonald, but it was not until 1881 that he began advertising himself as a literary agent.[12] Watt is credited with developing the basis of literary agenting as it is practiced today, establishing the standard commission fee (10 percent) for successful representation and acting as "scout" for material likely to profit both publisher and author. His skill lay in recognizing and perfecting the mediating role of the literary agent as arbiter and evaluator of literary property— or more precisely, as one commentator noted, "participating in, and in fact becoming the source of, the valuation of copyright."[13]

From early on, Watt specialized in serving as middleman between author and publisher, acting as "double agent" to meet specific demands of both ends of the market. In early correspondence with Blackwood's, he adopted a dual strategy of offering potential material while at the same time seeking to ascertain areas and material likely to fit the publisher's particular literary tastes and lists. When in 1894 he approached Blackwood's with a work by the editor of *Atlantic Monthly*, for example, Watt delicately hinted that he would be willing to tailor his search for appropriate material if William Blackwood so desired: "I shall be very glad indeed," he wrote, "if I can assist you in any way to get the occasional works from the one or two writers you mentioned in your recent letter. If you will kindly let me have particulars as to exactly what it is you want and from whom, the matter will receive my immediate and most careful attention."[14] William Blackwood had initially been opposed to any such connections. As he commented in a memorandum in the late 1880s, agents such as Watt and W. Morris Colles were to be avoided, for "their business and interest is to get the highest possible price for their clients and these generally run far beyond what any old established self-respecting house would be justified in paying."[15]

By 1894, however, William was embracing those he had previously scorned. Thus, a week after Watt's letter he wrote with interest outlining his requests. "I am very glad indeed that you think you can help me in the way of getting an occasional work from the writers for whom I may have a particular fancy," he noted on 13 December, going on to present his wish list of works and clients represented by Watt. The list included poems by William Watson and John Davidson, novels by Stanley Weyman, and short stories by S. R. Crockett.[16] A work by John Davidson was promptly offered, but turned down because the price asked for (£25) was £15 more than Blackwood was willing to pay for an appearance in *Blackwood's Magazine*. Likewise works by Winston Churchill, Henry Rider Haggard, and Arthur Morrison were refused. John Davidson eventually made it into the pages of *Blackwood's* in December 1906 with "The Cake of Mithridates," not one of his best efforts.

Watt was not the only agent testing Blackwood's at this time; others included the formidably successful American agent Curtis Brown, who began working in London in 1899; the Literary Agency founded and run from 1899 by C. F. Cazenove and George Herbert Perris[17]; and William Morris Colles, founder of the Authors' Syndicate in 1890, an ineffectual collective closely allied with the Society of Authors and whose negotiations on behalf of the novelist Beatrice Harraden are dealt with later in this chapter. There was also James Brand Pinker, whose presence in the firm's history is inextricably linked with his role as agent for Joseph Conrad.

Pinker, born in 1863, a former newspaper and magazine editor, and at times abrasive and aggressive in negotiations and personal contact, began his agency in January 1896. While A. P. Watt had made his mark promoting established authors, such as Rider Haggard, Rudyard Kipling, Wilkie Collins, and Arthur Conan Doyle, Pinker concentrated on developing the careers of newly emerging authors, such as Joseph Conrad, Stephen Crane, Ford Madox Ford, D. H. Lawrence, James Joyce, and H. G. Wells. Until his death in 1922, he served as a prominent and imposing negotiator of literary property, a man of patience who, Conrad wrote, "has treated not only my moods but even my fancies with the greatest consideration."[18]

Like Watt, Pinker studied his markets, targeting and tailoring material to receptive publishing houses. Early letters in the Blackwood files show him seeking personal meetings to establish more precisely what type of work fitted the firm's tastes and perceived markets and audiences. "I should be very glad of an opportunity of meeting you," he wrote William Blackwood III early on in his career, "to discuss the possibilities of business with your House and learn what is most likely to suit the Magazine, and if I knew the suggestion were agreeable to you I would seize the earliest chance of going to Edinburgh."[19] Early successes in selling work to the firm by Jack London and Henry Lawson were matched by failures to place George Gissing, H. G. Wells, and Henry James. Within three years of initial contact in 1898, when Blackwood remarked that "this man has been sending some very fair mss lately though none of them have just been the thing," Pinker had become a major supplier of valued literary property for Blackwood's firm and its magazine.[20] We shall return to Pinker later in this chapter.

The bewildering range of new outlets for marketing literary property was often beyond the average capacity of publishers who were used to negotiating on relatively uncomplicated publishing terms. By 1925, for example, cases of agents negotiating more than twenty-six different rights to a book, including rights to playing-card and cigarette-packet pictures, were common.[21] In the face of such changes, the literary agent, hired to exploit these contradictions in favor of the author, was an easy target for blame by publishers. Faced with the multiplicity of markets competing for authors and their literary property, publishers resented the intrusion of agents questioning their estimation of the commercial value of authors and their literary property.

Economic power and control over literary property was shifting from publisher to author, with the author, via his agent, now seeking to control and determine his or her own market worth and economic value. Literary agents were accused of commercializing art, of turning authors into little more than saleable commodities by introducing Yankee-style sharp business practices, a particular complaint after the American Curtis Brown established himself as a major force in Britain after 1899. Ironically, American publishers were fond of observing that literary agents were a beneficial British invention, attributing their arrival to "the superior amicability and business wisdom of authors and publishers in this country."[22]

Likewise, publishers were not averse to using agents to seek commissioned work for their use. As noted earlier, Watt and Pinker frequently acted as "double agents," seeking to match specific requests from publishers while simultaneously using this information to target specific authors to publishers likely to be interested in their products. Yet despite this, many British publishers continued to remain suspicious of the value of literary agents to the book trade, generally agreeing with the trenchant note of William Blackwood III in 1904 that "these Literary Agents have reduced publishing to a level of a grocer's business without the profits."[23] That view was reiterated in 1963 by Ralph Arnold, who, recalling his days at Constable & Company, noted that letters from literary agents were often "red rags to a bull" to the managing director. "With a very few exceptions," Arnold added, "he hated literary agents, maintaining that they interposed an unnecessary and undesirable barrier between author and publisher."[24]

Such individual responses to the commercial evils of the literary agent could not mask the fact that, by 1914, the literary agent had become fully integrated into the publishing process. Indeed, they had become so entrenched that during the First World War they were recognized, co-opted, and utilized by the government, in this case in the prominent shape of the literary agent A. S. Watt. Between 1914 and 1918, as I have written elsewhere in connection with the wartime publications of Blackwood's, A. S. Watt, son of A. P. Watt, acted as the official conduit and mediator between authors, publishers, and government bureaus in the commission, production, and distribution of printed material for the highly secret propaganda war waged against Germany and Austria-Hungary at home and abroad, and in particular in the United States and Canada.[25] Watt commissioned and sought outlets for a variety of material from such authors as John Galsworthy, John Buchan, Thomas Hardy, Rudyard Kipling, and "Ian Hay," and also acted as intermediary between journalists, newspaper and journal editors, publishing and printing firms, and government ministries. Literary agency, and most certainly Watt's firm, emerged strengthened from the war as a permanent part of a changed literary marketplace, handling increasingly complex and diverse methods of marketing literary products.

The ensuing divergence in authorial representation between 1880 and 1920, from informed amateur to organized professional, the mixed results of such representations, and the general effect on author-publisher relations can be seen in a comparison of the diverging literary careers and commercial representations of three authors whose relationship with Blackwood's began roughly at the same time: Margaret Georgina Todd (or "Graham Travers"), Beatrice Harraden, and Joseph Conrad. The comparison raises interesting questions relating to gender and literary worth in the literary marketplace, and gives us insight into the process of change in literary agenting during this period from the informed amateur to the commercially astute professional.

Margaret Georgina Todd (1859–1918), doctor and novelist, Scotland-born daughter of a businessman with Indian connections, was educated in medical schools in Edinburgh, Berlin, Brussels, and London before settling in Edinburgh as a resident doctor at the Edinburgh Hospital for Women and Children, founded by the pioneering female physician, feminist activist, and suffragette Sophia Jex-Blake. *Mona MacLean*, Todd's first and most popular novel, of which more than sixteen editions in various formats (three-decker, six-shilling, 2/6 shilling, and six-penny editions) were published by Blackwood's under the pseudonym "Graham Travers" between 1892 and 1906, betrays its autobiographical origins in its depiction of a Scottish country lass battling prejudice and self-doubt to gain eventually a medical degree. Happiness is achieved in the end when she marries a fellow doctor and sets up with him as co-partner in a medical practice. In reality, happiness was found working on similar terms with her long-term companion Sophia Jex-Blake from the late 1880s until Sophia's death in 1912. (Jex-Blake features in *Mona MacLean* as the earnest, reformist medical student Miss Lascelles, "a tiny figure scarcely bigger than a child, yet full of character and dignity.")[26] This relationship remains unnoted in current appraisals of Jex-Blake, owing to the simple fact that it was left unrecorded in the standard 1918 biography of Jex-Blake, suppressed by its author, Margaret Todd.

Margaret Todd developed two careers, combining medical practice and social activism (campaigning for women's rights) with literary work. She wrote articles for *Blackwood's Magazine* and other literary journals, and five novels and collections of short stories between 1892 and 1908, before retiring to Sussex. Most were published by William Blackwood & Sons, and most were negotiated for by Todd's partner Sophia Jex-Blake. Jex-Blake, known for her pioneering work in medicine, for leading the first attempt (unsuccessful) by women to gain medical qualifications in Britain at the University of Edinburgh from 1869 to 1873, and for becoming the first British woman to register for medical practice following changes in the law in 1876, spent her life practicing medicine and running training hospitals for women in London and Edinburgh. Unknown until now has been her equally fervent role as literary agent for Margaret Todd, a role recorded in unpublished letters in the archives of the Edinburgh publishing firm William Blackwood & Sons in the National Library of Scotland.

Between 1892 and 1903 Jex-Blake negotiated sales rights on behalf of Margaret Todd with Blackwood's for three novels (*Mona MacLean* [1892], *Windyhaugh* [1898], and *The Way of Escape* [1902]), for a collection of short stories published as *Fellow Travellers* (1896), and for stories and articles in *Blackwood's Magazine*. Differences with Blackwood's, caused mainly by Jex-Blake's attempts to dictate publishing terms to Blackwood on behalf of Todd, resulted in a different publisher issuing her final novel, *Growth*, in 1906.

Jex-Blake first approached William Blackwood on behalf of "Graham Cameron" sometime in late July 1892 regarding the publishing of *Mona MacLean*, a romance centered on the trials and tribulations of a female medical student living in a small town on the east coast of Scotland. The choice of publishers was apt, as one of Blackwood's publishing interests at the time, and indeed well into the twentieth-century, was popular fiction by women, particularly romances set in Scotland and the colonies. Prominent in the Blackwood lists in this and subsequent years were authors such as Maud Diver (author of romances set in India), "Sydney Grier" (pseudonymous female author of Eastern-set popular romances), Katherine Cecil Thurston (author of the 1904 sensation novel *John Chilcote, M.P.*), Lucy B. Walford, and Beatrice Allhusen. The books of such authors, many of whose names and literary reputations are now all but forgotten, sold by the thousands during the first twenty years of the century and were a mainstay of the Blackwood catalog, sitting alongside colonial tales by Henry Lawson, Joseph Conrad, and Hugh Clifford; Scottish tales by Ian Hay, Neil Munro, and John Buchan; and endless reprints of George Eliot, Margaret Oliphant, and James Hogg.

William Blackwood responded to Jex-Blake in early August with a long and initially lukewarm critique of the work, calling it "a fairly good and readable novel, though judging by the highest standards, certainly not one of the highest order of fiction, though quite above the average of the general run of novels."[27] Despite his initial reservations, he made the firm's standard offer to untried authors to publish the work in three volumes, priced 25/6, with either a half-share of sales profits or a low royalty on all copies sold. Jex-Blake was not impressed, and made this clear in a brusque style that was to remain the hallmark of her correspondence with the firm: "I find that 'Graham Cameron' agrees with me in thinking the proposals in your favour of 11th inst. not very liberal, but she tells me that she will be contented with whatever arrangements I think fair, and she asks me to negociate [sic] in the matter exactly as if the book were my own."[28]

Further face-to-face discussions between Jex-Blake and Blackwood resulted in a slightly more enhanced offer, in this case a royalty of four shillings on every copy sold, but a refusal by Jex-Blake to agree on reprint offers before gauging the success of Todd's first work. What is telling in this small exchange is the manner in which Jex-Blake from the start assumed quite firmly the role of commercial mediator—"my honorary agent," as Todd jokingly noted—controlling the relationship and balance of power between authorial interest and publisher intentions.[29] William Blackwood believed, like his uncle John before him, that loyalty and personal links with authors were the keys to a successful publishing relationship, a point seen in his nurturing of Joseph Conrad, discussed later. Despite this personal approach to publishing on the part of William Blackwood, Jex-Blake (like J. B. Pinker, the literary agent whose takeover of Conrad's finances in 1903 disrupted such personal alliances but whose management of Conrad's career yielded him much success in subsequent years) maintained a commercial distance for Todd in order to negotiate more firmly for her work. Care was taken to shield initially the identity of the author and to keep Todd separate from all commercial negotiations. Todd, known first as "Graham Cameron" and subsequently as "Graham Travers," remained hidden behind the negotiating figure of Jex-Blake for several years, only emerging finally to establish a warm personal correspondence with William Blackwood in 1894. "My first letter from Miss Todd," William Blackwood noted significantly on her first missive dated 29 August 1894.[30] Subsequent exchanges were often friendly and personal, centering on literary ideas, holiday activities, and decidedly uncommercial matters.

Todd's friendliness with Blackwood was in direct contrast to Jex-Blake's frequently abrasive negotiations with the firm, illustrating what publishers disliked most about the increasing commercial accountability demanded on behalf of authors by their representatives. Jex-Blake proved to be a tough negotiator on behalf of Todd, questioning all figures, demanding increased royalties as Todd's reputation increased and further editions and new works appeared. Her lack of knowledge of the publishing business, however, did prove costly at one stage, illustrating how the separation between author, agent, and publisher could at times work at cross-purposes. Following the success of two separate three-volume editions of *Mona MacLean*, a deal was negotiated to reprint the work in a sixpenny one-volume edition. The royalties negotiated were quite low compared with ones we see later being negotiated for Harraden and Conrad, in this case a royalty of one shilling and sixpence per copy sold, and five pence per copy sold in the colonies, with Blackwood slipping in a standard house clause that copies sold were to be counted under trade discounting rules as equaling twelve copies for every thirteen sold. More than 18,000 six-shilling volumes were printed and sold in twelve editions between 1893 and 1899, and 7,300 were sold in two colonial editions.

This prompted William Blackwood to suggest casually to Todd in late December 1899 that the firm might profitably issue a popular sixpenny edition of *Mona MacLean*. "In the early part of this year there was quite a boom on sixpenny issues of popular books," he wrote in justifying the suggestion, "and although towards the end of the summer such issues seemed to be rather overdone, I believe there is still a field for a moderate number of popular novels issued in this form in a limited edition."[31] Todd responded enthusiastically, noting, "I very much like the idea of a cheap edition of *Mona*. . . . So many people have *enquired* about a six-penny *Mona*, that I think she should stand a good chance."[32] Nevertheless, Blackwood was referred to Jex-Blake for further discussions.

Blackwood wrote to Jex-Blake in early January 1900 outlining his ideas. He suggested publishing an edition of 100,000 copies, with the hope that "this issue of a popular edition of Mona MacLean will not only bring that book before a larger circle of the reading public, but that it will also direct more attention to the author and her other books."[33] He proposed a royalty of 10 percent on the selling price, noting it was a formula offered successfully to G. W. Steevens for the best-selling *With Kitchener to Khartum* (a transaction handled by Pinker) as well as to George Eliot's trustees for successive issues of her work. Jex-Blake's response, however, was unexpectedly negative. Blackwood's initial offer was received coldly, and after further discussions, in which Blackwood estimated the author's profit would run to around £240, taking into account sales of £75 from advertisements to be placed at the beginning and end of the work, Jex-Blake rejected the offer as not enough, in brusque terms quite in contrast to Todd's earlier enthusiasm. "I think it will probably be better to drop the idea for the present," she wrote on 13 January 1900. "Personally I have no great wish for a 6d edition, & should think it wiser to publish at a shilling an edition from present plates, in a stiff cover, & in fact practically like the one you issued ditto colonial, with a red cover instead of brown. This would involve infinitely less expense, & even a much smaller sale would be more remunerative."[34] She ended with an aesthetic critique curiously inconsistent with the strongly commercial tone of her negotiations with Blackwood's: "I see you speak of advertisements on the cover—I should strongly object to anything not literary—e.g. Pears Soap etc."[35]

In place of the rejected sixpenny edition, Jex-Blake negotiated the printing of a 2/6 edition of 5,200 copies in April 1900, which sold rather poorly (2,900 copies by 31 December 1901. The idea of a sixpenny popular edition remained dormant until June 1906, when it was finally issued in a print run of 26,250 copies. It was a great success, and within two years Blackwood's had sold more than 25,000 copies. In this case, Jex-Blake's judgment of literary value and worth, based on a faulty appraisal of the market, colored by an inherent distaste for "popular editions" (which in her mind equated to an inferior product), and influenced by the fact the edition had initially been suggested by the publisher, a person she mistrusted on principle, damaged rather than enhanced material prospects for Todd.

William Morris Colles's negotiations on behalf of Beatrice Harraden are also instructive of the evolving patterns of commercial behavior in the literary marketplace. Colles, a qualified barrister, began his commercial career by acting as legal counsel to, and member of, the executive committee of the Society of Authors in the 1880s. With the support of Walter Besant, he began the Authors' Syndicate in early 1890, a literary agency run as a type of authors' cooperative. It remained loosely affiliated with the Society of Authors for the first eight years of its life, sharing office space at the Society's premises on 4 Portugal Street, London, until 1898, when the firm cut ties with the Society and moved to a new site.[36]

Unlike other literary agents, Colles's fees were low (5 percent commission on placed work). Like Watt, however, Colles tended to concentrate on promoting established authors. His was not a very successful career, though. As Robert A. Colby notes, Colles did not have a head for business, for "his genteel style and somewhat Parnassian view of the literary profession inevitably left him behind his more astute competitors."[37] Colles's work on behalf of Beatrice Harraden reveals the manner in which his lack of business acumen could cause more problems for his authors than they anticipated.

Beatrice Harraden (1864–1936), novelist and suffragist, born in London and educated in Dresden, Cheltenham, and London University, began her writing career in the 1880s under the wing of novelist and journalist Eliza Lynn Linton. Harraden's first major publication was a children's book, *Things Will Take a Turn*, published in 1889. That year also marked the beginning of her connection with Blackwood's, when he published the short story "About the Umbrella-Menders: A Study" in the July 1889 issue of *Blackwood's Magazine*.

It was her first literary success, and short stories were published in quick succession in such literary journals as the *English Illustrated Magazine* and *The Graphic*. Blackwood's rejected her next major offering, *Ships That Pass in the Night*, a romantic novel of doomed love in the Alps, because he objected to the pessimistic tone and tragic ending of the work. (The heroine, after much travail, wins the love of the male protagonist, "the Disagreeable Man," but is then dispatched by a fatal street accident, run down by a wagon.) As he put it, "The morbid character of the tale, and the dismal picture of a vain struggle for happiness and brightness amid the overpowering hardships and sorrows of life does not make for very pleasant reading, and would not I fear make a popular novel, especially with its futile ending. To be a powerful or a successful book such a plot should have reached the degree of tragedy, and unfortunately the Disagreeable Man falls short of it."[38] He concluded, "Pessimism in fiction too has been so much vulgarized of late that the public are getting tired of it."[39]

Blackwood's aesthetic concerns reflected his view of what constituted successful and best-selling fiction, a perspective grounded in past experiences of sales of "Blackwood" products. That William Blackwood was getting out of touch with contemporary concerns and interests in the literary marketplace was proven when Harraden, with the help of Dr. Richard Garnett (keeper of printed books in the British Museum), subsequently placed the work for publication with the small publishing firm Lawrence & Bullen (a firm with connections to W. M. Colles) in 1893. It was an immediate best-seller, going through more than fifteen editions and remaining in print for the next twenty years.

In early 1894, flush with the success of *Ships*, Harraden wrote to William Backwood offering for consideration both a short story for Maga and a second novel. "About my second novel," she asked, "have you any wish to publish it just as it is (or rather I should say, will be, for it won't be ready for several months)."[40] (This was to be eventually her novella *Hilda Strafford*.) Teasingly reminding him of his failure to snap up her best-seller ("You remember you did not care for "Ships," which is now in its 10th edition, & sailing along merrily"), she concluded by offering him first refusal of the new work and, in recognition of his role in starting her career, noted, "I naturally turn to you first."[41]

William Blackwood was now keen to retrieve his connection with Harraden. Having made the mistake of passing her first work up, which confounded his expectations of readership tastes, he was now quick to note his interest in adding this next book to his lists, even going so far as to forgo his usual habit of reading the manuscript before making a decision. "I should indeed very much like to publish it," he wrote hurriedly the day he received the letter, "and am willing to take it as it is. When you send me the ms. I shall have some calculations made and perhaps you will tell me whether you would prefer a royalty or a share of the profits."[42] His enthusiasm brought a response from Harraden that promised even more work for him, in this case an offer to consider issuing a collection of short stories, as "following on the success of Ships, it would of course sell splendidly."[43] The question was whether it was wise to do so before or after the publication of the new novel, and she asked William Blackwood's advice on this matter. He responded with the suggestion that they wait until after the novel had appeared, a point duly noted by Harraden. In the end, however, this was not to be the case.

At this stage Harraden, who suffered from chronic ill health, intimated that she planned to travel to California to recuperate with friends who owned horses and property in El Cajon ("My lemon farm," she called it). William Blackwood encouraged her to do so, offered her exercise tips ("There is nothing so delightful in a warm climate as riding about to see the country"), inquired as to which boat she planned to sail across ("so that I may gratify my interest in your voyage"), and asked whether he could send her any particular works to read on the voyage.[44] It is an example of the style of publishing management William Blackwood had learned from his uncle John, the interest and care he took to foster personal relations with his authors to maintain one of the many "Blackwoodian" ecumenes or circles of this period. In this case, it was a circle of London-based popular women novelists (many graduates of London University) who formed the core of his literary production in the 1890s and 1900s, people like Margaret Todd (whom Harraden knew and wrote about to Blackwood on occasion), Katherine Cecil Thurston, and "Sydney Grier" (Hilda Gregg).

More significant, Harraden's ill health, her impending trip, and her disinterest in tackling the business arrangements and complications that success now demanded she attend prompted the entrance of William Morris Colles as her literary manager. Colles would take care of matters she no longer understood, she explained, saying that entrusting him with her business arrangements was necessary because "so many perplexities have arisen from the success of Ships, and I have been so greatly worried in consequence, that I feel I must keep my mind free from business details and reserve my little bit of strength for my writing."[45]

Colles got straight to the point in his first letter to Blackwood's about Harraden. Announcing that he was now her agent, he asked Blackwood's what terms he had in mind for her new work. "Could you put the offer in a substantive form?" he concluded.[46] The response on 30 January was one Blackwood had conveyed earlier to Harraden, mainly that he was willing to publish the work either for a fixed royalty or a two-thirds share of the profits, depending on the length of the final publication. By this time, with Harraden struggling to work on her novel while preparing for her trip to California, negotiations were shifting to account first for the collection of short stories Harraden had suggested to Blackwood's, which was to be called *In Varying Moods*.

Colles took time to consult Harraden before countering on 15 February 1894 with a sliding-scale offer: If published in three volumes, royalties were to be calculated at six shillings a copy; if published in one or two volumes and sold at six shillings, royalties were to be calculated at 20 percent of the published price; if sold in editions priced at less than six shillings, royalties would be calculated at two pence per shilling of the published price. Finally, Colles requested an advance of £100 on delivery of the manuscript.[47]

As we can see, the royalty rates were higher than those commanded for Margaret Todd, primarily because Colles knew the general patterns of royalty returns one could demand in these cases. That William Blackwood was willing to pay substantially more for Harraden's short-story collection than in the case of Margaret Todd's novel was not surprising; after all, Harraden was now a successful author, a known quantity, and his initial mistake in rejecting her work made him all the more eager to recoup lost ground, despite his usual reservations about short-story collections. "I am quite willing to publish the work on the terms you quote," he wrote back to Colles on 21 February, "so this settles the matter so far."[48]

But the matter was not settled. Further discussions in March over length and format led to concessions and difficulties. The work was to be published in a one-volume, three-shilling and sixpence edition. While William Blackwood agreed to pay two pence in the shilling for every copy sold, and Colles conceded in allowing the advance to drop to £50, Blackwood balked at increasing the royalties to 20 percent on the published price if sales exceeded 10,000 copies. In a letter now lost, Blackwood's set down his refusal and made unspecified charges against Colles that he was unduly profiting under these circumstances. Colles rejected the claim, believing the rates were perfectly reasonable and noting rather threateningly, "I should be very glad to hear wherein by whom it was stated that I am 'making a fortune.' If there is any innuendo attached or attachable I might be advised to give the person responsible an opportunity of justifying the innuendo."[49] In other words, desist or see you in court! Meetings were held over the following week to smooth out these differences, and by the end of the month Blackwood was able to report to Harraden that he had given way to Colles's demands.

The exchange of draft contracts in early April provoked another objection from Colles, this time to Blackwood's calculation of royalties based on thirteen copies selling as twelve, in line with the standard trade discounts Blackwood's had always offered. Quick to move, Colles struck out the clause, exclaiming in slighting manner on 10 April, "I have looked into the matter with some care and I cannot ascertain that it is the practice with first class publishers to account for copies of books sold on royalty agreements 13 as 12."[50] A scant four days before the official launch of the work, Blackwood's gave in and sent from his London office a revised agreement for final signatures on 16 April, Blackwood's calmly noting to Colles, "I still quite disagree with you as to the odd book, and it has never been our custom to do what you say the first class Publishers here do, but as Miss Harraden informs you she did not anticipate any such deduction from her receipts, I am ready to fall in with the arrangement though I think it is a very unfair one to the Publisher."[51]

Initial sales of *In Varying Moods* were quite brisk. Within a fortnight of publication, Blackwood's had sold more than 3,000 copies of the work, a fact that caught him by surprise. As he confessed to Harraden, "It is quite a new experience to me as for years past the public and trade never 'took' to a collection of any author's short stories; the tide must have & I hope will go on flowing freely in your favour."[52] By June 1896 it had gone through thirteen editions priced at 13/6, sold more than 12,000 copies, and netted a profit of £651 for publisher and author—making it one of Blackwood's publishing successes for that year.

Having shrewdly assessed Harraden's obvious worth to the firm, and in order to forestall further misunderstandings regarding Harraden's future work, Blackwood's met with her just after the publication of *In Varying Moods*. The result of this friendly meeting was a classic example of the triangular relationship that injecting the literary agent into the negotiation process could create. Blackwood's warm relations with Harraden, which extended to mutual family visits when either was in London or Edinburgh, created an unstated undercurrent in Blackwood's dealings with Colles, the professional intruder.

Blackwood's meeting with Harraden in late April 1894 established the real reason why Blackwood's had given way to Colles in negotiating for *In Varying Moods*. Having done so, he was able to confirm, as had always been the intention before Colles had become involved in Harraden's business affairs, that Blackwood's would retain first refusal of her next work once it was finished. In return, she was to instruct Colles before sailing off to the United States that he was not to enter into negotiations with any other firm for publication rights until Blackwood had a chance to read the finished product. On the one hand, it gave Harraden "mental freedom," as she called it, to complete the work without concerning herself with major negotiations, secure that her friendly publisher would be at hand to offer her a reasonable deal. On the other hand, William Blackwood was now assured that he would not miss out on an opportunity to secure her work, circumventing any action Colles might take to secure a better advance agreement for Harraden elsewhere.

Blackwood's letter to Colles on 20 April 1894 innocuously informed him: "I saw Miss Harraden yesterday & agreed with her that the signing of the formal Agreement for her new novel should be postponed until her return, so as to pass over any difficulty as to the lines on which it should be drafted."[53] It is not surprising that Colles reacted furiously when he received this and a missive from Harraden indicating that this informal agreement had been reached without his knowledge. As he saw it, if his job was to secure the best rates possible for his authors, he could not have Harraden wandering off to negotiate private understandings without his consent. The result was an extraordinary missive where Colles withdrew Harraden from circulation and declared all future negotiations for her work at an end:

> In reply to your letter of 21st inst. I beg to say that the obvious difficulty created by a private understandings between yourself and Miss Harraden relating to arrangements which appear on the correspondence of the Authors' Syndicate renders it necessary for me as responsible for the correspondence to say that I regard all arrangements regarding Miss Harraden's novel as at an end. She is perfectly free and you are perfectly free in the matter, and any further negotiations must begin *de nous*. I think this should be distinctly stated to avoid future misunderstanding.[54]

Colles's reaction illustrates the uncomfortable role of the literary agent in this period of change. While authors hired them to relieve themselves of having to negotiate for literary property, asking only in return that agents achieve the best agreements possible for their work, they did not necessarily leave all such commercial matters completely in the agent's hands. Colles's overreaction illustrated his understanding that personal loyalty was a currency of little consequence if he was to take advantage of Harraden's rising popularity to negotiate more lucrative deals for her. Blackwood's use of the privileged position of publisher friend to circumvent the literary agent threatened Colles's position as primary arbiter and negotiator of literary worth.

Blackwood, taken aback by this aggressive reaction to what he thought was a perfectly reasonable suggestion, threw the problem back at Colles and suggested that any difficulties regarding negotiating for Harraden's new work were due to Colles's inability to draft an agreement acceptable to all parties, hence the decision to delay such negotiations until the literary property at stake was completed. But in saying this Blackwood was also establishing that he was not prepared to negotiate solely on the basis of Harraden's name and reputation. For him, name was not enough; he wanted a tangible product, a finished text, before he would draw up a final agreement. As Blackwood's Edinburgh manager, put it, the issue here was that "the publisher and the author have come together and by a friendly arrangement for the benefit of the latter have agreed to wait the completion of a work rather than bind themselves to a pig in a poke."[55] In other words, her past work may have been good, but who was to say how the next work was to turn out? Better to wait, secure in the knowledge the firm had the first option of refusal.

Colles, with his legal training, interpreted the matter differently. It was not so much the issue of whether or not Blackwood's could be allowed to bid for the work, it was the manner in which Blackwood's was legally binding Harraden into an agreement that interfered with Colles's ability to promote Harraden.

> I am responsible, and it is only on my correspondence that any written undertaking exists. I am therefore placed in an intolerable position by private understandings between yourself and the author to which I am not a party and I decline to recognise the existence of any contract whatever. Certainly Miss Harraden could not on the correspondence compel you to publish the book and certainly in my view you cannot compel her to ask your consent before "rescinding the contract."[56]

What we see here is a fundamental battle over literary worth, with Colles seeking to assert his role in the publishing process as the individual responsible for investing in and marketing authorial reputation, and negotiating property based on an intangible capital. William Blackwood, however, resisted this interpretation, seeing the relationship between author and publisher as one based on an exchange of views on and negotiations over tangible capital, in this case completed manuscripts and books. Blackwood's ambivalence regarding negotiating for "names" reflected a reluctance on his part to pay "fancy prices," as he put it, for works merely to secure literary status. It also demonstrated his inherent caution against taking too much risk, a point he stressed in his willingness to publish Harraden's *Ships That Pass in the Night* if it had been a three-volume work, because the guaranteed library sale would have minimized the risk involved. But with the demise of the three-decker novel format in 1894, business practices had to change. Blackwood's attempts to reach a private understanding with Harraden was one method of coping with new uncertainties.

The result was a standoff, not resolved until Harraden, dissatisfied with the manner in which Colles had acted in spite of her declared wishes, transferred her business interests to A. P. Watt. By December 1896, negotiations were completed between Blackwood's and Watt for the new work, published in early 1897 as *Hilda Strafford and the Remittance Man: Two California Stories*. It is interesting that Watt succeeded where Colles failed, negotiating better rates (20 percent royalties on all sales) and a larger advance (£200) for Harraden's new publication (sums far greater than those negotiated by the amateur agent Jex-Blake for her friend Margaret Todd). Watt continued to represent Harraden for the rest of her long career.

In similar fashion, Conrad's relationship with his publisher William Blackwood and with literary agent James Brand Pinker (Fig. 7) reflects the changing nature of and tensions within British publishing practices at the turn of the century. Like Todd, and initially Harraden, the activities of Conrad's agent were ultimately to lead to estrangement with Blackwood. Unlike Todd, however, Conrad and to a certain extent Harraden were to gain greater material success due to the work of their literary agents.

Conrad's literary connections with William Blackwood & Sons are well known. Edward Garnett's advice to Conrad that "Karain: A Memory" was "destined by Providence" for the pages of *Blackwood's Magazine* led to his first publication with the firm in 1897.[57] Over the next six years, with William Blackwood's encouragement and, more important, the support of the firm's literary advisor, David Storrar Meldrum, Conrad published "Youth," "Heart of Darkness," "Lord Jim," and "The End of the Tether" in the magazine, as well as *Lord Jim* and *Youth* in book form.

Fig. 7 Literary agent James Brand Pinker (1863–1922). As well as acting for Joseph Conrad, Pinker represented such authors as Arnold Bennett, Stephen Crane, John Galsworthy, James Joyce, and H. G. Wells.

Meldrum's role in securing Conrad's loyalty and respect for the firm is an important one in this story, an example of the role that a publisher's reader and literary advisor played in the evolutionary chain linking the eighteenth-century bookseller/patron, the nineteenth-century publisher, and the twentieth-century literary agent/promoter. Both Meldrum and Garnett were literary middlemen, servicing publishers yet keenly aware of literary potential. Meldrum's role with Conrad blurred the lines between friendship and commercial interests, serving as a buffer between author and publisher. Meldrum's activities on behalf of Conrad, as Peter Keating succinctly notes, went far beyond his role as advisor to the firm. Urging Conrad's genius on Blackwood, warning him of attempts of other publishers to entice him away, and supporting Conrad's pleas for money with the arguments that publishing Conrad would establish Blackwood's reputation for posterity, Meldrum acted as protector of Conrad as well as his confidant. The result was that "Conrad gave his trust in return for Meldrum's sympathetic admiration."[58] But Meldrum could not, in the end, provide the all-embracing financial security Conrad needed, and in 1903 Pinker stepped in to become a major player in Conrad's world.

For Conrad, James Brand Pinker's assumption of financial control over his literary production in 1903 did not bring immediate material profit. It did, however, bring him financial stability, while before he had been dependent on the grace, good nature, and active support of publishers and friends to enable his work to progress. When Pinker made his initial approach to Conrad in 1899, he had been firmly rejected at first. Conrad wrote apologetically at the time, "My method of writing is so unbusiness-like that I don't think you could have any use for such an unsatisfactory person. I generally sell a work before it is begun, get paid when it is half done and don't do the other half till the spirit moves me. I must add that I have no control whatever over the spirit -neither has the man who has paid the money."[59] He concluded in humorous fashion: "I live in hopes of reformation and whenever that takes place you and you alone shall have the working of the New Conrad."[60]

Pinker, former journalist, periodical editor, and, briefly, manuscript reader and advisor to a publishing house, was an impressive negotiator whom Frank Swinnerton described as a man who "knew the monetary secrets of authors and the weaknesses of publishers, terrified some of these last and was refused admittance by others, dominated editors, and of course enjoyed much power."[61] Not one to give up easily on potential clients, by 1903 Pinker had reformed Conrad sufficiently for him to recognize the value of this "rosy, round-faced clean-shaven grey-haired sphinx with a protrusive under-lip."[62] Over the succeeding years, Conrad became dependent on Pinker to provide him with financial security, and by 1908 he owed Pinker more than £1,600. Between 1903 and 1922, Pinker acted as Conrad's banker and financial manager, paying for hotel rooms and comestibles, advancing him money, cajoling and coaxing manuscripts from him.

Indeed, Pinker's role as manager at one stage led to a very public dispute and accusations in 1904 by William Heinemann against Pinker of unethical behaviour and deliberate impoverishment of Conrad. Conrad was moved to issue a public refutal of such charges, writing to Edmund Gosse not to believe such gossip because Pinker's actions "has not been of a mercenary character." Rather, he continued, "he has stepped gallantly into the breach left open by the collapse of my bank; and not only gallantly, but successfully as well."[63] The argument in fact revealed the degree to which Conrad entrusted Pinker with his financial affairs, and the level to which Pinker was protecting and supporting Conrad at this stage. As Pinker noted in a candid letter to H. G. Wells, the impression that Conrad was impoverished because of Pinker's inhumane business practices was unfounded and untrue: "As a matter of fact Conrad always borrows a sovereign when he comes in—even on his last visit (last Wednesday) when he was going to the bank to cash a cheque for £70 which I had just given him, he had the usual sov."[64] Pinker concluded, "In truth I have never refused Conrad any sum that he has asked for."[65] Not until 1912, and Pinker's major coup in negotiating major sums for the serialization of *Chance* in the *New York Herald*, did this investment begin to pay off for both men.

After Conrad notified William Blackwood in writing that Pinker had assumed agency duties as of 16 February 1903, negotiations for his work assumed an impersonal tone, with documents and discussions centering on costs, royalties, and copyright issues. Two further works of Conrad's appeared in the pages of *Blackwood's Magazine*, "In Captivity" in 1905 and "Initiation" in 1906. For "In Captivity," Pinker accepted the initial offer of £13 for serialization rights. His reply exemplified Pinker's deliberate detachment of Conrad from the negotiations process, quoting the author as a distant figure in the commercial transactions being incurred on his behalf. "I have since consulted Mr. Conrad, and while he feels disappointed that you do not think the article justifies a larger fee than £13, he is willing that the arrangement should stand as you suggest."[66] Pinker subsequently negotiated the larger fee of £22 for "Initiation." The firm published no more work by Conrad, having subsequently rejected the stories "The Brute" and "Freya" when offered. Success with and higher fees from other publishing sources soon meant that the Blackwood firm would be dropped from consideration for any further Conrad work. The literary criticism and notes of encouragement Conrad had often sought and received also ceased to flow as before.

Pinker's role as intermediary for Conrad, Colles's proprietorial negotiations for Harraden, and Jex-Blake's interventions on behalf of Magaret Todd illustrate quite clearly the changes in publishing practices that were still being resisted by publishers during this period. As many have pointed out, the interposition of Pinker between Conrad and Blackwood's led to an eventual estrangement and loss of the special relationship built up between Conrad, David S. Meldrum, and William Blackwood III. William M. Colles's heavy-handed interventions on behalf of Harraden led eventually to her dispensing with his services and turning to a less-antagonistic firm to represent her interests. In Todd's case, a personal friendship with Blackwood developed not only out of but also in spite of Jex-Blake's activities on her behalf.

Yet Jex-Blake, Colles, and Pinker ultimately provided a much-needed financial service that extended beyond the capabilities of the Blackwood firm and its directors. Pinker's mediation in and connections with markets larger than those serviced by the Blackwood firm, and his ability to negotiate lucrative serialization and syndication rights in foreign markets, extended Conrad's earning potential and ultimately provided financial success to place alongside less materially helpful but equally important critical praise and recognition. The well-intentioned negotiations of Colles and Jex-Blake, while not always successful, demonstrated that authors and their representatives at this time were increasingly aware of the need to maintain accountability in a trade that was both dependent on commercial success from aesthetic products and inexorably changing in the face of increased competition and expanding markets.

Conclusion

The death of William Blackwood III in 1912 inspired commemorative notices in most newspapers and journals of the day.[1] "In his person there passes away the doyen of 'the trade,'" exclaimed *The Times* at the start of a five-column obituary.[2] The liberal daily broadsheet *The Scotsman*, not one normally to praise the conservative credentials of the Blackwood family, nevertheless grudgingly acknowledged William's abilities. "He seemed, in short, to have inherited the true editorial *flair*," it noted, adding, "No great hand with the pen himself, he was a sure critic of literary work in others, and the soundness of his judgment was only equalled by the felicity of his suggestions and the warmth of his appreciation."[3]

Almost all these notices laid particular stress on the characteristics and values enshrined in the image of the firm and its director, counting among them continuity, conservatism, "sound criticism," and establishment values. "It is still noted," affirmed one commentator, "especially for the production of military and travel books, and no publishers give greater attention to the bringing out of new novelists."[4] William Blackwood was presented to readers as a traditionalist who spent his life upholding and adhering in his work to particular establishment values. "He maintained the standing of the house unimpaired, and it should be recorded to his credit that he deliberately set his face against issuing the dubious class of fiction now so common," concluded the *Times*,[5] while the *Scotsman* sniffed, "The novels which came from his press could be safely counted upon as fit for respectable people to read."[6]

How such values came to be associated with the firm, and how such an identity was formed and maintained over a crucial fifty-year period in the firm's history, has been the primary theme of this work. By focusing on the activities of the firm and its directors between 1860 and 1910, using unpublished archival material as well as information gained from a variety of published sources, it has been my intention to outline the firm's history from a point of preeminence in mid-nineteenth-century British publishing and cultural history through to a marginalized position as publisher of popular works for colonial and special-service interests audiences at the start of the twentieth century.

In the process, I have sought to understand and explain how John and William Blackwood III approached the business of publishing and textual production, and how a publishing firm very much constructed as a family enterprise established and operated within several determinative "fields" or "planes" of textual production. The "house" image that John Blackwood nurtured throughout the 1860s and 1870s, and that William Blackwood III maintained with little deviation from 1879 to 1912, was one applied to a variety of specific textual planes with specific results.

As the case studies in this book demonstrate, John and William Blackwood III took steps to mold, manipulate, and control work produced under the firm's imprint in order to conform to particular cultural values and perceived tastes in contemporary readers, whether in travel narratives (John Hanning Speke), fiction (Charles Reade), or nonfiction (Margaret Oliphant). The production of the firm's history in 1897 is a prime example of how even a commemorative text on the business of publishing was shaped and rendered by cultural evaluation and unseen conflict over aesthetics, economics, and personal ambitions. At the same time, both directors tried to foster an "ecumene" of "Blackwoodian" authors based on personal connections and relationships. The communities of readers they claimed to speak for and to serve to remind us that texts are inevitably products of a social transaction between producers and readers. It is an important point, and one reflected in the firm's determination to foster unique communities of readers and authors at various stages in its history.

What becomes obvious in retrospect is that the firm's history between 1860 and 1910 is a narrative of the rise and maintenance of a family firm during a period of social consolidation, coinciding with the rise and establishment of an affluent and middle-class reading public to whom the firm could cater. Between 1860 and 1879, under the direction of John Blackwood and supported by a dedicated team of directors and subordinate staff, the firm expanded and prospered. It did so by pursuing conservative policies (both in business and in politics) and by using personal contacts to establish close links with key figures and contributors from British political, cultural, and social establishments. During this period the firm published texts that shaped or supported significant sociopolitical and cultural spheres of influence. These ranged from hymnals for use in all Church of Scotland services, Scottish Legal Statutes, Acts of Parliament, and military officer training manuals, to significant literary and prose texts by George Eliot, Margaret Oliphant, Alexander Kinglake, and John Hanning Speke, among others.

Under the direction of William Blackwood III between 1879 and 1912, these links were maintained and protected in the face of subsequent major social, economic, and cultural changes affecting the publishing industry in Britain. At the same time, the business structures that had so ably supported the firm's developments began disappearing or fell under threat. The loss of key personnel in the early 1880s, and the failure to replace them until late in the century with similarly dedicated staff, hampered operations, as did the firm's failure to adapt quickly to new developments in business practices. The movement of the literary agent into the business of literary negotiation, and the introduction of new arenas of cultural production, such as radio and film, were not anticipated or dealt with well by William Blackwood III and his collaborators. The firm's lack of flexibility in gauging trends in literary and nonliterary fields led at the turn of the twentieth century to an inevitable stagnation and an overdependence in their lists on past publishing successes.

And yet the Blackwood firm was not simply a manufacturer turning handwriting into print, but also a complexly integrated commercial enterprise that "made" and "remade" authors and texts, exploited certain niches in the market and forwent others, and inflected its practices through consultation within and outside the organization. (The latter point is exemplified in the daily correspondence between the London and Edinburgh directors and office managers and in the vast archival collection of correspondence with authors.) The result for us, as Leslie Howsam astutely notes in a similar publishing study, is an appreciation that publishers then (as now) operated within a shifting and at times conflicting framework of economic profit and cultural evaluation. "Publishers were gate-keepers, or perhaps mediators," she adds, "for the culture they lived in. That is, that within financial constraints, market constraints, they had the power to select one text and reject another, and to frame the way that manuscripts appeared in published form."[7] The most useful way of studying mediations by Victorian publishers such as Blackwood's is to understand, appreciate, and evaluate the complex networks within which these firms operated. As this study makes clear, such economic, social, and cultural networks play a major part in the story of the Blackwood firm between 1860 and 1910.

Appendices

Appendices 1–3: Introduction

The appendices that follow have been compiled from the Publication Ledgers of the Edinburgh firm William Blackwood & Sons, located in the National Library of Scotland, manuscript numbers 30859 through to 30866. The manuscripts examined comprise eight of the eleven bound ledgers recording financial details of most of the works published by the firm from its inception in 1804 until 1920. These eight ledgers cover, in particular, works published between 1856 and 1920. Detailed listings of all works recorded as published between 1860 and 1910 were compiled, and information was extracted as required.

Appendix 1 lists the top-selling and most profitable publications of each decade from 1860 to 1910. Works generating profits of £800 or above during each period in question are noted, with relevant details. Appendix 2 lists *Blackwood's Magazine* sales, advertising costs, and profits generated between 1856 and 1915. Appendix 3 lists Margaret Oliphant's main works published with Blackwood's between 1860 and 1897 and indicates general sales and profits details of these works.

Appendix 1 (Blackwood & Sons Publishing Statistics, 1860–1910) and Appendix 3 (Margaret Oliphant Sales, 1860–1897)

Layout of information generated for both appendices is noted below, with the following provisos.

1. In order to arrive at an overall view of the sales impact and profits generated by general and specific texts produced by the firm in Appendix 1 and Appendix 3, it has proven impossible to represent distinct details and sales figures for each variation of a particular edition issued. For example, from the 1890s onward, the firm started printing sheets of new novels for subsequent binding and selling in three formats: cloth, paper, and colonial editions. Individual sales and profits from each were tallied together in the ledgers to produce overall details for use in calculating royalties and other payments to authors. I have reproduced these final figures rather than offering figures for individual editions.

2. Details and figures for Appendix 1 are given for texts by decade where possible. Thus one can track the general sales trends of continuing "best-sellers" over a period of time and compare these with corresponding new publications. This has meant compiling information from across several ledgers and creating final tallies based on multiple ledger record totals. In some cases, where a work was not reissued and sales languished until the account was finally closed some time later, the year is given in which the final tally or entry of details for the work was made. Note that, where possible, totals in profits and advertising costs columns in relevant appendices are noted at the very least in pounds and shillings, or when exact totals could be arrived at, in pounds, shillings, and pence. For those not familiar with this system of valuation, twelve pence equals one shilling, twenty shillings equal one pound, and twenty-one shillings equals one guinea. (The latter is not used in these appendices.)

Key to Categories for Appendix 1 and Appendix 3

1. Author of work
   Names of authors are given, when known, with surname first, followed by first name, if known. In the case of series, educational texts, or other multi- or anonymously authored texts, the field has been left blank.
2. Title of work or series
   Titles of works are given, along with details of editions, impressions, or volume numbers, if relevant. Abbreviations are used to indicate the following:

ed. = edition; imps. = impressions; vol. = volume; pop. = popular; col. = colonial; The differentiation between an edition and an impression is based on how the issue was reported in the ledgers. In most cases, impressions indicated a quick reprinting from original plates of the first issue, whereas an edition denoted a resetting or redating of new printings. In many cases, titles were issued at different times in different formats (for example, the multifarious issues of George Eliot in a variety of cheap editions and cheap formats); hence, some titles that are repeated and are recorded distinct from each other (for example, George Eliot's *Daniel Deronda*, or Kinglake's *Invasion of the Crimea*).

3. Volume numbers

   This indicates the number of volumes in which publications were issued, with corresponding changes in price.

4. Price

   Prices indicated are those noted in publication ledgers. Some ledgers record sales and details of multiformated and multipriced issues of the same text (George Eliot works, for example). The general prices of these are noted here.

5. Printed

   Where possible, the total number of copies printed for all relevant editions or impressions over the period indicated is given. In the case of multiple editions or impressions of continuing "best-sellers," the date of final tally is the one nearest the end of the decade in question, with details continued in the decade following.

6. Sold

   This category records the total number of copies sold by the final closing date noted in the relevant pages in the ledgers. As in the case of the copies printed section, where sales continue from decade to decade (unless related to an edition that failed to sell heavily enough to merit reprinting), the date of final tally is the one nearest the end of the decade in question, with details continued in the decade following.

7. Total profit

   This is a tally of profits generated by sales of the work as noted in ledgers after costs were deducted. In general, this was the total sum generated before any division of money as per any royalty agreement (if relevant) negotiated with authors. Once accounts had been finalized regarding the sales and profits generated, these details were "brought forward" for noting in the firm's "copyright ledgers," where the sums generated were then recalculated if relevant as per agreed contract rates and royalties.

8. Date issued

This category records the date in which a text was officially released for sale, or in the case of continuing editions and impressions, when the date of reprinting occurred.

9. Date tallied

This category indicates the date by which the details indicated in previous categories were tallied. For continuing editions and impressions, it notes the final date recorded in the tallying of relevant details for that decade.

Appendix 2 (*Blackwood's Magazine* Sales 1856–1915)

Key to Categories

1. Issue numbers

Issue numbers covered in the yearly return of sales and profits recorded in the ledgers for *Blackwood's Magazine*. Two exceptions in the annual calculations are issues between June 1860 and April 1861, which were calculated as a result of financial tallies following the death of Major William Blackwood II in early 1861, and issues between June 1878 and October 1879, a result of tallies undertaken after the death of John Blackwood in late 1879.

2. Regular sales

Total sales for issues tallied. These do not include American sales of *Blackwood's Magazine*, which until 1891 were handled exclusively by an American agent.

3. American sales

Total sales figures generated through American copies printed by Blackwood's from 1891 onward.

4. Ad costs

Annual advertising costs noted in financial ledgers. Such figures prove useful in gauging average expenditure in promoting the magazine over an extended period of time.

5. Profits

This is a tally of profits generated by sales of the work as noted in ledgers after costs were deducted.

6. Date tallied

This category indicates the month and year in which the totals indicated in previous categories were tallied.

Appendix 1

Blackwood & Sons Publishing Statistics, 1860–1910

1860–1869

Author	Title	Vol.	Price	Printed	Sold	Profit	Date Issued	Date Tallied
Kinglake, A.W.	History of the Crimea, vols. 1 & 2, 1–4th ed.	2	32/-	15,225	14,979	6,454.15.0	Jan 1863	Jul 1873
	Ancient Classics for English Readers	8			171,422	5,242.0.7	Dec 1869	Jun 1881
Eliot, George	The Mill on the Floss	3	31/6	6,574	6,066	4,442.11	Apr 1860	Apr 1861
Kinglake, A.W.	History of the Crimea, vols. 3 & 4, 1–2d ed.	2	34/-	6,000	5,879	4,107.6.2	Jun 1868	Dec 1874
Eliot, George	Felix Holt	3	31/6	5,252	4,708	3,436.17.3	Jun 1866	Jun 1873
Speke, John Hanning	Journal of the Discovery of the Source of the Nile	1	21/-	10,544	9,048	2,728.10.4	Dec 1863	Jun 1868
Stephens	Book of the Farm, 2d ed.	2	60/-		1,533	2,546.8.7	Apr 1861	Jun 1870
Wilson	Works	12	72/-		32,198	2,412.16.9	Apr 1861	Jun 1873
Eliot, George	Silas Marner, 1–6th ed.	1	12/-	8,181	7,871	2,201.17.2	Mar 1861	Jun 1863
	Tales from Blackwood, 1st ser.	12			159,342	1,685.12.11	Apr 1861	Jun 1891
Warren	Works	8			18,448	1,677.19.2	Jun 1861	Jun 1873
McIntosh	Book of the Garden	2	4.7.6		1,074	1,386.16.6	Apr 1861	Jun 1873
	Standard Novels	22	2/6, 2/-, 1/6, 1/-		129,557	1,376.15.2	Aug 1867	Jun 1881
	Scottish Hymnals	1	Various	184,777	181,976	1,243.12.7	Aug 1868	Dec 1871
Eliot, George	Eliot's Works	5			85,522	1,185.2.11	Jan 1867	Jun 1874
Martin, Theodore	Bon Gaultier Ballads, 7–10th ed.	1	8/6	8,589	7,471	1,121.09.2	Oct 1861	Mar 1870

Author	Title	Vol.	Price	Printed	Sold	Profit	Date Issued	Date Tallied
Hamley, E.B.	Operations of War, 1–2d ed.	1	28/-	2,545	2,343	1,089.0.7	May 1866	Mar 1873
	Public general statutes		Various		21,492	1,037.6.9	Apr 1861	Jun 1870
Alison, Archibald	History of Europe, continuation	9	6.7.6		4,041	955.16.3	Apr 1861	Jun 1873
Johnston	Chemistry of Common Life	2	11/6		6,666	872.19.11	Apr 1861	Jun 1873
Oliphant, M.O.W.	The Perpetual Curate	3	31/6	1,580	1,351	846.3.5	Oct 1864	Dec 1873
			1870–1879					
Eliot, George	Daniel Deronda, 8 pts., 4 vols. cl	8, 4	5/-, 42/-, 21/-	63,927	59,534	7,627.8.0	Jan 1876	Jun 1877
	Middlemarch, 8 pts., 4 vols.	4	5/-, 42/-	46,898	45,588	6,602.7.1	Nov 1871	Dec 1873
	Scottish Hymnals		Various		704,956	5,628.4.10	Dec 1871	Jun 1881
Stephens	Book of the Farm, 3d ed.	2	2.10.0		4,670	2,529.7.4	Apr 1871	Jun 1881
Eliot, George	Works, cheap ed. & cabinet ed.	8,24	Various		79,763	2,336.11.7	Jan 1877	Dec 1879
Lytton, Edward Bulwer	Kenelm Chillingly, 1–2d ed.	3	31/6	4,163	3,867	2,196.18.7	Mar 1873	Feb 1874
Eliot, George	Middlemarch	1	7/6, 8/6	25,000	24,706	2,084.15.5	Dec 1873	Jun 1880
Kinglake, A.W.	History of the Crimea, vol. 5	1	17/-	6,300	6,083	2,083.17.9	Jan 1875	Jan 1877
Eliot, George	Works, cabinet ed.	20	5.0.0	63,919	50,346	2,080.15.1	Jan 1877	Dec 1881
Hamley, E.B.	Operations of War, 3–4th ed.	1	28/-	3,413	3,347	2,140.12.7	Jan 1873	Dec 1889
Brougham, Lord	Memoirs of Lord Brougham	3	48/-	7,100	6,348	1,817.16.7	Feb 1871	Jun 1873
	Public general statutes		Various		39,576	1,794.3.2	Jul 1870	Jun 1881
Lytton, Edward Bulwer	Parisians	4	21/-	12,675	10,149	1,459.9.2	Oct 1873	Feb 1876
Eliot, George	Theophrastus Such, 1–4th ed.	1	10/6	6,190	6,069	1,422.16.1	May 1879	Dec 1881
Eliot, George	Daniel Deronda	1	7/6	10,504	10,446	1,408.6.10	Jun 1877	Jun 1880
Nicholson, H.A.	Manual of Zoology, 1–5th ed.	1	12/6	9,029	8,455	1,398.1.9	Dec 1870	Nov 1880
Kinglake, A.W.	History of the Crimea, cabinet ed.	6	36/-	34,650	32,768	1,834.8.2	Jan 1876	Oct 1879

Author	Work	No.	Price			Amount		
Eliot, George	Works	5			53,126	1,355.6.7	Jul 1874	Feb 1878
Mackay	Elements of Modern Geography, 8–21st ed.	1	3/-	27,300	27,007	1,322.3.1	Oct 1870	Dec 1880
Burton, John Hill	History of Scotland	9	63/-	18,219	14,313	1,233.8.4	Mar 1873	Dec 1880
Martin, Theodore	Bon Gaultier Ballads, 11–13th ed.	1	8/6	8,045	7,777	1,198.2.5	Mar 1870	Dec 1884
Aytoun, W.E.	Lays of the Cavaliers, 24–28th ed.	1	7/6	7,770	7,750	1,174.6.6	Jan 1874	Jun 1883
Hamilton	Metaphysics, 5–6th ed.	2	24/-	3,035	3,009	1,129.1.9	Jun 1870	Jun 1882
Chesney, George	Battle of Dorking	1	6d	110,550	108,252	1,058.17.7	Jun 1871	Apr 1872
Eliot, George	Works	6			22,866	931.4.0	Feb 1878	Jan 1880
	1880–1889							
Eliot, George	Works, cheap ed. & cabinet ed.	8;24	Various		49,726	14,081.14.11	Jan 1880	Dec 1889
	Scottish Hymnals Incorporated		2/6; 1/-; 6d; 3d; 1d		841,473	11,263.11.10	Jun 1885	Jun 1890
Meiklejohn	Educational Series	86	Various		118,958	5,408.6	Jun 1883	Jun 1890
Cross, John W.	George Eliot's Life, 1–3d ed.	3	42/-	5,558	5,323	5,262.18.10	Jan 1885	Jan 1886
Eliot, George	Middlemarch, 9 imps.	1	7/6	27,500	27,314	4,824.11.2	Mar 1880	Jun 1890
Eliot, George	Daniel Deronda, 8 imps.	1	7/6	24,300	24,296	4,314.2.9	May 1880	Dec 1891
	Scottish Hymnals		3/6; 1/6; 1/-; 6d; 2d; 1d		363,934	3,468.8.7	Jun 1881	Jun 1890
Stormonth	Dictionary, 6–10th ed.	1	7/6	24,150	24,019	3,302.11.2	Dec 1880	Nov 1892
Eliot, George	Works, cabinet ed.	20	5.0.0	44,079	33,666	2,252.4	Dec 1881	Jan 1884
	Acts of Parliament	1	Various		285,930	2,046.6.1	Jun 1888	Jun 1896
Trollope, Anthony	Autobiography	3	21/-	4,463	4,282	2,012.2.7	Oct 1883	Jun 1886
Kinglake, A.W.	History of the Crimea, cabinet ed.	6	36/-	28,695	21,510	1,969.12	May 1880	Jun 1890

Author	Title	Vol.	Price	Printed	Sold	Profit	Date Issued	Date Tallied
Eliot, George	Works, cabinet ed., vol. 1–6	6	5/-	55,055	44,890	1,693.7.9	Jan 1880	Dec 1881
	Ancient Classics for English Readers	24			52,191	3,779.10.7	Jun 1881	Jun 1886
	Public General Statutes		Various		17,681	1,625.4.7	Oct 1881	Jun 1891
Burton, John Hill	History of Scotland	8	63/-		9,379	1,327.8	Dec 1880	Jun 1894
Oliphant, Laurence	Altiora Peto, 1–5 imps.	2	21/-	13,895	8,674	1,270.17.5	Jun 1883	Jun 1884
Kinglake, A.W.	History of the Crimea, vol. 6	1	16/-	5,250	4,584	1,207.9.2	Sep 1880	Apr 1887
Hamley, E.B.	Operations of War, 5th ed.	1	30/-	1,575	1,572	1,131.13.6	Sep 1889	Aug 1900
Kinglake, A.W.	History of the Crimea, vols. 7 & 8	2	28/-	6,300	4,382	897.11.10	Dec 1887	Jun 1888
Mackay	Outlines of Geography	1	1/-	59,020	58,965	858.10.5	Mar 1880	Aug 1889
Nicholson, H.A.	Manual of Zoology, 6–7th ed.	1	14/-	5,244	4,398	810.4.0	Jul 1880	Dec 1895
Burton, John Hill	Book Hunter, new ed.	1		1,400	1,232	802.4.7	Jun 1882	Jun 1883
1890–1899								
Eliot, George	Works, cheap ed.	6	Various		276,644	13,756.15.9	Jun 1890	Jun 1902
Steevens, George	With Kitchener to Khartum, 1st & col. ed.	1	6/-; 2/-; 1/6	49,187	49,014	5,551.12.10	Jun 1898	Jun 1900
	Scottish Hymnals	1	Various		727,539	5,293.19.9	Jun 1890	Jun 1896
Eliot, George	Works, cheap ed. & cabinet ed.	8	Various		190,278	5,205.4.6	Jan 1890	Dec 1894
Ranjitsinhji	The Jubilee Book of Cricket, deluxe ed., pop. ed., col. ed.	1	5.5.0; 1.5.0; 6/-; 2/-; 1/6.	34,099	32,753	4,254.15.5	Aug 1897	Dec 1905
Eliot, George	Middlemarch, 7 imps.	1	7/6	22,175	22,152	3,640.6.9	Mar 1890	Dec 1900
Travers, Graham	Mona MacLean, 3–14th ed.	1	6/-	18,262	17,545	1,891.11.0	Apr 1893	Dec 1904
Harraden, Beatrice	The Fowler, 1–3d ed., col. ed.	1	6/-; 2/-; 1/6	18,944	18,077	1,852.0.10	Mar 1899	Dec 1901

Author	Title							
Eliot, George	Works, cabinet ed.	24			18,031	1,839.6	Jun 1892	Dec 1909
Oliphant, M.O.W.	Life of Laurence Oliphant, 1–9th ed.	2	21/-	3,981	3,734	1,562.6.5	Apr 1891	Dec 1892
Eliot, George	Daniel Deronda, 3 imps.	1	7/6	9,500	9,491	1,520.13.8	Feb 1891	Mar 1896
	Works, standard ed.	21			79,280	1,368.13.11	Jun 1895	Jun 1902
Stormonth	Dictionary, 11–15th ed.	1	7/6	10,075	10,053	1,345.7	Oct 1892	Aug 1901
Kinglake, A.W.	The Invasion of the Crimea	9	6/-		19,394	1,800.9.2	Jun 1890	Jun 1902
	Educational Series		Various		781,904	1,217.13.8	Jun 1890	Jun 1894
Oliphant & Porter	House of Blackwood	3	84/-; 42/-	4,220	3,140	1,173.8	Sep 1897	Jun 1905
	Life of the Earl of Iddesleigh, 1–3d imp.	2	31/6	2,112	1,851	1,073.18.3	Oct 1890	Mar 1891
Eliot, George	Daniel Deronda, 2 imps.	1	6/-	6,300	6,291	1,020.1.4	Mar 1896	Aug 1902
Steevens, George	With Kitchener to Khartum	1	6d	184,425	140,424	973.2.2	Mar 1899	Jun 1902
Travers, Graham	Windyhaugh, 1–4th ed., col. ed.	1	6/-; 2/-; 1/6	12,657	11,262	929.1.6	Oct 1898	Jun 1900

1900–1909

Author	Title							
Thurston, Katherine C.	John Chilcote, M.P., 1st & col. ed.	1	6/-, 2/-, 1/6	31,336	31,137	3,055.17.5	Sep 1904	Dec 1909
Synge	Readers	5	Various		92,237	2,244.2.1	Dec 1906	Dec 1910
Hamley, E.B.	Operations of War, new ed.	1	30/-	2,899	2,693	1,976.0.7	Aug 1907	Dec 1920
Diver, Maud	Candles in the Wind, 1–2nd imp.,col. ed.	1	6/-; 2/-; 1/6	20,111	19,806	1,901.19.2	Oct 1909	Dec 1911
	The Great Amulet, 1–7th imp.	1	1/-	137,307	131,501	1,870.2.7	Apr 1909	Dec 1914
Eliot, George	Works, Warwick ed.	14			135,022	1,836.12.3	Jun 1901	Jun 1906
Thurston, Katherine C.	The Fly on the Wheel, 1st & col. ed.	1	6/-, 2/-; 1/6	18,850	18,110	1,836.0.9	Mar 1908	Dec 1910
Steevens, George	Capetown to Ladysmith	1	3/6, 2/-; 1/6	33,769	33,553	1,780.1.4	Feb 1900	Jun 1902

Author	Title	Vol.	Price	Printed	Sold	Profit	Date Issued	Date Tallied
Eliot, George	Works, cheap ed.	8	3/6		40,052	2,105.7.0	Jun 1905	Dec 1912
	Works, cheap ed. & col. ed.	6	Various		33,748	1,631.15.2	Jun 1902	Jun 1905
Diver, Maud	Captain Desmond, 1-12th imp.	1	1/-	128,900	122,875	1,525.12.9	Sep 1908	Dec 1911
Harraden, Beatrice	Katharine Frensham, 1-2d ed., col. ed.	1	6/-; 2/-; 1/6	16,800	15,100	1,522.10.2	Oct 1903	Jun 1905
Grant	Words by an Eyewitness, 1-11th imp.	1	6/-	12,662	11,754	1,223.15.6	Oct 1901	Dec 1902
Thurston, Katherine C.	John Chilcote, M.P.	1	6d	143,916	143,755	978.3.8	Jul 1905	Oct 1908
Travers, Graham	The Way of Escape, 1-2d imp, col.ed.	1	6/-; 2/-; 1/6	13,569	13,416	895.3.3	Apr 1902	Jun 1903
Meiklejohn	Educational Series		Various		245,603	877.18.6	Jun 1905	Jun 1913
Eliot, George	Works, Warwick ed.	14	Various		18,271	864.8.4	Jun 1905	Dec 1909
Hamley, E.B.	Operations of War, 5th ed., 2d imp.	1	30/-	3,153	2,166	842.14.8	Aug 1900	Dec 1911
Lang	A History of Scotland, vols. 1-4	4			2,946	836.10.5	Jan 1905	Dec 1910
Munro, Neil	The Daft Days, 1-3d imp. & col. ed.	1	6/-, 2/-, 1/6	9,535	9,228	824.6.3	Apr 1907	Dec 1908

Blackwood's Magazine *Sales, 1856–1915*

Issue Nos.	Regular Sales	American Sales	Ad Costs	Profits	Date Tallied
490–501	78,556	0	337.18	4,686.08	Jun 1857
502–13	85,715	0	321.2	4,911.13	Jun 1858
514–25	88,331	0	323.5	5,280.19	Jun 1859
526–37	90,444	0	348.7	5,216.14	Jun 1860
538–46	64,522	0	244.17	3,616.11	Apr 1861
547–61	100,837	0	460.3.10	5,640.13.8	Jun 1862
562–73	79,353	0	338.7.3	5,039.0	Jun 1863
574–85	79,485	0	334.9.2	4,811.2.10	Jun 1864
586–97	79,300	0	355.4.3	5,013.6.6	Jun 1865
598–609	77,872	0	345.3.5	4,761.8.3	Jun 1866
610–21	73,327	0	332.4.8	4,250.18.11	Jun 1867
622–33	70,813	0	321.1.1	4,117.13.7	Jun 1868
634–45	68,982	0	350.11.3	3,911.13.9	Jun 1869
646–57	68,808	0	386.4.1	3,975.10.3	Jun 1870
658–69	67,125	0	412.17.9	3,830.3.10	Jun 1871
670–81	65,564	0	416.8.1	3,761.18.2	Jun 1872
682–93	68,564	0	387.2.4	3,758.17.8	Jun 1873
694–705	66,947	0	405.8.2	3,695.2.11	Jun 1874
706–17	67,510	0	417.11.1	3,806.9.10	Jun 1875
718–29	65,595	0	428.16.11	3,636.19.10	Jun 1876
730–41	68,988	0	447.12.1	3,967.16.1	Jun 1877
742–53	65,021	0	458.1.4	3,307.19.5	Jun 1878
754–69	85,481	0	586.19.11	4,568.1.9	Oct 1879
770–77	45,241	0	338.1.10	3,368.12	Jun 1880
778–89	65,937	0	545.6.4	3,727.4.1	Jun 1881
790–801	64,705	0	527.4.9	3,631.13.1	Jun 1882
802–13	63,249	0	618.0.1	3,565.12.5	Jun 1883
814–25	61,465	0	647.13.11	3,328.16	Jun 1884
826–37	60,130	0	735.5.5	3,174.14.11	Jun 1885
838–49	58,845	0	723.18.9	3,077.15.1	Jun 1886
850–61	57,176	0	718.13.4	2,992.14.11	Jun 1887
862–73	55,010	0	734.17.4	2,811.7.8	Jun 1888
874–85	53,912	0	692.11.8	2,488.7.8	Jun 1889
886–97	55,831	0	706.3	2,669.6.7	Jun 1890
898–909	54,328	11,700	691.18.11	3,048.5.8	Jun 1891
910–21	53,458	15,600	688.2.6	2,979.11.4	Jun 1892
922–33	50,890	14,700	612.4.3	2,778.14.5	Jun 1893
934–45	49,358	14,175	623.12.7	2,685.6.3	Jun 1894
946–57	50,033	13,500	740.2.7	2,436.3.1	Jun 1895
958–69	48,922	13,500	696.15.2	2,505.11.9	Jun 1896

Issue Nos.	Regular Sales	American Sales	Ad Costs	Profits	Date Tallied
970–81	49,111	12,900	492.19.1	2,725.5.3	Jun 1897
982–93	46,074	12,050	466.6.8	2,308	Jun 1898
994–1005	49,506	11,825	558.13.1	2,288.14.2	Jun 1899
1006–17	49,047	12,000	492.13	2,777.0.10	Jun 1900
1018–29	48,488	12,225	505.16.4	2,476.12.8	Jun 1901
1030–41	47,795	12,000	422.19.8	2,658.7	Jun 1902
1042–53	49,724	12,000	0	3,160.5.7	Jun 1903
1054–65	49,983	12,000	167.3.6	3,420.10.11	Jun 1904
1066–77	49,958	12,000	225.19.4	3,271.8.3	Jun 1905
1078–89	49,443	12,000	226.18.7	3,419.16.11	Jun 1906
1090–1101	49,648	12,000	249.0.4	3,271.4.1	Jun 1907
1102–13	47,967	12,000	286.11.6	3,058.12.4	Jun 1908
1114–25	49,905	12,000	368.3.7	3,136.9.11	Jun 1909
1126–37	50,140	12,000	354.17.6	3,134.4.3	Jun 1910
1138–49	51,639	12,000	364.2.11	3,204.12.7	Jun 1911
1150–61	54,226	12,000	451.11.6	3,600.9	Jun 1912
1162–73	55,908	12,000	583.6.8	3,624.6.7	Jun 1913
1174–85	64,200	12,000	664.3.8	3,788.4.1	Jun 1914
1186–97	76,685	12,000	442.11.4	5,072.7.11	Jun 1915

Appendix 3

Margaret Oliphant Sales, 1860–1897

Title	Vols.	Cost	No. Printed	No. Sold	Profit	Date Issued	Date Tallied
Salem Chapel	2	24/-	1,579	1,503	797.13.1	Feb 1863	May 1863
Salem Chapel, cheap ed., 3 imps.	1	5/-	2,066	2,055	95.2.5	May 1863	Oct 1865
The Rector	1	10/6	1,307	1,252	228.14.11	May 1863	Nov 1863
The Rector, cheap ed.	1	4/-	1,050	1,045	29.5.5	Oct 1863	Jun 1867
The Perpetual Curate	3	31/6	1,580	1,351	846.3.5	Oct 1864	Dec 1873
The Perpetual Curate, cheap ed.	1	6/-	1,560	1,164	42.5.8	Sep 1865	Dec 1873
Miss Marjoribanks	3	31/6	1,050	1,002	666.19.4	Apr 1866	Jun 1867
Miss Marjoribanks, cheap ed.	1	6/-	785	780	22.5.4	Aug 1866	Aug 1867
Brownlows	3	31/6	1,313	899	516.16.10	Feb 1868	Dec 1873
Historical Sketches of the Reign of George II	2	21/-	1,055	970	335.10	Oct 1869	May 1870
John	2	21/-	1,050	974	279.5.11	Jul 1870	Dec 1873
Memoir of Montalembert	2	24/-	1,575	1,276	554.19	Jul 1872	Jun 1876
Katie Stewart	1	2/6	1,050	1,044	14.2.4	Jan 1875	Mar 1875
Valentine and his Brothers	3	25/6	1,313	967	414.17.1	Feb 1875	Dec 1875
Valentine and His Brothers, cheap ed.	1	5/-	1,050	1,050	-41.11.1	Dec 1875	Dec 1889
The Ladies Lindores	3	18/6	1,313	1,014	389.17.4	Apr 1883	Dec 1887
Seen and Unseen	1	2/6	5,268	2,522	40.15	Dec 1884	Aug 1902
A House Divided Against Itself	3	25/6	1,050	668	174.6.1	Jul 1886	Feb 1890
Life of Principal Tulloch, 1–3d ed.	1	21/-	2,640	2,128	470.13.8	Oct 1888	Dec 1889
The Duke's Daughter	3	25/6	788	479	169.17.6	Mar 1890	Mar 1894
Sons and Daughters	1	3/6	1,050	979	26.2	Jul 1890	Dec 1890
Life of Laurence Oliphant, 1–9th ed.	2	21/-	3,981	3,734	1,562.6.5	Apr 1891	Dec 1892
Life of Laurence Oliphant, American ed.	2	21/-	2,000	2,000	433.10.11	Jun 1891	Jul 1891

Title	Vols.	Cost	No. Printed	No. Sold	Profit	Date Issued	Date Tallied
Life of Laurence Oliphant	1	7/6	1,576	1,419	54.4.8	Mar 1892	Jun 1906
Who was Lost and is Found, 1–2d ed.	1	6/-	2,110	2,021	61.5	Oct 1894	Dec 1904
Annals of a Publishing House	3	84/-; 42/-	4,220	3,140	1,173.08	Sep 1897	Jun 1905

Notes

References to manuscript material from the Blackwood archives will on occasion vary in noting folio numbers, page numbers, or no page or folio reference at all. This is because the archive consists of three different types of cataloged material:

1. Cataloged volumes of correspondence and other documents, bound, indexed, and with folio numbers
2. Cataloged ledgers and other material, unindexed but bound and with page numbers
3. Cataloged but unindexed material, loose in files and boxes, with no page or folio numbers

Notes to Chapter 1

1. Blackwood Inventory, Ms 30853, unfoliated document, National Library of Scotland, Edinburgh. Unless otherwise noted, all further references to the Blackwood Papers collection at the National Library of Scotland, Edinburgh, give only date, manuscript, and folio or page numbers.

2. For a detailed breakdown of numbers, see Maurice Milne, "The Management of a Nineteenth-Century Magazine: William Blackwood & Sons, 1827–1847," *Journal of Newspaper and Periodical History* 1 (Summer 1985): 32.

3. I am grateful to Michael Blackwood, former director of the firm and last editor of *Blackwood's Magazine*, for permission to use and quote from this document, a microfilm copy of which is on deposit in the National Library of Scotland.

4. Mark Rose, *Authors and Owners: The Invention of Copyright* (Cambridge, Mass.: Harvard University Press, 1993), 112.

5. Thomas Constable, *Archibald Constable and His Correspondents* (Edinburgh: Edmonston & Douglas, 1873), 7.

6. F. D. Tredrey, *The House of Blackwood, 1804–1954* (Edinburgh: William Blackwood & Sons, 1954), 18.

7. Maurice Milne, "The 'Veiled Editor' Unveiled: William Blackwood and His Magazine," *Publishing History* 16 (1984): 89.

8. John Blackwood to J. M. Langford, 28 December 1862, Blackwood Papers, MS 30862, p. 151.

9. Simon Eliot, *Some Patterns and Trends in British Publishing, 1800–1919* (London: The Bibliographical Society, 1994), 13–14.

10. N. N. Feltes, *Literary Capital and the Late Victorian Novel* (Madison: University of Wisconsin Press, 1993), xii, 12.

11. Donald W. Nichol, "Arthur Murphy's Law," *Times Literary Supplement* 19 (April 1996): 15–16.

12. Stuart Hall, Introduction to A. C. H. Smith, *Paper Voices: The Popular Press and Social Change, 1935–1965* (London: Chatto & Windus, 1975), 22.

13. Matthew Schneirov, *The Dream of a New Social Order: Popular Magazines in America, 1893–1914* (New York: Columbia University Press, 1994), 19.

14. Douglas Kellner, *Media Culture: Cultural Studies, Identity, and Politics Between the Modern and the Post-Modern* (New York and London: Routledge, 1995), 28.

15. Janice Radway, "Books and Reading in the Age of Mass Production," The Adam Helms Lecture 1996 (Stockholm: Swedish Publishers' Association and the Stockholm University Library, 1996), 24.

16. Ibid., 24.

Notes to Chapter 2

1. Simpson to John Blackwood, 23 March 1850, MS 4091, fol. 41.

2. Alexander Allardyce, former Anglo-Indian journalist and editor, was subsequently appointed to John Brown's old post, assuming over the next twenty years a similar role as confidant and commentator for William Blackwood III. See John Blackwood to Alexander Allardyce, 22 March 1877, MS 30034.

3. John Brown to John Blackwood, 24 June 1863, MS 30013.

4. See John Blackwood to John Brown, 30 June 1863, MS 30013, about salary raise.

5. Margaret Oliphant, *Annals of a Publishing House, William Blackwood and Sons*, vol. 2 (Edinburgh: William Blackwood & Sons, 1897), 417.

6. John Blackwood to George Simpson, 10 April 1850, MS 4087, fol. 249.

7. The sum amassed was quite substantial. On his death in 1894, Simpson left an estate valued at £8,500, which was subsequently distributed among several Edinburgh public institutions, including £2,000 each to the Royal Infirmary and the Scottish National Portrait Gallery. "Blackwoodiana," 9, Blackwood family collection of clippings, microfilm copy of which is in the National Library of Scotland.

8. John shared rooms with Delane when both began work in London in 1840 (Delane in the office of the *Times*, Blackwood as business manager of the London office). See Mary Porter, *Annals of a Publishing House: William Blackwood and Sons*, vol. 3 (Edinburgh: William Blackwood & Sons, 1898), 16–18, for further details. John is one of the first to hear of Delane's promotion to editor in 1841: "By Jove, John, what do you think has happened?" Delane is said to have exclaimed upon bursting into their shared lodgings on St. James Street early one morning. "I am editor of *The Times*" (Porter, *Annals of a Publishing House*, 3:17; A. I. Dasent, *John Thadeus Delane, Editor of "The Times": His Life and Correspondence*, vol. 1 [London: John Murray, 1908], 26).

9. *Minutes of the Evidence Taken Before the Royal Commission on Copyright* (London: Eyre & Spottiswoode, 1878), 41. The commission did not issue its report until two years after evidence had been taken. Trollope played a leading role in its activities, but the results were negligible. See N. John Hall, *Trollope: A Biography* (Oxford: Oxford University Press, 1993), 421, for commentary on Trollope's stint on the commission.

10. *Minutes of the Evidence Taken Before the Royal Commission on Copyright*, 40.

11. William Blackwood III to John Blackwood, 24 April 1865, MS 4196, fol. 7.

12. Tredrey, *House of Blackwood*, 117–18, 125.

13. For more on Oliphant, see Anne Taylor, *Laurence Oliphant, 1829–1888* (Oxford: Oxford University Press, 1982).

14. In a letter dated 23 August 1872, John Blackwood thanked Stanley for his interest in publishing with Blackwood, but suggested that John Murray, as main publisher of Livingstone, would be more suitable for his work (MS 30364, p. 177). John also wrote Laurence Oliphant thanking him for his work on the firm's behalf and concluding, "It is so like the kind consideration I have so often seen on your part in doing anything you may think likely to be useful to your friend" (7 August 1872, MS 30364, pp. 178–79).

15. *Edinburgh Evening Courant*, 17 August 1871, 4.

16. Gordon Haight's work on George Eliot is central to understanding Eliot's financial and personal connections with the Blackwood firm. See, for example, his *George Eliot: A Biography* (Oxford:

Oxford University Press, 1968) and *The George Eliot Letters*, vols. 1–9 (Oxford: Oxford University Press, 1954–78). See also Roland F. Anderson, "George Eliot Provoked: John Blackwood and Chapter Seventeen of *Adam Bede*," *Modern Philology* 71 (August 1973): 39–47; Anderson, "Negotiating for the *Mill on the Floss*," *Publishing History* 2 (1978): 27–40; Rosemarie Bodenheimer, *The Real Life of Mary Ann Evans: George Eliot, Her Letters and Fiction* (Ithaca: Cornell University Press, 1994); and Carol A. Martin, *George Eliot's Serial Fiction* (Columbus: Ohio State University Press, 1994).

17. For a detailed analysis of the negotiations and subsequent publication of *Romola*, see Roland Anderson, "'Things Wisely Ordered': John Blackwood, George Eliot, and the Publication of *Romola*," *Publishing History* 11 (1982): 5–39; and Haight, *George Eliot: A Biography*, 354–74.

18. Joseph Langford to John Blackwood, 23 May 1862, MS 4171, fols. 151–52. A minor transcription error in this sentence in Gordon Haight's epic edition of George Eliot's letters (he substitutes "flirt" for "flint") has resulted in misquoting Langford's comment in all subsequent accounts of this incident. See Haight, *George Eliot Letters*, vol. 4: *1862–1868* (Oxford: Oxford University Press, 1956), 38.

19. Joseph Langford to John Blackwood, 23 May 1862, MS 4171, fols. 151–52; and Haight, *George Eliot Letters*, 4:38.

20. William Blackwood III to John Blackwood, 24 May 1862, MS 4167, fols. 132–33.

21. Ibid.

22. Haight, *George Eliot Letters*, 4:38.

23. E. H. Nolan, *History of the War Against Russia* (London: J. S. Virtue, 1857), quoted in Robert Wilkinson-Latham, *From Our Special Correspondent: Victorian War Correspondents and Their Campaigns* (London: Hodder & Stoughton, 1979), 50.

24. John Blackwood to George Simpson, 3 September 1862, MS 30360, p. 270.

25. George Paston, *At John Murray's: Records of a Literary Circle, 1843–1892* (London: John Murray, 1932), 153.

26. Henry Drummond Wolff to John Blackwood, 21 August 1862, MS 4175, fol. 164.

27. John Blackwood to H. Drummond Wolff, 22 August 1862, MS 30360, p. 263.

28. John Blackwood to George Simpson, 3 September 1862, MS 30360, pp. 270–71.

29. A. W. Kinglake to John Blackwood, 6 September 1862, MS 4171, fol. 108.

30. A. W. Kinglake to John Blackwood, 10 September 1862, MS 4171, fol. 111.

31. John Blackwood, 15 September 1862, MS 30013.

32. Later a royalty of one shilling and four pence per copy sold above and beyond the initial print run would be agreed on. See MS 30843, Memoranda on Copyrights, p. 39.

33. Further if slightly misleading details can be found in Porter, *Annals of a Publishing House*, 3:88–118; and Tredrey, *House of Blackwood*, 123–27.

34. William Blackwood III to John Blackwood, 12 May 1868, MS 4229, fols. 81–82.

35. William Blackwood to III John Blackwood, 14 May 1868, MS 4229, fols. 87–88.

36. See, for example, Robert Colby and Vineta Colby, *The Equivocal Virtue: Mrs. Oliphant and the Victorian Literary Market Place* (New York: Archon Books, 1966); Elisabeth Jay, *Mrs. Oliphant, "A Fiction to Herself": A Literary Life* (Oxford: Clarendon Press, 1995).

37. Jay, *Mrs. Oliphant, "A Fiction to Herself,"* 248.

38. Quoted in ibid.

39. John Blackwood to William Blackwood III, 26 May 1866, MS 4206, fol. 181–82.

40. In her study of Oliphant's negotiations in 1866 for *Miss Marjoribanks*, J. A. Haythornthwaite misreads ledger accounts to suggest that *Miss Marjoribanks* earned a profit of £336.12.2 1/2. See J. A. Haythornthwaite, "The Wages of Success: 'Miss Marjoribanks,' Margaret Oliphant, and the House of Blackwood," *Publishing History* 15 (1984): 102. As the ledger accounts she then reproduces demonstrate, though, *Marjoribanks* in fact earned a profit of £666.19.4, almost twice the sum assumed. *Salem Chapel* generated profits of slightly more than £797.

41. Colby and Colby, *The Equivocal Virtue*, 56.

42. Among reasons suggested for this include the firm's doubts about the "three-decker" style of fiction Oliphant seemed to represent to them, and the firm's shift toward literary work of such

authors as George Eliot, George Chesney, F. Marion Crawford, and Graham Travers (see ibid., 68, and n. 28, 255).

43. Edward M. Spiers, *The Late Victorian Army, 1868–1902* (Manchester: Manchester University Press, 1992), 246. Tredrey notes that after Hamley's death in 1893 the revised version (by General Aston) continued to be on the Staff College reading list until the 1930s (*House of Blackwood*, 128).

44. As recounted by Sam Kinnear to an acquaintance, *Scotsman*, 16 August 1916, 46.

45. Sam Kinnear in a 1897 letter to the *Scotsman*, in "Blackwoodiana," 1, Blackwood family collection of clippings, microfilm copy of which is in the National Library of Scotland. See also Tredrey, *House of Blackwood*, 180–81, for more commentary from this source.

46. Ibid.

47. Sian Reynolds, *Britannica's Typesetters: Women Compositors in Edinburgh* (Edinburgh: Edinburgh University Press, 1989), 39.

48. Ian MacDougall, ed., *The Minutes of the Edinburgh Trades Council, 1859–1873* (Edinburgh: T. & A. Constable, 1968).

49. Reynolds, *Britannica's Typesetters*.

50. Ibid., 41.

51. Sarah C. Gillespie, *A Hundred Years of Progress: The Record of the Scottish Typographical Association, 1853–1952* (Glasgow: Robert Maclehose & Co.), 1953, 118.

52. William Blackwood III to John Blackwood, 17 October 1872, MS 4286, fols. 174–75.

53. William Blackwood III to John Blackwood, 1 November 1872, MS 4286, fols. 197–98.

54. William Blackwood III to John Blackwood, 15 November 1872, MS 4286, fols. 216–17.

55. Ibid., fol. 215.

56. This is confirmed in the Minute Books of the Edinburgh Typographical Association strike committee, which records on 25 November 1872: "Letter read from Mr. A. Wilson, Reader, Blackwood's, thanking Executives of Society for offering him pecuniary reward on receiving his notice for refusing to go to case" (Accession 4068, no. 39, p. 20, National Library of Scotland).

57. William Blackwood III to John Blackwood, 11 November 1872, MS 4286, fols. 207–8.

58. John Blackwood to G. H. Lewes, 22 November 1872, MS 30364, pp. 206–7.

59. Reynolds, *Britannica's Typesetters*, 42.

60. John Blackwood to William Blackwood III, 21 February 1873, MS 4299, fol. 172.

61. Reynolds, *Britannica's Typesetters*, 45–46.

62. Accession 4068, no. 87, *Edinburgh Typographical Association, Index to Members, 1871–1881*, National Library of Scotland.

63. John Blackwood to William Blackwood III, 18 November 1872, MS 4285, fols. 185–86.

64. John Blackwood to William Blackwood III, 24 October 1872, MS 4285, fols. 168–69.

65. Tredrey, *House of Blackwood*, 189.

66. Gillespie, *Hundred Years of Progress*, 155. In 1908, for example, they finally and successfully negotiate workweeks of fifty hours and an increase in wages on time rates beyond the rates established previously.

67. For further information and statistical details supporting this point, see my article "'The Secret': British Publishers and Mudie's Struggle for Survival, 1861–1864," *Publishing History* 34 (1993): 21–50.

68. Ibid., 35, 39–42.

69. See John Sutherland, *Victorian Novelists and Publishers* (Chicago: University of Chicago Press, 1978), 13–40;

70. Finkelstein, "'The Secret.'" See also Guinever L. Griest, *Mudie's Circulating Library and the Victorian Novel* (Bloomington: Indiana University Press, 1970).

71. Ibid., 23–25.

72. Ibid., 34.

73. William Blackwood III to John Blackwood, 11 December 1863, MS 4178, fol. 241.

74. Joseph Langford to William Blackwood III, 5 December 1864, MS 4190, fol. 129.

75. Bill Bell, "'Pioneers of Literature': The Commercial Traveller in the Early Nineteenth Century," in Peter Isaac and Barry McKay, eds., *The Reach of Print: Making, Selling, and Using Books* (Winchester: St. Paul's Bibliographies, 1998), 121.

76. Ibid.

77. William Blackwood III to John Blackwood, 17 July 1862, MS 4167, fol. 184.

78. William Blackwood III to John Blackwood, 12 July 1862, MS 4167, fols. 175–76.

79. See William B. Todd and Ann Bowden, *Tauchnitz International Editions in English, 1841–1955: A Bibliographical History* (New York: Bibliographical Society of America and Oak Knoll Press, 1984).

80. The Blackwood letters are sprinkled with examples of the firm negotiating payment with Harper's for U.S. publication of British authors, as, for example, a letter to Margaret Oliphant in 1883 in which William Blackwood III writes: "We today received payment from Messr Harper for the advance sheets of 'The Ladies Lindores' £30 and as promised I have the pleasure of enclosing you the honorarium. It ought to have been double the amount but it is difficult now to get even £10 or £15 from the pirates except by writing for their Magazines which I suppose you have found out when I understand they pay sums old Maga even could not dream of" (William Blackwood III to Margaret Oliphant, 8 June 1883, MS 30369, pp. 391–92).

Notes to Chapter 3

1. Alan Moorehead, *The White Nile* (Harmondsworth: Penguin Books, 1973), 12.

2. William Blackwood III to John Blackwood, MS 4178, fol. 36.

3. A guinea was equivalent to one pound and one shilling, or twenty-one shillings. Thus the sum was in effect 42,000 shillings, or 2,200 pounds.

4. John Blackwood to William Blackwood II, 20 June 1863, MS 4177, fol. 58. The offer had been relayed to Speke via Sir Roderick Impey Murchison (1792–1871), a well-known member and past president of the Royal Geographical Society. This is confirmed in a letter from John Murray in the Murray archives, addressed to Murchison: "My dear Sir Roderick, As the publisher of the *Travels of Livingstone*, Du Chaillu etc., as well as of the Geographical Society's Journal, you may judge how anxious I am to have also the honor of publishing Captn. Speke's Discovery of the Source of the Nile. Captn. Speke may arrive any day or hour. You will have much to say to and hear from him, but it would be a favor added to many others conferred on me, if you could find an opportunity to state this my anxious wish—& that if he is able to place his m.s.s. in my hands, I am prepared to treat him as I did Livingstone i.e. give him 2/3rds of all the profits of the work & guarantee to him in the first instance two thousand guineas, as part of them" (from Murray Letter Books, 1858–68, p. 184).

5. John Blackwood to William Blackwood III, 20 June 1863, MS 4177, fol. 58.

6. John Blackwood to William Blackwood III, 20 December 1863, MS 4177, fol. 137.

7. Grant's diary notes, in fact, meetings with both parties on the same day: "22 [June]. Illustrated Newsman, Blackwood, Langford all here" (J. A. Grant Papers, National Library of Scotland, MS 17915, p. 315).

8. William Blackwood III to John Blackwood, 9 July 1863, MS 4178, fol. 98.

9. William Blackwood III to John Blackwood, 10 July 1863, MS 4178, fol. 101.

10. John Blackwood to William Blackwood III, 22 July 1863, MS 4177, fol. 73.

11. Ibid.

12. William Blackwood III to John Blackwood, 23 July 1863, MS 4178, fols. 118–19.

13. William Blackwood III to John Blackwood, 25 July 1863, MS 4178, fols. 128–29.

14. Journal entry, MS 4872, p. 366. Final published version, *Journal of the Discovery of the Source of the Nile* (Edinburgh: William Blackwood & Sons, 1863), 400.

15. Journal entry, MS 4872, p. 48; published version p. 20.

16. Journal entry, 368; published version p. 296.

17. William Blackwood III to John Blackwood, 26 July 1863, MS 4178, fol. 130.
18. Ibid.
19. Margaret Oliphant to John Blackwood, 26 July 1863, MS 4184, fols. 60–61.
20. John Blackwood to William Blackwood III, 26 July 1863, MS 4177, fol. 74.
21. William Blackwood III to John Blackwood, 26 July 1863, MS 4178, fol. 137. Fifteen years after, Margaret Oliphant was called upon to edit an influential series of "Foreign Classics," which featured contributions from such authors as George Henry Lewes, Henry Trollope (son of Anthony), and Henry Reeve (editor of the *Edinburgh Review*).
22. John Blackwood to William Blackwood III, 30 July 1863, MS 4177, fol. 79.
23. Ibid., fol. 80.
24. William Blackwood III to John Blackwood, 31 July 1863, MS 4178, fol. 138.
25. William Blackwood III to John Blackwood, 3 August 1863, MS 4178, fols. 141–42.
26. John Blackwood to William Blackwood III, 4 August 1863, MS 4177, fol. 84.
27. Ibid.
28. William Blackwood III to John Blackwood, 4 August 1863, MS 4178, fol. 146.
29. Ibid.
30. Ibid., fol. 147.
31. John Blackwood to William Blackwood III, 13 August 1863, MS 4177, fol. 88.
32. George Simpson to J. M. Langford, date illegible, approximately mid-August 1863, MS 30322, p. 79.
33. George Simpson to J. M. Langford, 15 August 1863, MS 4185, fol. 149.
34. John Blackwood to J. M. Langford, 28 August 1863, MS 4177, fol. 91.
35. John Speke to John Blackwood, undated, MS 4185, fol. 268.
36. John Blackwood to J. M. Langford, 28 August 1863, MS 4177, fol. 91.
37. William Blackwood III to John Blackwood, 8 September 1863, MS 4178, fol. 162.
38. J. M. Langford to George Simpson, 14 July 1863, MS 30970, fols. 3–4.
39. George Simpson to J. M. Langford, 15 July 1863, MS 30322, fol. 73.
40. Ibid.
41. Ibid., fol. 74.
42. Ibid.
43. George Simpson to J. M. Langford, MS 30322, fol. 79.
44. Original journal entry, MS 4872, p. 314.
45. *Journal of the Discovery of the Source of the Nile*, 292.
46. Original journal entry, MS 4872, pp. 127–28.
47. *Journal*, 109–10.
48. Original journal entry, MS 4872, p. 1.
49. Original journal entry, MS 4873, p. 1; *Journal of the Discovery of the Source of the Nile*, xiii.
50. Original journal entry, MS 4872, p. 40.
51. *Journal of the Discovery of the Source of the Nile*, 18.
52. Ibid., xxii.
53. Ibid., xxv.
54. Ibid., xxvii.
55. Original journal entry, MS 4872, p. 1; *Journal of the Discovery of the Source of the Nile*, xiii.
56. Christine Bolt, *Victorian Attitudes to Race* (London: Routledge & Kegan Paul, 1971), 109–57.
57. William Blackwood III to John Blackwood, 25 October 1863, MS 4178, fol. 222.
58. John Blackwood to John Delane, 7 December 1863, MS 30361, pp. 38–39. Also in Porter, *Annals of a Publishing House*, 3:97.
59. Ibid.
60. Ibid.
61. John Blackwood to (unknown), 20 November 1863, MS 30361, p. 29.
62. John Blackwood to John Burton, 21 December 1863, MS 30361, pp. 42–43.
63. Ibid.

64. John Blackwood to John Delane, 7 December 1863, MS 30361, pp. 38–39.
65. John Blackwood to John Burton, 18 September 1864, MS 30361, p. 180.

Notes to Chapter 4

1. Malcolm Elwin, *Charles Reade: A Biography* (London: Jonathan Cape, 1931), 291.
2. E. Moberly Bell, *Storming the Citadel: The Rise of the Woman Doctor* (London: Constable & Co., 1953), 23. Bell cites Salerno's medical school, founded in the eleventh century, as one of the earliest to admit women as teachers and students.
3. Juliet Mitchell and Ann Oakley, eds., *The Rights and Wrongs of Women* (Harmondsworth: Penguin Books,1976), 37.
4. *Life of Sir Robert Christison*, vol. 2 (Edinburgh: William Blackwood & Sons, 1885–86), 49–50.
5. Edythe Lutzker, "Medical Education for Women in Great Britain" (Ph.D. diss., Columbia University, 1959), 3.
6. Bell, *Storming the Citadel*, 45.
7. *Medical Times and Gazette*, 23 February 1867, 199, quoted in Lutzker, "Medical Education for Women in Great Britain," 5.
8. Jean Donnison, *Midwives and Medical Men* (London: Historical Publications, 1988), 76.
9. Lutzker, "Medical Education for Women in Great Britain," 5.
10. Quoted in Patricia Hollis, ed., *Women in Public, 1850–1900* (London: George Allen & Unwin, 1979), 101.
11. Quoted in Lutzker, "Medical Education for Women in Great Britain," 43.
12. Ibid., 59.
13. In 1863 Charles Dickens paid £3,000 to serialize *Hard Cash in All the Year Round*, while in 1869–70 George Smith paid £4,000 to serialize *Put Yourself in His Place* in the *Cornhill Magazine*. In an 1865 review, Henry James stated of George Eliot: "She has the microscopic observation, not a myriad of whose keen notations are worth a single one of those great sympathetic guesses with which a real master attacks the truth, and which, by their occasional occurrence in the stories of Mr. Charles Reade (the much abused "Griffith Gaunt" included), make him, to our mind, the most readable of living English novelists, and prove him a distant kinsman of Shakespeare" (quoted in Wayne Burns, *Charles Reade: A Study in Victorian Authorship* [New York: Bookman Associates, 1961], 11).
14. Elwin, *Charles Reade*, 291. The work cleared a massive 2,700 copies in two days when published as a cheap edition.
15. J. M. Langford to John Blackwood, 12 February 1876, MS 4347, fol. 146.
16. As early as 1861, Langford had proposed securing Reade's work for *Blackwood's Magazine*. Although John Blackwood did not discourage the idea, his comments then reflected a negative appraisal of Reade's work, which did not change over the years. "I do not like the style or tone of his stories generally," he wrote Langford, "but it is a great pity that an undoubtedly clever fellow who you tell me is also a good one should continue plunging on always putting his foot in it, & if he does send me anything I shall look at it with the disposition to do the best I can for both parties" (Blackwood to Langford, 15 April 1861, MS 4156, fol. 190).
17. J. M. Langford to John Blackwood, 28 March 1865, MS 4200, fols. 11–12.
18. Blackwood later changed his mind about the quality of *Griffith Gaunt*. On its publication as a three-volume novel in 1866, Blackwood commented to Langford, "When I read the first part of Griffith Gaunt I thought *very highly* of it but now that I have read the complete novel I am truly glad I had nothing to do with it" (Blackwood to Langford, 3 December 1866, MS 4206, fol. 235–40).
19. J. M. Langford to John Blackwood, 12 February 1876, MS 4347, fols. 146–47.
20. Recent works such as John Sutherland's *Victorian Novelists and Publishers* (Chicago: University of Chicago Press, 1978); N. N. Feltes, *Modes of Production of Victorian Novels* (Chicago: University of Chicago Press, 1986) and *Literary Capital and the Late Victorian Novel* (Madison: University of Wisconsin Press, 1993); and Peter Keating *The Haunted Study* (London: Secker & Warburg, 1989),

explore these issues in greater detail. See also Griest, *Mudie's Circulating Library*, 140–55, for a detailed discussion of Charles Mudie's censoring effect on the production of mid-century texts.

21. John Sutherland gives details, for example, of Richard Bentley's exploitation of Reade's works in *Victorian Novelists and Publishers*, 87–89.

22. John Blackwood to J. M. Langford, 15 February 1876, MS 30365, pp. 291–92.

23. Charles Reade to John Blackwood, 19 February 1876, MS 4726, fols. 39–42.

24. J. M. Langford to John Blackwood, 16 February 1876, MS 4347, fols. 150–51.

25. Charles Reade to John Blackwood, 19 February 1876, MS 4726, fols. 39–42.

26. J. M. Langford to William Blackwood III, 3 April 1876, MS 4347, fols. 166–67.

27. Elwin, *Charles Reade*, 295.

28. Compton Reade, *Charles Reade: A Memoir*, vol. 2 (London: Chapman & Hall, 1887), 243.

29. Charles Reade to John Blackwood, 19 February 1876, MS 4726, fols. 39–42.

30. Charles Reade, "A Woman Hater," *Blackwood's Magazine*, November 1876, 555. Hereafter references to the magazine are noted in the text in parentheses.

31. Margaret Todd, *The Life of Sophia Jex-Blake* (London: Macmillan & Co., 1918), 435.

32. Charles Reade to John Blackwood, 31 March [1876], MS 4726, fols. 53–54.

33. John Blackwood to J. M. Langford, 9 March 1876, MS 4341, fols. 198–99.

34. John Blackwood to J. M. Langford, 13 March 1876, MS 4341, fol. 200.

35. J. M. Langford to John Blackwood, 14 March 1876, MS 4347, fol. 157.

36. Charles Reade to John Blackwood, 21 March 1876, MS 4726, fols. 151–52.

37. Ibid.

38. Ibid.

39. Ibid.

40. Ibid.

41. John Blackwood to Charles Reade, 27 March 1876, MS 30365, p. 323.

42. John Blackwood to Charles Reade, 30 March 1876, MS 30365, p. 326.

43. Charles Reade to John Blackwood, 31 March [1876], MS 4726, fol. 54.

44. J. M. Langford to John Blackwood, 3 April 1876, MS 4347, fol. 166.

45. John Blackwood to Charles Reade, 28 June 1876, MS 30365, p. 380.

46. Ibid.

47. Mrs. Harry Coghill, ed., *Autobiography and Letters of Mrs. Margaret Oliphant*, 2nd ed. (Leicester: Leicester University Press, 1974), 259.

48. John Blackwood to Charles Reade, 28 June 1876, MS 30365, p. 381.

49. Todd, *Life of Sophia Jex-Blake*, 435.

50. [Hilda Gregg], "The Medical Woman in Fiction," *Blackwood's Magazine*, July 1898, 95.

51. Sophia Jex-Blake, "Medical Women in Fiction," *The Nineteenth Century*, January–June 1873, 262.

52. J. M. Langford to William Blackwood III, 13 July 1876, MS 4347, fols. 192–93.

53. J. M. Langford to William Blackwood III, 13 October 1876, MS 4347, fols. 232–33.

54. J. M. Langford to William Blackwood III, 30 October 1876, MS 4347, fol. 246.

55. J. M. Langford to William Blackwood III, 13 October 1876, MS 4347, fols. 232–33.

56. John Blackwood to Charles Reade, 10 July 1876, MS 30365, p. 385.

57. Ibid.

58. Ibid.

59. Charles Reade to William Blackwood III 4 July 1876, MS 4726, fols. 71–72.

60. John Blackwood to William Blackwood III, 8 October 1876, MS 4341, fols. 291–92. An ironic comment, considering John Blackwood's similar qualms over and initial resistance to portions of Eliot's *Scenes of Clerical Life* and *Adam Bede*. Further details can be found in Martin, *George Eliot's Serial Fiction*.

61. John Blackwood to Charles Reade, 11 October 1876, MS 30365, pp. 440–41, and 20 October 1876, MS 30365, pp. 447–48.

62. John Blackwood to Charles Reade, 20 October 1876, MS 30365, pp. 447–48.

63. Charles Reade to John Blackwood, 21 October 1876, MS 4726, fols. 86–87.

64. Charles Reade to John Blackwood, 7 October 1876, MS 4726, fols. 84–85. The family misfortunes referred to included the death of Reade's favorite nephew, novelist and African explorer Winwood Reade. Also deflecting Reade's attention during this period was a costly and lengthy lawsuit against the *Glasgow Herald* for infringement of copyright on his work *A Hero and a Martyr*, which necessitated frequent and tiring trips to Glaswegian courts. See Elwin, *Charles Reade*, 288–314, for a short account of Reade's life during this troubled period and a misleading discussion of his difficulties with Blackwood over *A Woman Hater*.

65. John Blackwood to William Blackwood III, 22 October 1876, MS 4341, fol. 295.

66. J. M. Langford to William Blackwood III, 24 October 1876, MS 4347, fol. 242.

67. Burns, *Charles Reade*, 132.

68. Ibid., 133.

69. John Blackwood to Charles Reade, 10 July 1876, MS 30365, p. 384.

70. Lutzker, "Medical Education for Women in Great Britain," 65.

71. John Blackwood to Charles Reade, 28 November 1876, MS 30365, pp. 472–73.

72. John Blackwood to Charles Reade, 27 February 1877, MS 30365, pp. 553–54.

Notes to Chapter 5

1. David Lyell to Joseph M. Langford, 7 February 1880, MS 30039.

2. William Blackwood III to Joseph M. Langford, 10 May 1878, MS 4370, fols. 90–91.

3. David Bryce Burn to William Blackwood III, 6 November 1880, MS 30039.

4. William Blackwood III to William Lucas Collins, 21 June 1882, private letter in hands of author.

5. R. J. Haldane to William Blackwood III, 30 June 1896, MS 30067, fols. 146–48.

6. For a brief comment on Langford's theater work noted by Herman Melville, who was entertained by Langford on a London visit in 1849, see Eleanor Melville Metcalf, *Herman Melville, Cycle and Epicycle: Journal of a Visit to London and the Continent by Herman Melville, 1849–1850* (Cambridge: Cambridge University Press, 1948), n. 8, 180–81.

7. For further information regarding this episode, see my article, "*Immaturity* Considered: George Bernard Shaw and His Dealings with William Blackwood & Sons," *Notes and Queries*, n.s., 40 (March 1993): 61–63.

8. For a discussion of Hardy's connection with the Blackwood firm, see F. B. Pinion, "The Composition of 'The Return of the Native,'" *Times Literary Supplement* 21 (August 1970): 931.

9. As F. D. Tredrey points out, Doyle attempted to publish with Blackwood's over a period of eight years, from 1882 to 1890. William took only a short story, "A Physiologist's Wife," rejecting Doyle's novel *Micah Clarke* and several short tales and missing out on the chance to publish *The White Company* (Tredrey, *House of Blackwood*, 167–68). William, while friendly enough in his rejection of Conan Doyle during this period, was to feel less charitable in his later years, writing of him in 1907 to Charles Whibley, "He has always seemed to me a pretentious chap spoilt by public success. His only redeeming points are his views on Imperialism and Tariff Reform but these do not excuse his weakness in regards to books" (William Blackwood III to Charles Whibley, 12 December 1907, MS 30395, p. 428).

10. William Blackwood III turned down two works of Wells offered by the literary agent James Brand Pinker, *The Great Prospectus* and *The Sea Lady*. See J. B. Pinker to William Blackwood III, 26 March 1900, MS 4705, p. 100; and William Blackwood III to J. B. Pinker, 19 June 1901, MS 30389, p. 308.

11. DeLancey Ferguson and Marshall Waingrow, eds., *RLS: Stevenson's Letters to Charles Baxter* (New Haven: Yale University Press, 1956), 314.

12. William Blackwood III, undated memorandum, MS 30071.

13. Eliot, *Some Patterns and Trends in British Publishing*, 13–14; Feltes, *Literary Capital and the Late Victorian Novel*, xii, 12. For a case study on publishers' uses of innovative strategies of syndication and

multiple use of copyright to generate income during this period, see Alexis Weedon, "From Three-Deckers to Film Rights: A Turn in British Publishing Strategies, 1870–1930," *Book History* 2 (1999): 188–206.

14. Quoted in Barbara Quinn Schmidt, "Novelists, Publishers, and Fiction in Middle-Class Magazines, 1860–1880," *Victorian Periodicals Review* 17 (Winter 1984): 143.

15. Charles Whibley, "A Retrospect," *Blackwood's Magazine* 201 (April 1917): 433.

16. For more on the Chace Act, see Simon Nowell-Smith, *International Copyright Law and the Publisher in the Reign of Queen Victoria* (Oxford: Clarendon Press, 1968); and Feltes, *Literary Capital and the Late Victorian Novel*, 56–57.

17. William Blackwood III to the Leonard Scott Publication Company, 24 April 1894, MS 30334, p. 99.

18. For further analysis of the magazine's role in British cultural formations during the First World War, see my "Literature, Propaganda, and the First World War: The Case of *Blackwood's Magazine*," in Jeremy Treglown and Bridget Bennett, eds., *Grub Street and the Ivory Tower: Essays on the Relations Between Literary Journalism and Literary Scholarship* (Oxford: Oxford University Press, 1998), 91–111.

19. Willliam Blackwood III, undated memorandum, MS 30071.

20. Ibid.

21. Alvin Sullivan, ed., *British Literary Magazines: The Victorian and Edwardian Age, 1837–1913* (Westport, Conn.: Greenwood Press, 1984), 242.

22. Quoted in ibid., 242.

23. Ibid., 244.

24. Ibid., 243.

25. Robert Blake, *The Conservative Party from Peel to Churchill* (London: Eyre & Spottiswood, 1970), 24.

26. For further information on the role of Blackwood's in shaping Tory economic policies, see Frank W. Fetter, "The Economic Articles in Blackwood's Edinburgh Magazine and Their Authors, 1817–1853," *Scottish Journal of Political Economy* 7 (1960): 85–107, 213–31; and Salim Rashid, "David Robinson and the Tory Macroeconomics of Blackwood's *Edinburgh Magazine*," *History of Political Economy* 10, no. 2 (1978): 259–70.

27. William Blackwood III to Sir Henry Stafford Northcote, 13 February 1883, MS 30369, pp. 283–85.

28. William Blackwood III to Lord John Manners, 23 February 1883, MS 30369, pp. 311–12.

29. Joseph M. Langford to William Blackwood III, 21 December 1883, MS 4446, fol. 234.

30. William Blackwood III to John Skelton, 1 March 1883, MS 30369, pp. 317–18.

31. William Blackwood III to George T. Chesney, 3 April 1883, MS 30369, pp. 369–70.

32. J. Lewis May, *John Lane in the Nineties* (London: Bodley Head, 1936), 206–7, quoted in Peter McDonald, *British Literary Culture and Publishing Practice, 1880–1914* (Cambridge: Cambridge University Press, 1997), 75.

33. See, for example, N. N. Feltes, *Modes of Production of Victorian Novels* (Chicago: University of Chicago Press, 1986) and also his *Literary Capital*.

34. Nowell-Smith, *International Copyright Law*, 94. For more information on Murray's Colonial Library series, see Angus Fraser, "John Murray's Colonial and Home Library," *Papers of the Bibliographical Society of America* 91 (September 1997): 339–408; and Priya Joshi, "Culture and Consumption: Fiction, the Reading Public, and the British Novel in Colonial India," *Book History* 1 (1998): 206–7.

35. In connection with these discussions, Joseph Langford wrote John Blackwood on 7 April 1858: "I had some talk with Smith, Elder and Co. about Bookselling in India and mentioned your views about the probable increase of the sale of books in which they agree. They think too that there will be a large demand for school books there and are preparing to be early in the market. For this purpose they want to have our Atlases and other school books at advantageous terms. I think this worthy consideration as by taking the field early with our books they might establish them there" (Joseph Langford to John Blackwood, 7 April 1858, MS 4132, fol. 100).

36. Quoted in Margaret Diane Stetz, "Sex, Lies, and Printed Cloth: Bookselling at the Bodley Head in the Eighteen-Nineties," *Victorian Studies* 35 (Autumn 1991): 80–81. For a comprehensive discussion of Murray's and Macmillan's Colonial Libraries, see Graeme Johanson, *Study of Colonial Editions in Australia, 1843–1872* (Wellington, N.Z.: Elibank Press, 2000).

37. For a brief discussion of the establishment of the Net Book Agreement, see John Feather, *A History of Publishing* (London: Routledge, 1988), 145–48.

38. See correspondence between William Blackwood III and James Brand Pinker, 19 June 1899, MS 30387, pp. 102–3; 5 December 1899, MS 4693, p. 120; 7 December 1899, MS 30387, pp. 418–21; and 28 December 1899, MS 30387, p. 457.

39. William Blackwood III to E. M. Forster, 14 January 1907, MS 30350, p. 358.

40. E. M. Forster to R. C. Trevelyan, 27 January 1907, EMF/ACF, Envelope 3, 1902–11, King's College Archive, Cambridge.

41. William Blackwood & Sons to E. M. Forster, 24 December 1906, MS 30350, p. 336; 7 January 1907, MS 30350, pp. 349–50; 28 January 1907, MS 30350, pp. 374–75.

42. The serialization coincided with the conclusion of long-serving Blackwood employee Alexander Allardyce's novel *Earlscourt*, which ran from January 1893 to January 1894 and was subsequently issued in December 1893 as one of the last three-volume novels published by the firm.

43. William Blackwood III to David Storrar Meldrum, 28 December 1893, MS 30380, pp. 119–20.

44. James Hugh Blackwood (1878–1951) had joined the firm fresh from Eton College in 1898, and by 1901 he was deemed experienced enough to begin undertaking management of the financial aspects of London Office business, while Meldrum continued to handle literary and commissioning aspects. (F. D. Tredrey, in his survey of the firm, notes only that "in 1901 James had taken over the managership of the London Office and, in company with Meldrum, met Conrad, Galsworthy, Buchan, Garnett, and others who were in correspondence with Edinburgh" [*House of Blackwood*, 190–91]. But in saying this he ignores the evidence of legal partnership subsequently established between Meldrum and William, George, and James Blackwood from 1903 to 1910.)

45. Quoted in Douglas Blackburn, ed., *Joseph Conrad: Letters to William Blackwood and David S. Meldrum* (Cambridge: Cambridge University Press, 1958), xiv: "And in April of 1897, when Conrad seemed at a loss to know what to do with his short story 'Karain: A Memory,' Garnett spoke with sudden inspiration and authority: it was 'destined by Providence,' he said, for *Blackwood's Magazine*."

46. William Blackwood III to David Storrar Meldrum, 27 May 1896, MS 30392, pp. 461–62.

47. Further information regarding Conrad and Casement is noted in Hunt Hawkins, "Joseph Conrad, Roger Casement, and the Congo Reform Movement," *Journal of Modern Literature* 9, no. 1 (1981–82): 65–80. See also Jeffrey Meyers, "Conrad and Roger Casement," *Conradiana* 5, no. 3 (1973): 64–69.

48. Conrad, *Last Essays*, 1926, 161, quoted in Hawkins, "Joseph Conrad, Roger Casement, and the Congo Reform Movement," 67.

49. Jessie Conrad, *Joseph Conrad and His Circle* (New York: E. P. Dutton & Co., 1935), 103, quoted in Hawkins, "Joseph Conrad, Roger Casement, and the Congo Reform Movement," 79.

50. Stephen Gwynn to William Blackwood III, 29 July 1905, MS 30113.

51. Stephen Gwynn to William Blackwood III, 9 August 1905, MS 30113.

52. William Blackwood III to Roger Casement, 4 September 1905, MS 30393, p. 161.

53. Roger Casement to William Blackwood III, 5 September 1905, 22 September 1905, MS 30111.

54. William Blackwood III to Roger Casement, 23 October 1905, MS 30393, p. 231.

55. See, for example, Jane Ford, "An African Encounter, a British Traitor, and *Heart of Darkness*," *Conradiana* 27 (1995): 123–34; and Meyers, "Conrad and Roger Casement." I am indebted to Linda Dryden and Gene Moore for pointing out these sources to me.

56. Roger Casement to William Blackwood III, 22 September 1905, MS 30111.

57. For references to Gwynn's views on Somerville and Ross, see Gifford Lewis, *Somerville and Ross: The World of the Irish R.M.* (Harmondsworth: Penguin Books, 1985), 108, 118, 170–72, 178–79.

58. McDonald, *British Literary Culture and Publishing Practice*, 66–67.

59. Quoted in Blackburn, ed., *Joseph Conrad: Letters to Blackwood and Meldrum*, 17.

60. Frederick R. Karl and Laurence Davies, eds., *The Collected Letters of Joseph Conrad*, vol. 4: *1908–1911* (Cambridge: Cambridge University Press, 1990), 130.

61. Stephen Gwynn, *The Irish Statesman*, 10 November 1923, 279.

62. Stetz, "Sex, Lies, and Printed Cloth," 82.

Notes to Chapter 6

The author would like to thank Dale J. Trela for the opportunity to use his extensive transcription of Margaret Oliphant's letters in the National Library of Scotland, without which he would not have been able to piece together a portion of this chapter.

1. Margaret Oliphant to William Blackwood III, 27 July 1894, MS 4621, fols. 201–2.

2. William Blackwood III to Margaret Oliphant, 24 August 1894, MS 30380, pp. 581–82.

3. Ibid.

4. Margaret Oliphant to William Blackwood III, 3 November 1894, MS 4621, fols. 211–12.

5. William Chambers, *Memoirs of Robert Chambers, with Autobiographical Reminiscences of William Chambers* (Edinburgh and London: W. & R. Chambers, 1872), 103.

6. Ibid., 103–4.

7. Nicholas Phillipson, quoted in Peter Womack, *Improvement and Romance: Constructing the Myth of the Highlands* (Basingstoke: Macmillan Press, 1989), 147.

8. Fintan O'Toole, "Imagining Scotland," *Granta* 56 (Winter 1996): 72.

9. Chambers, *Memoirs*, v.

10. Ibid., 352.

11. Thomas Hughes, *Memoir of Daniel Macmillan* (London: Macmillan & Co., 1882), vii.

12. Ibid., 3–4.

13. Ibid., x–xi.

14. William Blackwood III to Margaret Oliphant, 5 December 1894, MS 30381, p. 207.

15. Margaret Oliphant to William Blackwood III, 3 November 1894, MS 4621, fols. 413–14.

16. Margaret Oliphant to William Blackwood III, 1 January 1895, MS 4635, fols. 214–15.

17. Ibid.

18. William Blackwood III to Mary Porter, 31 December 1894, MS 30381, pp. 288–89.

19. William Blackwood III to Mary Porter, 31 December 1894, MS 30381, p. 290.

20. Margaret Oliphant to William Blackwood III, 1 February 1895, MS 4635, fols. 220–21.

21. Margaret Oliphant to Mary Porter, February 1895, MS 4635, fols. 226–27.

22. Margaret Oliphant to William Blackwood III, 19 March 1895, MS 4635, fols. 231–32.

23. Ibid.

24. Margaret Oliphant to William Blackwood III, 1 June 1895, MS 4635, fols. 239–40.

25. Margaret Oliphant to William Blackwood III, 10 September 1895, MS 4635, fols. 243–44.

26. Ibid.

27. Margaret Oliphant to McCall Smith, 8 January 1896, MS 4650, fols. 110–11.

28. William Blackwood III to Margaret Oliphant, 5 May 1897, MS 30384, pp. 237–38.

29. Ibid., p. 238.

30. Margaret Oliphant to William Blackwood III, 7 May 1897, MS 4650, fols. 196–97.

31. William Blackwood III, to Margaret Oliphant, 13 May 1897, MS 30384, pp. 259–60.

32. Margaret Oliphant, *Annals of a Publishing House: William Blackwood and Sons*, vol. 1 (Edinburgh: William Blackwood & Sons, 1897), 25.

33. Margaret Oliphant to William Blackwood III, 1 March 1897, MS 4664, fols. 174–75.

34. William Blackwood III to Mary Porter, MS 30394, 3 March 1897, pp. 89–90.

35. Margaret Oliphant to William Blackwood III, 19 March 1897, MS 4664, fols. 179–80.

36. Ibid.
37. William Blackwood III to Mary Porter, 19 November 1897, MS 30385, p. 121.
38. Ibid., 120–21.
39. Porter, *Annals of a Publishing House*, 3:195–96.
40. Ibid., 262.

Notes to Chapter 7

1. James Hepburn, *The Author's Empty Purse and the Rise of the Literary Agent* (Oxford: Oxford University Press, 1968), 2.
2. Donald Sheehan, *This Was Publishing* (Bloomington: Indiana University Press, 1952), 75.
3. William Blackwood III, undated memorandum, MS 30071.
4. Frederick Whyte, *William Heinemann: A Memoir* (London: Jonathan Cape, 1928), 124.
5. William Blackwood III, undated memorandum (see note 3).
6. Hepburn, *The Author's Empty Purse*, 98.
7. Keating, *The Haunted Study*, 71.
8. Hepburn, *The Author's Empty Purse*, 26.
9. Robert Patten, *Dickens and His Publishers* (Santa Cruz: The Dickens Project, 1991), 80.
10. Hepburn, *The Author's Empty Purse*, 26.
11. For further information on this, see James J. Barnes and Patience B. Barnes, "Thomas Aspinwall: First Transatlantic Literary Agent," *Papers of the Bibliographical Society of America* 78, no. 3 (1984): 321–32.
12. Mary Ann Gillies, "A. P. Watt, Literary Agent," *Publishing Research Quarterly* 9 (Spring 1993): 21.
13. Ibid., 22.
14. A. P. Watt to William Blackwood III, 7 December 1894, MS 4625, fols. 139.
15. William Blackwood III, undated memorandum, MS 30071.
16. William Blackwood III to A. P. Watt, 13 December 1894, MS 30381, 247–48.
17. For more information on the activities of the Literary Agency, see Robert Gomme, "Edward Thomas and the Literary Agency of London," *The Book Collector* 47 (Spring 1998): 67–78.
18. Hepburn, *The Author's Empty Purse*, 58.
19. J. B. Pinker to William Blackwood III, 1 July 1898, MS 4664, 14.
20. J. B. Pinker to William Blackwood III, addendum, 1 July 1898, MS 4664, 14.
21. Michael Joseph, *The Commercial Side of Literature* (London: Hutchinson & Co., 1925), 92–93.
22. Sheehan, *This Was Publishing*, 74.
23. William Blackwood III to Charles Whibley, 21 September 1904, MS 30392, 283.
24. Ralph Arnold, *Orange Street and Brickhole Lane* (London: Rupert Hart-Davis, 1963), 46.
25. See David Finkelstein, "Literature, Propaganda, and the First World War: The Case of *Blackwood's Magazine*," 91–112, in Jeremy Treglown and Bridget Bennett, eds., *Grub Street and the Ivory Tower: Essays on the Relations Between Literary Journalism and Literary Scholarship* (Oxford: Oxford University Press), 1998.
26. Travers, *Mona MacLean*, 14th ed. (Edinburgh: William Blackwood & Sons, 1899), 369. In a letter to William Blackwood III in early 1894 (1 January 1894, MS 4615, fol. 133), Todd's contemporary Beatrice Harraden writes, "I met Graham Travers' friend the other day: the friend who figures in Mona MacLean as Miss Lascelles." Having made her mentor Eliza Lynn Linton read Mona, Harraden then notes that the work "did not regenerate" this conservative and notoriously antireformist novelist: "She seems to think that all modern women ought to be annihilated, but she does not understand them, or rather does not know them."
27. William Blackwood III to Sophia Jex-Blake, 2 August 1892, MS 30378, 528–29.
28. Sophia Jex-Blake to William Blackwood III, 16 August 1892, MS 4584, 216–17.
29. Margaret Todd to William Blackwood III, 27 December 1899, MS 4695, 240.

30. Margaret Todd to William Blackwood III, 29 August 1894, MS 4624, 175–76.

31. William Blackwood III to Margaret Todd, 16 December 1899, MS 30387, 436.

32. Margaret Todd to William Blackwood III, 27 December 1899, MS 4695, 239.

33. William Blackwood III to Sophia Jex-Blake, 4 January 1900, MS 30387, 470–71.

34. Sophia Jex-Blake to William Blackwood III, 13 January 1900, MS 4697, 134–35.

35. Sophia Jex-Blake, 13 January 1900, MS 4697, 135.

36. Further information on the Authors' Syndicate can be found in Robert A. Colby, "'What Fools Authors Be!': The Authors' Syndicate, 1890–1920," *Library Chronicle of the University of Texas* 35 (1986): 60–87.

37. Ibid., 84.

38. William Blackwood III to Beatrice Harraden, 9 September 1892, MS 30379, pp. 10–12.

39. Ibid., 11.

40. Beatrice Harraden to William Blackwood III, 1 January 1894, MS 4615, fol. 132.

41. Ibid., fol. 133.

42. William Blackwood III to Beatrice Harraden, 2 January 1894, MS 30380, p. 130.

43. Beatrice Harraden to William Blackwood III, 3 January 1894, MS 4615, fols. 134–35.

44. William Blackwood III to Beatrice Harraden, 8 January 1894, MS 30380, pp. 143–44.

45. Beatrice Harraden to William Blackwood III, 18 January 1894, MS 30064, fols. 33–34.

46. W. Morris Colles to William Blackwood III, 24 January 1894, MS 30064, fol. 101.

47. W. Morris Colles to William Blackwood III, 15 February 1894, MS 30064, fol. 86.

48. William Blackwood III to W. Morris Colles, 21 February 1894, MS 30380, p. 275.

49. W. Morris Colles to William Blackwood III, 22 March 1894, MS 30064, fol. 139.

50. W. Morris Colles to William Blackwood III, 10 April 1894, MS 30064, fol. 182.

51. William Blackwood III to W. Morris Colles, 16 April 1894, MS 30380, pp. 360–61.

52. William Blackwood III to Beatrice Harraden, 4 May 1894, MS 30380, p. 419.

53. William Blackwood III to W. Morris Colles, 20 April 1894, MS 30380, p. 366.

54. W. Morris Colles to William Blackwood III, 21 April 1894, MS 30064, fols. 228–29.

55. G. R. Morton to William Blackwood III, 2 May 1894, MS 30064, fol. 255.

56. W. Morris Colles to William Blackwood III, 1 May 1894, MS 30064, fols. 244–45.

57. Blackburn, ed., *Joseph Conrad: Letters to Blackwood and Meldrum*, xiv. Further information about Garnett's role in Conrad's career can be found in Cedric Watts, "Edward Garnett's Influence on Conrad," *The Conradian* 21 (Spring 1996): 79–92.

58. Keating, *The Haunted Study*, 67.

59. Karl and Davies, *Collected Letters of Joseph Conrad*, 2:195.

60. Ibid.

61. James Hepburn, ed., *Letters of Arnold Bennett*, vol. 1: *Letters to J. B. Pinker* (Oxford: Oxford University Press, 1966), 27.

62. Ibid.

63. Frederick Karl and Laurence Davies, eds., *The Collected Letters of Joseph Conrad*, vol. 3 (Cambridge: Cambridge University Press, 1991), 154.

64. J. H. Stape and Owen Knowles, eds., *A Portrait in Letters: Correspondence To and About Conrad*, special monograph issue of *The Conradian* 19, nos. 1–2 (1995): 43–44.

65. Ibid., 44.

66. Blackburn, ed., *Conrad: Letters to Blackwood and Meldrum*, 197.

Conclusion

1. Journals in which notices appeared included *The Athenaeum, The Book Monthly, The British Weekly, The Church Family Newspaper, The Daily Chronicle, The Glasgow Herald, The Illustrated London News, The Morning Post, The Pall Mall Gazette, The Scotsman,* and *The Times.*

2. *The Times,* 11 November 1912.

3. *The Scotsman*, 11 November 1912.

4. *The Church Family Newspaper*, 15 November 1912.

5. *The Times*, 11 November 1912.

6. *The Scotsman*, 11 November 1912.

7. Leslie Howsam, *Kegan Paul: A Victorian Imprint* (Toronto: University of Toronto Press, 1998), 14.

Bibliography

Primary Sources

Blackwood Papers. National Library of Scotland, Edinburgh.
Forster Papers. King's College Archive, Cambridge.
Murray Letter Books. John Murray Archive, London.

The Annual Register, new series. London: Rivingtons, 1872.
Edinburgh Typographical Association, Index to Members, 1871–1881. National Library of
    Scotland, Edinburgh
Minutes of the Evidence Taken Before the Royal Commission on Copyright. London: Eyre &
    Spottiswoode, 1878.

The Church Family Newspaper, 15 November 1912.
Edinburgh Evening Courant, 17 August 1871.
The Globe, 1 May 1871.
The Graphic, 13 May 1871.
Pall Mall Gazette, 3 May, 29 June 1871.
The Publishers' Circular, 1 September 1871.
Punch, 20 May 1871.
Saturday Review, 6 May 1871.
Scotsman, 11 November 1912, 16 August 1916.
The Spectator, 13 May, 27 May, 3 June 1871.
The Times, 26 June 1871, 11 November 1912.

Secondary Sources

Anderson, Roland F. "George Eliot Provoked: John Blackwood and Chapter Seventeen
    of *Adam Bede*." *Modern Philology* 71 (August 1973): 39–47.
———. "Negotiating for the *Mill on the Floss*." *Publishing History* 2 (1978): 27–40.
———. "'Things Wisely Ordered': John Blackwood, George Eliot, and the Publication
    of Romola." *Publishing History* 11 (1982): 5–39.
Anon. *Life of Sir Robert Christison*. 2 vols. Edinburgh: William Blackwood & Sons,
    1885–86.
Arnold, Ralph. *Orange Street and Brickhole Lane*. London: Rupert Hart-Davis, 1963.
Barnes, James J., and Patience B. Barnes. "Thomas Aspinwall: First Transatlantic Literary
    Agent." *The Papers of the Bibliographical Society of America* 78, no. 3 (1984): 321–32.

Bell, E. Moberly. *Storming the Citadel: The Rise of the Woman Doctor.* London: Constable & Co., 1953.

Blackburn, William, ed. *Joseph Conrad: Letters to William Blackwood and David S. Meldrum.* Cambridge: Cambridge University Press, 1958.

Blake, Robert. *The Conservative Party from Peel to Churchill.* London: Eyre & Spottiswood, 1970.

Bodenheimer, Rosemarie. *The Real Life of Mary Ann Evans: George Eliot, Her Letters and Fiction.* Ithaca, N.Y.: Cornell University Press, 1994.

Bolt, Christine. *Victorian Attitudes to Race.* London: Routledge & Kegan Paul, 1971.

Burns, Wayne. *Charles Reade: A Study in Victorian Authorship.* New York: Bookman Associates, 1961.

Chambers, William. *Memoirs of Robert Chambers, with Autobiographical Reminiscences of William Chambers.* Edinburgh and London: W. & R. Chambers, 1872.

Chesney, George. *The Battle of Dorking.* Edinburgh: William Blackwood & Sons, 1871.

Clarke, I. F. *Voices Prophesying War.* 2nd ed. Oxford: Oxford University Press, 1992.

Coghill, Mrs. Harry, ed. *Autobiography and Letters of Mrs. Margaret Oliphant.* 2nd ed. Leicester: Leicester University Press, 1974.

Colby, Robert A. "'What Fools Authors Be!': The Authors' Syndicate, 1890–1920." *Library Chronicle of the University of Texas* 35 (1986): 60–87.

Colby, Robert, and Vineta Colby. *The Equivocal Virtue: Mrs. Oliphant and the Victorian Literary Market Place.* New York: Archon Books, 1966.

Conrad, Jessie. *Joseph Conrad and His Circle.* New York: E. P. Dutton & Co., 1935.

Constable, Thomas. *Archibald Constable and His Correspondents.* Edinburgh: Edmonston & Douglas, 1873.

Dasent, A. I. *John Thadeus Delane, Editor of "The Times": His Life and Correspondence.* 2 vols. London: John Murray, 1908.

Donnison, Jean. *Midwives and Medical Men.* London: Historical Publications, 1988.

Eliot, Simon. *Some Patterns and Trends in British Publishing, 1800–1919.* London: The Bibliographical Society, 1994.

Elwin, Malcolm. *Charles Reade: A Biography.* London: Jonathan Cape, 1931.

Feather, John. *A History of Publishing.* London: Routledge, 1988.

Feltes, N. N. *Literary Capital and the Late Victorian Novel.* Madison: University of Wisconsin Press, 1993.

———. *Modes of Production of Victorian Novels.* Chicago: University of Chicago Press, 1986.

Ferguson, DeLancey, and Marshall Waingrow, eds. *RLS: Stevenson's Letters to Charles Baxter.* New Haven: Yale University Press, 1956.

Fetter, Frank W. "The Economic Articles in Blackwood's Edinburgh Magazine and Their Authors, 1817–1853." *Scottish Journal of Political Economy* 7 (1960): 85–107, 213–31.

Finkelstein, David. "*Immaturity* Considered: George Bernard Shaw and His Dealings with William Blackwood & Sons." *Notes and Queries,* new series, 40 (March 1993): 61–63.

———. *An Index to Blackwood's Magazine, 1901–1980.* Aldershot: Scolar Press, 1995.

———. "Literature, Propaganda, and the First World War: The Case of *Blackwood's Magazine.*" In Jeremy Treglown and Bridget Bennett, eds., *Grub Street and the Ivory Tower: Essays on the Relations Between Literary Journalism and Literary Scholarship,* 91–111. Oxford: Oxford University Press, 1998.

———. "'The Secret': British Publishers and Mudie's Struggle for Survival, 1861–1864." *Publishing History* 34 (1993): 21–50.

Ford, Jane. "An African Encounter, a British Traitor, and *Heart of Darkness*." *Conradiana* 27 (1995): 123–34.

Fraser, Angus. "John Murray's Colonial and Home Library." *Papers of the Bibliographical Society of America* 91(September 1997): 339–408.

Gillespie, Sarah C. *A Hundred Years of Progress: The Record of the Scottish Typographical Association, 1853–1952.* Glasgow: Robert Maclehose & Co., 1953.

Gillies, Mary Ann. "A. P. Watt, Literary Agent." *Publishing Research Quarterly* 9 (Spring 1993): 20–34.

Gomme, Robert. "Edward Thomas and the Literary Agency of London." *The Book Collector* 47 (Spring 1998): 67–78.

[Gregg, Hilda]. "The Medical Woman in Fiction." *Blackwood's Magazine*, July 1898, 94–109.

Griest, Guinever L. *Mudie's Circulating Library and the Victorian Novel.* Bloomington: Indiana University Press, 1970.

Gwynn, Stephen. *The Irish Statesman*, November 10, 1923, 279.

Haight, Gordon. *George Eliot: A Biography.* Oxford: Oxford University Press, 1968.

———. *The George Eliot Letters.* Vols. 1–9. Oxford: Oxford University Press, 1954–78.

Hall, N. John. *Trollope: A Biography.* Oxford: Oxford University Press, 1993.

Hawkins, Hunt. "Joseph Conrad, Roger Casement, and the Congo Reform Movement." *Journal of Modern Literature* 9.1 (1981–82): 65–80.

Haythornthwaite, J. A. "The Wages of Success: 'Miss Marjoribanks,' Margaret Oliphant, and the House of Blackwood." *Publishing History* 15 (1984): 91–107.

Hepburn, James. *The Author's Empty Purse and the Rise of the Literary Agent.* London: Oxford University Press, 1968.

———, ed. *Letters of Arnold Bennett*, vol. 1: *Letters to J. B. Pinker.* London: Oxford University Press, 1966.

Hollis, Patricia, ed. *Women in Public, 1850–1900.* London: George Allen & Unwin, 1979.

Howsam, Leslie. *Kegan Paul—A Victorian Imprint.* University of Toronto Press, 1998.

Hughes, Thomas. *Memoir of Daniel Macmillan.* London: Macmillan & Co., 1882.

Isaac, Peter, and Barry McKay, eds. *The Reach of Print: Making, Selling and Using Books.* Winchester: St. Paul's Bibliographies, 1998.

Jay, Elisabeth. *Mrs. Oliphant: "A Fiction to Herself," A Literary Life.* Oxford: Clarendon Press, 1995.

Jex-Blake, Sophia. "Medical Women in Fiction." *The Nineteenth Century*, January–June 1873.

Joseph, Michael. *The Commercial Side of Literature.* London: Hutchinson & Co., 1925.

Joshi, Priya. "Culture and Consumption: Fiction, the Reading Public, and the British Novel in Colonial India." *Book History* 1 (1998): 206–7.

Karl, Frederick R., and Laurence Davies, eds. *The Collected Letters of Joseph Conrad*, vols. 1–4. Cambridge: Cambridge University Press, 1986–91.

Keating, Peter. *The Haunted Study.* London: Secker & Warburg, 1989.

Kellner, Douglas. *Media Culture: Cultural Studies, Identity and Politics Between the Modern and the Post-Modern.* New York & London: Routledge, 1995.

Lewis, Gifford. *The Selected Letters of Somerville and Ross.* London: Faber & Faber, 1989.

———. *Somerville and Ross: The World of the Irish R.M.* Harmondsworth: Penguin Books, 1985.

Lutzker, Edythe. *Medical Education for Women in Great Britain*. Ph.D. dissertation, Columbia University, 1959.

MacDougall, Ian, ed. *The Minutes of the Edinburgh Trades Council, 1859–1873*. Edinburgh: T. & A. Constable, 1968.

Martin, Carol A. *George Eliot's Serial Fiction*. Columbus: Ohio State University Press, 1994.

Matthew, H. C. G., ed. *The Gladstone Diaries*. Vol. 7. Oxford: Oxford University Press, 1982.

May, J. Lewis. *John Lane in the Nineties*. London: Bodley Head, 1936.

McDonald, Peter. *British Literary Culture and Publishing Practice, 1880–1914*. Cambridge: Cambridge University Press, 1997.

Metcalf, Eleanor Melville. *Herman Melville, Cycle and Epicycle: Journal of a Visit to London and the Continent by Herman Melville, 1849–1850*. Cambridge: Cambridge University Press, 1948.

Meyers, Jeffrey. "Conrad and Roger Casement." *Conradiana* 5, no. 3 (1973): 64–69.

Milne, Maurice. "The Management of a Nineteenth-Century Magazine: William Blackwood & Sons, 1827–1847." *Journal of Newspaper and Periodical History* 1 (Summer 1985): 24–33.

———. "The 'Veiled Editor' Unveiled: William Blackwood and His Magazine." *Publishing History* 16 (1984): 87–103.

Mitchell, Juliet, and Ann Oakley, eds. *The Rights and Wrongs of Women*. Harmondsworth: Penguin Books, 1976.

Moorehead, Alan. *The White Nile*. Harmondsworth: Penguin Books, 1973.

Nichol, Donald W. "Arthur Murphy's Law." *Times Literary Supplement*, 19 April 1996, 15–16.

Nolan, E. H. *History of the War Against Russia*. London: J. S. Virtue, 1857.

Nowell-Smith, Simon. *International Copyright Law and the Publisher in the Reign of Queen Victoria*. Oxford: Oxford University Press, 1968.

Oliphant, Margaret. *Annals of a Publishing House*. Vols. 1 and 2. Edinburgh: William Blackwood & Sons, 1897.

O'Toole, Fintan. "Imagining Scotland." *Granta* 56 (Winter 1996): 59–76.

Paston, George. *At John Murray's: Records of a Literary Circle, 1843–1892*. London: John Murray, 1932.

Patten, Robert. *Dickens and His Publishers*. Santa Cruz: The Dickens Project, 1991.

Pinion, F. B. "The Composition of 'The Return of the Native.'" *Times Literary Supplement*, 21 August 1970, 931.

Porter, Mary. *Annals of a Publishing House*. Vol. 3. William Blackwood & Sons, 1898.

Radway, Janice. "Books and Reading in the Age of Mass Production." *The Adam Helms Lecture 1996*. Stockholm: Swedish Publishers' Association and the Stockholm University Library, 1996.

Rashid, Salim. "David Robinson and the Tory Macroeconomics of Blackwood's Edinburgh Magazine." *History of Political Economy* 10, no. 2 (1978): 259–70.

Reade, Compton. *Charles Reade: A Memoir*. 2 vols. London: Chapman & Hall, 1887.

Reynolds, Sian. *Britannica's Typesetters: Women Compositors in Edinburgh*. Edinburgh: Edinburgh University Press, 1989.

Rose, Mark. *Authors and Owners: The Invention of Copyright*. Harvard University Press, 1993.

Schmidt, Barbara Quinn. "Novelists, Publishers, and Fiction in Middle-Class Magazines: 1860–1880." *Victorian Periodicals Review* 17 (Winter 1984): 142–52.

Schneirov, Matthew. *The Dream of a New Social Order: Popular Magazines in America, 1893–1914.* New York: Columbia University Press, 1994.

Sheehan, Donald. *This Was Publishing.* Bloomington: Indiana University Press, 1952.

Smith, A. C. H. *Paper Voices: The Popular Press and Social Change, 1935–1965.* London: Chatto & Windus, 1975.

Speke, John Hanning. *Journal of the Discovery of the Source of the Nile.* Edinburgh: William Blackwood & Sons, 1863.

Spiers, Edward M. *The Late Victorian Army, 1868–1902.* Manchester: Manchester University Press, 1992.

Stape, J. H., and Owen Knowles, eds. *A Portrait in Letters: Correspondence To and About Conrad,* special monograph issue of The Conradian 19, nos. 1–2 (1995).

Stetz, Margaret Diane. "Sex, Lies, and Printed Cloth: Bookselling at the Bodley Head in the Eighteen-Nineties." *Victorian Studies* 35 (Autumn 1991): 71–86.

Sullivan, Alvin, ed. *British Literary Magazines: The Victorian and Edwardian Age, 1837–1913.* Westport, Conn.: Greenwood Press, 1984.

Sutherland, John. *Victorian Novelists and Publishers.* Chicago: University of Chicago Press, 1978.

Taylor, Anne. *Laurence Oliphant, 1829–1888.* Oxford: Oxford University Press, 1982.

Todd, Margaret. *The Life of Sophia Jex-Blake.* London: Macmillan & Co., 1918.

——— [Graham Travers]. *Mona MacLean.* 14th edition. Edinburgh: William Blackwood & Sons, 1899.

Tredrey, F. D. *The House of Blackwood, 1804–1954.* Edinburgh: William Blackwood & Sons, 1954.

Watts, Cedric. "Edward Garnett's Influence on Conrad." *The Conradian* 21 (Spring 1996): 79–92.

Weedon, Alexis. "From Three-Deckers to Film Rights: A Turn in British Publishing Strategies, 1870–1930." *Book History* 2 (1999): 188–206.

Whibley, Charles. "A Retrospect." *Blackwood's Magazine* 201 (April 1917): 433–46.

Whyte, Frederick. *William Heinemann: A Memoir.* London: Jonathan Cape, 1928.

Wilkinson-Latham, Robert. *From Our Special Correspondent: Victorian War Correspondents and Their Campaigns.* London: Hodder & Stoughton, 1979.

Womack, Peter. *Improvement and Romance: Constructing the Myth of the Highlands.* Basingstoke: Macmillan Press, 1989.

Index

Printed in Great Britain
by Amazon

13692503R00119